COSMOPOLITAN CAPITALISTS

COSMOPOLITAN CAPITALISTS

Hong Kong and the Chinese Diaspora at the End of the 20th Century

Edited by

Gary G. Hamilton

University of Washington Press

Seattle and London

This publication was supported in part by the
Donald R. Ellegood International Publications Endowment.

Copyright © 1999 by the University of Washington Press
Printed in the United States of America

Library of Congress Cataloging-in-Publication Data

Cosmopolitan Capitalists: Hong Kong and the Chinese diaspora at the end of
   the twentieth century / edited by Gary Hamilton.
     p. cm.
   Includes index.
   ISBN 0-295-97803-1 (alk. paper)
   1. Hong Kong (China)—Economic conditions. 2.Capitalism—China—
Hong Kong. 3. Hong Kong (China)—Emigration and immigration.
4. Chinese—Foreign countries. I. Hamilton, Gary G.
HC470.3.C67 1999
330.95125'06--dc21   98-52535
                                        CIP

Contents

v

Acknowledgments

I would like to thank a number of people who helped make this book a reality. Most importantly, I want to thank those who helped me develop and run the seminar series from which these essays emerged. Resat Kasaba, the Director of the Center for International Studies, asked me to organize the seminar series and supported it generously. Additional and equally generous support also came from David Bachman, Director of the Center for Chinese Studies, and Susan Jeffords, Divisional Dean of the Social Sciences. I also want to thank the students in the graduate course on ethnicity and nationalism (SIS 522) that ran concurrently with the seminar series. They read and commented on each of the essays presented, and their advice was conveyed to the authors for their consideration during the revision process.

The book would not have been possible without two other people: Michael Duckworth at the University of Washington Press, who promoted an unfinished project and then pushed for the final manuscript, and Jarrett Paschel, who cheerfully learned Pagemaker in order to format the revisions as soon as they came in. Finally I want to thank Eleanor Hamilton, who read and commented on several chapters.

GARY HAMILTON

COSMOPOLITAN CAPITALISTS

Introduction

GARY HAMILTON

At the stroke of midnight on the 30th of June 1997, in a convention center built for the occasion, Prince Charles, the next king of England, symbolically handed the sovereignty of Hong Kong to Jiang Zemin, the President of the People's Republic of China. From that moment forward, Hong Kong was officially a Chinese city. Journalists hailed this transfer of sovereignty as an extraordinary historical event, signifying the end of British colonial presence in Asia and the beginning of a new Asian era. In apparent agreement, several hundred thousand persons descended on Hong Kong—former civil servants, past residents, tourists—all wanting to be there to witness "history being made."

Great events, such as this change of government in Hong Kong, do indeed cause history "to be made," in part because they blur, if they do not actually distort, historical perspective. Such moments capture the public imagination, sometimes by crystallizing widely held anxieties about the future. Public figures and the mass media seize on these events and try to turn them into collective representations, symbols capable of creating a shared cultural space that spreads beyond a specific time and place. Like a black hole, the seeming gravity of great events compresses all strands of history, pulling them into a common core and redefining them in the light of the moment. From now on, many analysts will find it appropriate, if not necessary, to make all paths from Hong Kong's pre-1997 past lead inexorably to the handover and to make all post-1997 changes the inevitable outcomes of the change in government.

One should not minimize the importance of momentous occasions, but such events should be placed in the context of history, rather than placing history in the context of big events. The type of history I have in mind here is not a linear, unitary succession of happenings, but rather the multiplex, non-linear histories of the type that Fernand Braudel (1976, 1984) so eloquently described. Different spheres of human society possess different structural parameters and hence move with different rhythms and with different consequences for the society as a whole. Human demography, for instance, has a different history than politics; the growth and spread of technology has a different history than popular culture and social movements. Obviously demography, politics, technology, and popular culture are all interrelated, but the significant events in one set of histories would not necessarily be equally significant in another set.

Indeed, it is equally obvious that all the histories that might be written about Hong Kong do not converge on a timeline dictated by the 99-year lease for the peninsula jutting out from China's mainland toward Hong Kong Island, which was signed by the imperial Chinese and British Governments in 1898. The lease for this land, known as the New Territories, may have established some loose parameters for political relations between England and the government of China, by setting June 30, 1997, as its ending date. But had the lease been for 50 years, or 150 years for that matter, political decision making about what to do when the lease expired would have worked out quite differently. As it was, when the British and Chinese began to negotiate in the early 1980s, they did so in the context of a Hong Kong that was then in the midst of a most profound capitalist transformation, along with the rest of East Asia.

In the four decades before the handover, Hong Kong changed from a struggling entrepôt to one of the core areas of global capitalist expansion. The transformation is apparent in Hong Kong's skyline, in the fashionable clothes that its people wear, in nearly every aspect of life in Hong Kong, all of which seems to be updated every year. A colonial backwater in the 1950s, Hong Kong became, successively, one of the main manufacturing, financial, and service centers of East Asian capitalism. But more than that, Hong Kong became the center of so much of Asia's vitality. A producer of more movies than Hollywood, a fashion center nearly as important as Paris, and a tourist mecca, Hong Kong is Asia's New York, Paris, and Los Angeles all rolled into one city.

Hong Kong's metamorphosis took place in an unbelievably short period, in the span of less than two generations. Those were heady times, for it seemed that the successes would never end. Economic, political, and social triumphs followed one after the other and built on one another so naturally that continuing good fortune seemed inevitable.

The Asian business crisis has, of course, broken Hong Kong's string of successes, at least for the moment. Less than a year after the handover, immersed in a severe economic downturn, Hong Kong stumbled from one unfortunate incident to another: floods, a mysterious and deadly flu carried by chickens, a red tide that killed great quantities of fish, a precipitous decline in tourism, serious snafus at the new airport, a property market that fell by 40 percent, and a stock market that fell by over 50 percent. On the eve of the new millennium, instead of anticipating the arrival of the Pacific Century, Hongkongers are braced for the worst yet to come.

But, unlike the current crisis of confidence, a century ago, in the last years of the Qing dynasty, China was awash in adversity and pervasive uncertainty. Losing every war, embattled on nearly every front, the Qing government found itself ceding and leasing bits and pieces of Chinese soil merely to remain in power. This was the period during which the New Territories became part of the Colony of Hong Kong. In 1898, the year the lease was signed, the British could not have foreseen a capitalist transformation anywhere along the China coast, let alone one centered in Hong Kong. At the time, Westerners wrote mainly about China's poverty and backwardness. In fact, as late as the 1950s, observers did not sense any economic development in the region, even though, in retrospect, the beginnings of growth were evident even earlier. By the early 1980s, however, British and Chinese negotiators both saw what they interpreted to be a long-term capitalist trajectory, and projecting that trajectory into the future, they wrote and signed the Sino-British Joint Declaration. The secret and relatively brief negotiations were followed by an abrupt announcement giving all of the colony, and not just the New Territories, back to China. It was a clear case of making a quick political judgment based on an interpretation of what Braudel (1979, 1984) calls *"La longue durée"*.

La longue durée, duration over the long term, refers to those background factors and very long-term historical phenomena that structure events but do not actually cause them. In explaining the rise of Western capitalism, for instance, Braudel (1977: 6f) argues that "mankind is more than waist-deep in daily routine." These mundane routines are the "structures of daily life" that change only slowly but nonetheless prepare the way for patterns of shorter duration, such as cycles of political leaders and their regimes, without determining the concatenation of events. Distant first causes and a chain of fate, therefore, cannot effectively explain the world we know today. Equally, the explanation of our times cannot be set adrift in a sea of current events, so that only historical accidents and proximate causes can account for human destiny. Obviously, some combination of long-term trends and immediate and short-run conditions best explains the twists and turns of our times. With this in mind, when we look at Hong Kong at the turn of millennium—at its splendor as a world city, its centrality as a primary node in the global economy, and the ups and downs that go along with its position in the world—we would do well to keep in mind the multiple, complex trajectories that, through their conjuncture, make up the constantly surprising world that we see represented there today.

This book examines some of the most important trajectories and background factors influencing contemporary Hong Kong. The nine chapters, which began as presentations in a lecture series, place contemporary Hong Kong in a number of diverse historical and comparative perspectives that cumulatively build a complex, multileveled portrait of Hong Kong and Hongkongers at the end of the twentieth century. The essays are arranged to move from the more general and historical topics to the more immediate and contemporary ones. The authors of these chapters locate multiple perspectives that illuminate trends shaping Hong Kong today. With some oversimplification, these perspectives can be arranged into three categories: the patterned flows of people, products, and capital; the changing dynamics of how people identify themselves; and the politics of creating a new order.

FLOWS OF PEOPLE, PRODUCTS, AND CAPITAL

When most people conceptualize Asian capitalism, they think of Asia as a set of discrete economies lined up one after another. The first and most often-cited lineup consists of Japan, South Korea, Taiwan, Hong Kong, and Singapore. Later, in the 1980s and 1990s, as economic growth spread throughout Asia, China and most of the countries in Southeast Asia joined the list. The listed countries are known by their acronyms (NICs and NIEs) or by bestial metaphors (dragons, tigers, and geese). Collected country by country, economic statistics also support the view that each national economy is discrete, measurable, and in the process of becoming capitalist.

In truth, however, political and economic boundaries rarely coincide, and they certainly do not coincide in Hong Kong, which has one of the world's most globally networked economies. Moreover, capitalism is not a stable and readily identifiable configuration that, like a flower, suddenly bursts forth in bloom. Instead, capitalism is merely a term that covers an extremely wide range of diverse economic activities organized in the context of competitive markets and whose institutional conditions include private ownership and non-state decision making. Economic statistics only represent an aggregation of individual and collective actions compiled according to predetermined categories. The contents and limits of these actions, however, are determined, not by a politically sanctioned line on the ground or even by the categories of their classification, but rather by the most diverse and intersecting conditions imaginable—some global, some national, some local. As I describe in the first chapter, instead of equating it with national economies, capitalism is best conceptualized in terms of the organized economic activities and institutional conditions that constitute it, and countries are best conceptualized as locations where specific activities occur.

Once capitalism is viewed in terms of the organized activities, then it is obvious that national borders do not necessarily contain these activities. Most economic activities involve the movements of people, products, and capital, and in the case of Hong Kong, almost all of these movements are organized internationally. Before World War II, Hong Kong served as the main port of demarcation for the global migration of Chinese merchants and laborers, but the people living in Hong Kong at the time were not the main organizers of this migration. Also in the pre-war years, Hong Kong was the center for the transshipment of goods coming from or going to China, but again the people of Hong Kong were not the primary organizers of the trade. After World War II, local industrialists turned Hong Kong into a key manufacturing site, but they served largely as suppliers and subcontractors for retail outlets and brand-name merchandisers located in the United States and Europe, such as those specializing in mass-produced fashion garments (e.g., Anne Klein, Esprit, and the Gap). Both before and after the war, Hong Kong was a financial center, in the earlier period handling remittances sent to villages in South China from Chinese emigrants living outside of China and in the later period funneling international money into and out of Asian capitalist projects. Even in the last several decades when entrepreneurs in Hong Kong began to play key roles in organizing the economy of South China and linking it to the rest of the world, Hong Kong's economy became more and not less globally networked.

Hong Kong's intense and long-term involvement in the global economy means that its trajectories of change are actually aspects of larger Asian and global trends. Since its founding, to paraphrase Manuel Castells (1996: 376–428), Hong Kong has been a place in the "space of flows," an urban funnel through which people, products, and capital move. Hong Kong takes its economic life from the capitalist world in which it exists. There have been many explanations for Hong Kong's economic development, most of which emphasize its divergence from the "East Asian development model," economies developed through the intervention of strong states.[1] This model has always been overdone (Orrù, Biggart, and Hamilton 1997). But even the most laissez-faire-oriented explanations fail to explain the extent to which Hong Kong is entangled in the world economy and reflects (even as it helps to create) the current conditions of global capitalism.

The important thing to recognize about these global flows is that they are rarely in sync, and in fact are often at odds with one another. In the most recent decades, the flow of products through Hong Kong links global retailing and merchandising chains with local manufacturing in Hong Kong's hinterland. Western buyers work with Hong Kong and Taiwanese entrepreneurs who coordinate the manufacturing and distribution networks for an array of products. The Taiwanese tend to specialize in the manufacture of shoes and bicycles (Hsing 1998) and the Hongkongers in fashion garments (Bonacich et al. 1994), but in many other arenas, such as property development, they also compete with each other. Even as they sign contracts with Western buyers, manufacturers in Hong Kong and Taiwan also try to build their own brand names, in order to reduce their reliance on merchandising chains over which they have no control.

A similar tension is present in financial markets. The flow of Chinese capital into and out of Hong Kong takes advantage of what Barry Naughton (Chapter 4) calls Hong Kong's "property-rights regime," a secure haven for privatizing control over assets owned collectively in China. This tactic has drawn into Hong Kong vast sums of money that circulate quite differently from the capital that European and American entrepreneurs and portfolio managers moved to and through Hong Kong financial markets. However, none of the financial markets are aligned with the flow of products, a disjuncture that is one of the underlying causes of the Asian business crisis. Moreover, as Wong Siu-lun's and Katharyne Mitchell's chapters show, the migratory flows of people from Hong Kong do not overlap with the primary flows of either products or capital. All of these examples demonstrate that there are no precise ways to characterize Hong Kong's current economy, and it is impossible to predict which of the current trends will prove the most significant historically.

Given the complexity of Hong Kong's current situation, it seems worthwhile to ask the following questions. What are the relations between local actions and global trajectories? Do local entrepreneurs, not daring or knowing how to disembark, merely ride the backs of these global trends? Or have Hong Kong's capitalists attained sufficient economic power and global significance to stand their own ground and shape their own future? At the end of the twentieth century, these are open questions. But one thing is certain from the essays in this book: The decisions and actions of people do make a difference historically.

In the nineteenth century, for instance, Western gunboat diplomacy forcibly opened Asian economies to outside influences. Taking advantage of these events, the Chinese and Japanese, each in very different ways, forged separate capitalist trajectories that still shape (but do not determine) the actions of entrepreneurs today. Edgar Wickberg's essay (Chapter 2) gives a similar historical lesson in regard to the global migration of the Chinese in the last half of the nineteenth century. While Chinese migrants responded largely to opportunities created by the spread of European and American capitalism, they used their own peculiar social institutions to organize themselves in ways that gave them economic advantages vis-à-vis the local population. Descendants of these migrants still control a significant portion of the economies of Southeast Asia.

The large-scale movement of middle-and upper-class Chinese migrants from Hong Kong, as well as from other predominantly Chinese societies, parallels the great Chinese Diaspora of the last half of the nineteenth century. Pushed by politics and by the uncertainties surrounding the handover, many well-off Chinese decided to establish homes in developed, English-speaking capitalist regions, such as Canada and Australia. Both Wong Siu-lun (Chapter 7) and Katharyne Mitchell

(Chapter 8) demonstrate that these decisions have already started to reshape—and surely will continue to influence—economic, social, and political relationships throughout the Pacific Rim. These chapters, together with chapter 4, reveal the similarities to and the differences from earlier Chinese migrations.

Hong Kong's global integration is assured through its economic and social linkages to the rest of the world. However, to understand this global integration, it is important to grasp Hong Kong's regional integration with China as well. G. William Skinner (Chapter 3) meticulously demonstrates that Hong Kong is already well along in the process of becoming a "Chinese" city, a city that is integrated into its macroregion and shares the characteristics of other cities similarly ranked in other macroregions. This point is a subtle one, but is so crucial to understanding Hong Kong today. Hong Kong is no longer a city-state cut off from its hinterland, as it was as recently as 1980, but is now the central city in the Guangzhou region as well as a place that integrates the Chinese economy more generally. Barry Naughton (Chapter 4) adds considerable detail describing exactly how and why Hong Kong has become integrated into the greater Chinese economy. His chapter surveys developments since the 1978 Chinese economic reform and shows that in only 20 years Hong Kong has been transformed into a city at the core of the Chinese economy, particularly as that economy is integrated into global economy. Naughton's analysis frames the distinctive roles that Hong Kong is playing in the industrialization of China, as a service and value-added center for the export-oriented economy of South China and as a financial safe haven that allows for the conversion of public assets into private advantage. In both of these roles, entrepreneurs from Hong Kong and China have forged a new path where there was none before. In this regard, past actions create precedents for those living in the present, but not necessarily destinies.

THE AMBIGUITIES OF SELF-DEFINITION

Hong Kong is a place where many different people with very different interests and livelihoods collectively pursue a range of organized activities. The operative word here is "collectively." Although people may make decisions individually or jointly in small groups, such as within the family, they live in a world of established institutions and shared meanings. This experience of living together in a shared world leads diverse people to make separate decisions conjointly. What people do at any one point in time is therefore not randomly distributed across all possible courses of action but is oriented instead to situationally real conditions. Where to live? What to do for a livelihood? What to buy? How to make money? What movie to watch? What clothes to wear? What emotions to feel? These and so many other facets of life are carried on with a high degree of mutuality. At any one point in time, there is considerable agreement on the parameters for answers—

if not the exact answers—to these and other similar questions.

Middle-and short-term trends are best understood as trajectories of situationally real conditions and of decisions made with reference to them. The "realness quotient" of these conditions can change rather quickly. What is certain is that Hong Kong is at the vortex of a continuing Asian transformation. Socially, economically, and politically, Hong Kong is in flux, pushed and pulled by many forces. These forces, however, are not impersonal but are aspects of a lived-in world that people simultaneously experience and create through their own actions. Indeed, to the people who live in Hong Kong, the changes they confront and the perceived reality they act upon, including the handover and the later economic crisis, reflect a set of extraordinary personal events. For instance, the transfer of sovereignty itself not only requires a transfer of nationality but also a reorientation of life and livelihood. If we now put the quandaries facing those in Hong Kong today within a broader historical perspective, then we can see just how profound these personal changes have been. Throughout the twentieth century, virtually every new generation of people living in Hong Kong has experienced an Asia remade.

In just the past 50 years, the people of Hong Kong have also changed from being resident migrants who trace their origins to nearby districts in South China to "Hongkongers," people who identify deeply with the locale and its urbane outlook. The driving force behind Hong Kong's outward orientation to the world is mainly business, and the integration of this business into the mainstream of global capitalism. Hong Kong's colonial status kept politics in the background and brought to the fore the considerable abilities of the Chinese to make money for themselves and for their families and friends.

As a consequence of the 30-year break with the mainland, Hong Kong's wealthy entrepreneurs and professional middle classes are now caught in the great dilemma of this historical moment. They are the ones who have the most global outlook, who owe their very successes to their economic and professional connections to the world outside of China. But they are also the ones who now must assess whether the risks of being grounded in China, politically if not economically, outweigh the opportunities that might ensue from becoming China's broker to the world. In the years leading up to the handover, many Hongkongers decided that the risks outweigh the opportunities, uprooted themselves, and moved everything to a new country. Others decided to stay and made no provisions for migrating in the future, even should the occasion call for it. But a great many, perhaps the majority of the upper echelons of Hong Kong society, decided to do both—to stay and to migrate at the same time. These Hongkongers maintain their lives and livelihoods in Hong Kong but have also spread assets and family members around the world. They have purchased apartments in London and condos in Vancouver, invested in firms in both Guangzhou and Thailand, enrolled their children in boarding schools in Europe, the United States, and Australia, and maintain passport options in one or several countries besides the Special Administrative Region (SAR) of Hong Kong. They have transformed a cosmopolitan outlook into a global presence.

Unlike the Chinese migrants in the nineteenth century, who were mainly peasants and petty merchants from South China, the migrants in the new Chinese Diaspora are, by world standards, wealthy and highly educated people. In this global migration, Hongkongers lead the way, but Chinese from other locations join in—Chinese from Taiwan who also worry about their future and political autonomy; Chinese from Southeast Asia who have loosened their attachments to their host countries in order to participate in accelerating economic opportunities that cut across national boundaries; and, increasingly, Chinese from the People's Republic of China who find the economic opportunities and personal advantages outside the PRC so much more lucrative than those within. These up-market migrants have created a new group of global cosmopolitans, Chinese whose identities and residences do not necessarily match. They have created a world where Hongkongers can live as Hongkongers in North America, Australia, and Europe, as well as in Hong Kong itself, or where Taiwanese can be equally at home in Monterey Park, California, or in Taipei.

The crucial point here is that Chinese identities are curiously ambiguous. In examining Hong Kong's political location at the margins of empires, Helen Siu (Chapter 5) argues that the Chinese of Hong Kong have always been able to create the vibrant world in which they live by avoiding rigidly defined identities, by learning how to be flexible in themselves, and by maneuvering in political spaces where sovereignty is ambiguous.

Wang Gungwu (Chapter 6) adds to these insights by showing that Chineseness is a flexible category of identification that is re-created situationally however and wherever people accepting that label migrate. A key theme that runs through Wang's analysis is that the "Hongkonger" identity is similar to the role played by the Shanghainese in the pre–World War II period, that of projecting to other Chinese throughout China and the rest of the world the image of "fundamental modernity." This quintessentially Chinese identity is very different from the ethnic Chinese identity that the Chinese in North American and Southeast Asia construct for themselves.

Even within this quintessential modernity, however, there is room to embrace a range of diverse identities. Based on extensive surveys of those living in Hong Kong before the handover, Wong Siu-lun (Chapter 7) probes the agonies of those Hong Kong residents deciding whether to leave, stay, or move back and forth without making a final decision. He discovers that the ways in which people identify themselves—whether as primarily Chinese or primarily Hongkonger—deeply influence their decisions regarding migration, and that the very ability of middle-class "yuppie" Hongkongers to manage multiple identities simultaneously increases their agonies manifold.

THE POLITICS OF SELF-REALIZATION

The ambiguities of personal identity also make for uncertainties in the day-to-day politics of creating a new political order. On July 1, 1997, a millionaire business-man, Tung Chee Hwa, became the Chief Executive of the Hong Kong Special Administrative Region Government. In December of the previous year, a 400-member Selection Committee picked Tung for this post. Chinese officials nudged the Selection Committee to make this choice after the Chinese President, Jiang Zemin, had auspiciously shaken Tung's hand at a ceremonial gathering of the Pre-paratory Committee in Beijing in January 1996 (Gilley 1996: 22–23). Despite this indication, pollsters continued to report, almost weekly for the rest of 1996, on the persons Hongkongers allegedly wanted for their leader.

In the two years leading up to the handover, the political scene turned mercu-rial and partisan. On one side, the liberal and pro-democracy factions aligned them-selves with Christopher Patten, the last British-appointed governor of Hong Kong, in their enthusiastic support for rapidly expanding the voting franchise to full and equal participation. On the other side, the more conservative and pro-Beijing fac-tions demanded that the colonial government keep the political order as it was at the time the Joint Declaration was signed. This political pulling and pushing "put the already divided civil society of the Hong Kong Chinese in disarray" (Tsang 1998: 47).

These political divisions were apparent in the 1995 elections for the Hong Kong Legislative Council. The pro-democracy forces won by a landslide even though the Chinese government promised that there would be no "through train" for leg-islators elected in 1995. True to its promise, as soon as the new SAR government was in office, it dismissed those people elected in 1995 and appointed a new slate of legislators. However, in the legislative elections in 1998, which were held un-der rules that reduced democratic participation from the 1995 level, the people of Hong Kong voted in record numbers despite a torrential downpour and put back into office many of those pro-democracy politicians the new government had booted out.

And so it goes. As in most places, the politics of Hong Kong and Hongkongers involve daily struggles to define the identity and direction of the collective. This struggle is clearly present in Vancouver, British Columbia, where very large num-bers of Hong Kong emigrants have established homes. As Katharyne Mitchell describes in Chapter 8, the newcomers redefined local politics by being more demo-cratic than the local, mainly Caucasian, upper-and middle-class voters. The same democratic tactics, however, did not allow the Hong Kong migrants to win out against the Vancouver Chinese community, which had arisen largely from pre–World War II migration. The newcomers were accused of not respecting the old relationships that were so crucial to the social makeup of the previous generations of Chinese migrants.

The stakes of these political struggles, however, are particularly high in Hong Kong because there are no historical precedents for the new SAR government to fall back on. For guidance, the new government really has only the optimism contained in Deng Xiaoping's famous formula pledging that for 50 years after the handover China and Hong Kong would be "one country, two systems." By guaranteeing 50 years of autonomy for Hong Kong, this formula holds out the promise that the projections of Hong Kong's capitalist future will come to fruition. At the time the Joint Declaration was signed, the British negotiators, as well as the Hong Kong onlookers, further hoped that during these 50 years China, following Hong Kong's example, would go through its own capitalist transformation and experience the same political liberalization that occurred in Hong Kong in the two decades before the handover. In the best of all possible futures, at the end of the 50 years, in the year 2047, China and Hong Kong would converge at the same place along the same trajectory and would seamlessly merge to become "one country, one system."

But this dream for the future collides with the reality of everyday politics. Political leaders must continually respond to the moment—must decide about quarantines to protect against the spread of the chicken flu, must respond to money speculators trying to break the ties of Hong Kong's currency to the U.S. dollar, must increase the supply of low-cost housing to gradually deflate a very expensive property market. Short-term goals, political expediency, historical accidents—these make up the world to which politicians respond.

But a continuing recognition of the linkages to the past and to the future is also a part of this world of constant crisis management. The perception of global migration as a way of life, the reemergence of Hong Kong as an entrepôt and a center of global capitalism, the significance of cosmopolitan urban centers in setting standards for modernity in China and beyond, the flexibility of Chinese identities, and the importance of sovereignty at the edge of empires—all these structural patterns connect the Hong Kong of today with its nineteenth–century past. In the midst of the extraordinary changes that Hong Kong now faces, these patterned continuities provide some bearing by which to chart the future. The negotiators of the Joint Declaration may have formulated an impossible goal for Hong Kong's politicians, but the politics of the next 50 years will use the Joint Declaration as a compass by which to search for what might be possible.

It is fitting, therefore, that the last words in this book are those of the Honorable Rosanna Yick-ming Wong. Unlike the rest of the contributors, the author of the last chapter is not a practicing academic but a person intimately involved in the day-to-day politics of Hong Kong. Although no stranger to the academy, she is currently the executive director of the Hong Kong Housing Authority, the world's largest public housing project. She is also one of only two members of the last Executive Council under British rule to be selected as members for the first Executive Council led by Tung Chee Hwa. In her essay, Rosanna Wong focuses on the shifting foundations of sovereignty during the colonial period, which progressively allowed Hong Kong's Chinese elite greater political participation. With passion and commitment, she argues that the trends of the past must be acknowledged in the reality of Hong Kong politics today. This chapter illustrates the theme of ambivalent identities and the politics of new beginnings. Potent identities are in the process of being constructed for the sake of politics at the start of this new era. Could there be any better ending for this book than her concluding sentence? "The truths of which historians will someday write are the truths that we must now create. The people of Hong Kong can and must grasp their own future today and every day to come."

NOTE

1. For excellent reviews of this exceptionalist literature on Hong Kong's development, as well as careful analyses of Hong Kong's economic growth, see Chiu (1996) and Chiu, Ho, and Lui (1997). For key works formulating the Asian development model, see Amsden (1989), Deyo (1987), Evans (1995), Johnson (1982), and Wade (1990).

REFERENCES

Amsden, Alice H. 1989. *Asia's Next Giant: South Korea and Late Industrialization*. New York: Oxford University Press.

Bonacich, Edna, Lucie Cheng, Norma Chinchilla, Nora Hamilton, and Paul Ong. 1994. *Global Production, The Apparel Industry in the Pacific Rim*. Philadelphia: Temple University Press.

Braudel, Fernand. [1966] 1976. *The Mediterranean and the Mediterranean World in the Age of Philip II*. Trans. Sean Reynolds. 2 vols. New York: Harper and Row.

———. [1977] *Afterthoughts on Material Civilization and Capitalism*. Baltimore: Johns Hopkins Press.

———. [1979] 1984. *Civilization and Capitalism: 15th–18th Century*. Volume 3 *The Perspective of the World. Translated by Sean Reynolds*. New York: Harper and Row.

Castells, Manuel. 1996. *The Rise of the Network Society*. Oxford: Blackwell.

Chiu, Stephen W.K. 1996. "Unraveling Hong Kong's Exceptionalism: The Politics of Laissez-Faire in the Industrial Takeoff," *Political Power and Social Theory 10: 229–256.*

Chiu, Stephen W.K., K.C. Ho, and Tai-Lok Lui. 1997. *City-States in the Global Economy: Industrial Restructuring in Hong Kong and Singapore.* Boulder, Colo.:Westview Press.

Deyo, Frederic C., ed. 1987. *The Political Economy of the New Asian Industrialism.* Ithaca, N.Y.: Cornell University Press.

Evans, Peter B. 1995. *Embedded Autonomy: States and Industrial Transformation.* Princeton, N.J.: Princeton University Press.

Gilley, Bruce. 1996. "Playing Favorites," *Far Eastern Economic Review,* February 8, 1966, pp. 22–23.

Hsing, You-tien. 1998. *Making Capitalism in China: The Taiwan Connection.* New York: Oxford University Press.

Johnson, Chalmers. 1982. *MITI and the Japanese Miracle.* Stanford, California: Stanford University Press.

Orru, Marco, Nicole Woolsey Biggart, and Gary G. Hamilton. 1997. *The Economic Organization of East Asian Capitalism.* Thousand Hills, C.A.: Sage Publications.

Tsang, Wing-kwong. 1998. "Skeptical, Dissenting, and Disorganized Spectators: The Political Orientations and Attitudes of Hong Kong Voters in the Run-up to 1997." Paper presented at the annual meeting of the American Sociological Association, San Francisco, August 21–25.

Wade, Robert. 1990. *Governing the Market: Economic Theory and the Role of Government in East Asian Industrialization.* Princeton, N.J.: Princeton University Press.

1 / Hong Kong and the Rise
of Capitalism in Asia

GARY HAMILTON

In the early 1980s, British and Chinese diplomats began secret negotiations that would lead to the signing of the Sino-British Joint Declaration in 1984. This agreement set the route by which the two governments and the people of Hong Kong would travel in the 13-year journey to 1997. The backdrop to these negotiations, as well as this unprecedented change of sovereignty, has been Hong Kong's status as one of the world's premier cities in the global economy. Any understanding of Hong Kong today has to begin with the capitalist transformation that has made it the global city that it has now become. Most writers treat Hong Kong's rise to prominence as strictly a post–World War II phenomenon and explain its success as a triumph of free-market capitalism. In this initial chapter, however, I want to argue that Hong Kong's role in the global economy needs to be situated in history and understood as integral to Asia's capitalist trajectories, which developed in the nineteenth century.

This topic is large and complex enough that I will be able to develop only a broad outline of a single theme in this chapter. Before I summarize this theme, however, please consider the two key terms that underlie this chapter, and indeed the book: capitalism and Hong Kong. For capitalism, keep in mind three dimensions. First, don't think of capitalism in terms of countries, but rather think of capitalism in terms of people, firms, money, products, industries, and the interrelationships among these. Second, think of capitalism as ever-changing movements of these things in time and space, as having historical and geographical characteristics. Third, think of capitalism, this movement in time and space, as complex economic activities that people try to control in some fashion. Entrepreneurs try to organize these activities, often in competition with one another; workers want to limit them so they don't dominate their lives too much; government officials try to regulate them, usually in opposition to somebody; bankers try to channel them, always to their own advantage. The idea, of course, is that capitalism represents contested economic movements in time and space that are always organized to some degree.

Now consider Hong Kong. Do not think of Hong Kong as a NIC, a NIE, an Asian tiger, a little dragon, or one of the flying geese. All these acronyms and metaphors that are used to characterize Hong Kong are so biological, so functional in the sense of a closed system, that they make Hong Kong seem like a type of economic species that was born or hatched and may grow to maturity someday. Instead, think about Hong Kong as a place where there is an ever changing mix and an ever contested but still organized movement of people, firms, money, products, and industries.

Having conceptualized capitalism and Hong Kong in these ways, I now want to put before you the following thesis, which summarizes my understanding of Asia's capitalist transformation and of Hong Kong's roles in this transformation: There are two indigenous "great traditions" of organized capitalist development in East and Southeast Asia that began in the nineteenth century with the opening of East Asia to a Western-dominated world economy. These two great traditions are the Japanese and Chinese modes of organizing and controlling the economic opportunities in the region. As I will explain, the Japanese mode is one of corporatized political economy, and the Chinese is one of entrepreneurial deal making. These two modes of economic organization have led to two broad, path-dependent trajectories of development. Path dependence, a currently fashionable term, means that history makes a difference. Where you end up depends very much on where you start. This thesis is especially accurate in collective endeavors. Past patterns of collective action always shape but do not necessarily determine the present, as well as future patterns of action. Chinese and Japanese modes of seizing economic opportunities in the nineteenth century launched two distinct, more or less organized capitalist trajectories of economic development. Greatly altered by World War II and its aftermath, these trajectories, I maintain, nevertheless re-emerged in the second half of the twentieth century.

I will argue that Hong Kong, as a place, was and continues to be at the organizing center of Chinese-led capitalism. Hong Kong assumed this role shortly after its founding in the nineteenth century and continued it until World War II. Then after the war and the Chinese revolution, Hong Kong was the first location where Chinese capitalism reemerged, although in a somewhat changed form.

In the bulk of this chapter, I will give some supporting evidence for this thesis. In arguing that history makes a difference, I will concentrate mainly on the pre–World War II period. Then in the last section of the chapter, I will discuss in what ways Asia's post-war industrial boom represents a continuation of pre-war trajectories. Edgar Wickberg's discussion in Chapter 2 amplifies my discussion of pre–

World War II migration, and Barry Naughton's analysis in Chapter 4 greatly extends my brief survey of Hong Kong's post-war economy.

TWO TRAJECTORIES OF ASIAN CAPITALISM[1]

Most people date the development of Asian capitalism in areas outside of Japan to the period after World War II. Certainly, this is the era in which we see Hong Kong, Singapore, and Taiwan begin their rapid industrial ascent. But let me argue that such a dating ignores the fact that the groundwork for this ascent was prepared well in advance of the war. Chinese entrepreneurs throughout the region were already "capitalistic," if by this we mean that they were already aggressively profit-oriented in their private pursuits and were eager to seize opportunities to make more money. This capitalistic acquisitiveness was in place before the skylines of Hong Kong, Singapore, and Taipei filled with skyscrapers; these cities— the cities that we see today—are the consequences, not the causes, of capitalist development throughout the entire region.

The post-war dating also ignores another fact. The economic changes in these locations were not isolated events, but rather occurred in a rapidly developing capitalist world economy that was producing economic changes in many locations. In fact, the success of capitalism in Chines and ethnic Chinese–dominated economies outside the People's Republic of China—the economies of Taiwan, Hong Kong, Singapore, and many Southeast Asian countries—cannot be understood apart from the dynamics of this global economy. Because Chinese modes of capitalist acquisition are based on bottom-up individual and family-based strategies of seizing opportunities wherever they exist, rather than on top-down corporatist strategies of linking state administrative capabilities with elite economic opportunities, Chinese capitalism is integral to world capitalism itself.

It is the absence of a politically framed domestic economy that makes Chinese forms of capitalism so elusive. Most interpreters of Asia's recent past see no genuine capitalistic development in late-nineteenth and early-twentieth-century China. In fact, it is conventional to argue that whereas Japan industrialized in the late nineteenth and early twentieth centuries, China remained economically backward. To substantiate this thesis, most scholars simply point to the obvious early industrial capacity of the Japanese—particularly in heavy industries such as iron and steel, and in the related products such as ships, trains, trucks, and automobiles— and the lack of these industries in China. With these industries, so the interpretation goes, the Japanese developed modern armies and navies that won wars against the Chinese in 1895 and against the Russians in 1905. By contrast, the Chinese attempt to industrialize did not fare so well. While it is true that the Chinese developed some state-owned, merchant-run heavy industries in the nineteenth century, these industries were not particularly successful (Liu 1962; Feuerwerker 1958), and besides the Chinese lost every war they fought with an outside power from the time of the Opium Wars in the 1840s until World War II, when it was outside circumstances that defeated the Japanese.[2] Based upon these obvious comparisons, the Japanese industrialized and the Chinese did not.

But if we take another look at these "obvious" comparisons, I want to show you that they are not very persuasive because the time frame is too narrow and the definition of capitalism too rigid. If we made exactly the same comparisons today, that of industrial capacity based upon heavy industry, we would reach nearly the same conclusions: Japan is an industrial power, whereas Taiwan, Hong Kong, and Singapore are relatively undeveloped. The three Chinese-dominated economies do not have much in the way of heavy industries. But does that mean that today they are not industrialized or capitalistic? This is, of course, nonsense. Even so, it is still true that none of these locations has made a car for export.[3]

Chinese-dominated areas in the world economy are not characterized by heavy industries; by comparison, the Chinese manufacturers specialize in small and medium-sized firms. These modest-sized factories normally make consumer nondurables—products such clothes, shoes, TV sets, calculators, computers—manufactured items that fill houses throughout the United States and Europe, in addition to Asia. Economists know that one cannot compute a country's rate of economic growth and its GNP based only on the output of one or two industrial sectors. Why then should historians and sociologists, with their comparisons between Japanese and Chinese economies, implicitly do that for the nineteenth and early twentieth centuries?

Even if we take all the sectors into account, the historical comparison between Japan and China would still be clouded by the political dimension. China neither won its wars nor developed a successful political economy, and therefore, so the judgment goes, failed as an industrializing society.

This point brings us to a key question: Is political power, in the form of a strong state in war and peace, necessary for or even synonymous with capitalism, with the economic movement of people, firms, capital, products? Many analysts of economic development confidently conclude that centralized political power and capitalistic success are causally interrelated.[4] Indeed one can list numerous examples in which the two are interrelated, such as the capitalist development of South Korea, but can one not also envision successful forms of capitalism without a state structure and without an integrated political economy? Let me submit to you that the Chinese forms of acquisitiveness represent such a case.

Consider again the two Asian cases—Japan and China in the late nineteenth and early twentieth centuries. What we see in this contrast is not the presence of capitalism in the one and the absence of capitalism in the other. Rather, I would argue that we see two different versions of capitalism emerging more or less simultaneously with the opening of these economies to global economic and political influences. These two versions of capitalism have intensified and have taken their places among the dominant forms of global capitalism in the late twentieth century.

JAPAN'S CORPORATIZED POLITICAL ECONOMY

Let me compare the institutional beginnings of these two forms of capitalism, so that their differences are clear. Japanese capitalism is largely an indigenous transformation. It is a product of political economy. The record is absolutely clear on this score. For instance, during the Meiji era (1868–1912), the political elites of Japan formulated a comprehensive development plan, 30 volumes covering every aspect of the Japanese economy (Tu et al. 1991: pp. 79–80). Published in 1884, the plan was based on a thorough investigation of European economic and corporate institutions undertaken by elite Japanese who went to Europe, lived there for a while, observed, asked questions, and returned to Japan to develop an economic plan to catch up to the West, the first plan of its kind in the world. Even more amazing than the plan itself is the fact that most of the plan's 10-year targets "were in fact accomplished" (Tu et al. 1991: 79).

Another and even more impressive example of changes in the Meiji period comes from Eleanor Westney (1987), in her book *Imitation and Innovation, The Transfer of Western Organizational Patterns to Meiji Japan*. Westney shows that in the first 15 years of the Meiji period (roughly from 1868 to 1883), the Japanese political and economic elites organizationally transformed the Japanese state and society. They created among other things, Western-style armies and navies, postal and telegraph systems, an educational system ranging from primary schools to universities, a unified banking system, and a national police force organized bureaucratically. With each of these organizational innovations, Japanese government officials and private elites imitated Western practices, borrowing freely, sometimes exactly, sometimes loosely. As Westney (1987: 6) insightfully points out, "the distinction between copying and inventing, between imitation and innovation, are false dichotomies: the successful imitation of foreign organization patterns requires innovation." By the end of the Meiji period, Japan was on its way toward becoming an explicitly, self-consciously organized society, literally a society of organizations, and 100 percent Japanese.

In this context, it is important to see that Japanese industrialization was part of an evolving but always coordinated political policy. A part of this policy was the creation of an industrial structure made up of competing enterprise groups, each composed of large quasi-independent firms organized collectively, known as the *zaibatsu*. Mitsui, Mitsubishi and Sumitomo, among others, had all developed diversified holdings, systematic interlinkages among firms, and administrative management techniques before the end of the nineteenth century (Morikawa 1992).

In every arena—in politics, in business, in education—Japanese elites had sufficient authority within Japanese society to implement their policies successfully. This ability rested on a system of internal controls that permeated the social order. This system of social control relied on intricate intersecting relationships that created, beyond kinship, intense structurally embedded duties and obligations, which, from the participants' points of view, were demanding, even oppressive, but not necessarily centralized and authoritarian. This system of control gave the Japanese elites the ability to mobilize and manipulate vast human and material resources. At this point in time, in those early years of global change, this ability to mobilize also gave the Japanese an opening, a passageway by which to propel themselves collectively into the global scene, economically as well as politically.

Why did the Japanese elites pursue this route? Professor Hamashita (1988) of Tokyo University presents the convincing thesis that Japanese officials selected this course of action because they recognized their own limitations vis-a-vis their chief opponents in Asia, the Chinese. In the middle of the nineteenth century, with the Qing Dynasty still holding firm, Japanese officials felt that commercial expansion in Asia was not a viable strategy. Largely due to the Sinocentric tribute system that existed throughout Asia until the middle of the nineteenth century, Chinese merchants controlled commercial exchanges in almost every Asian port, including those in Japan. The Japanese determined that they could not beat the Chinese at their own game of being Asia's chief merchants, so they began instead to develop internally, using their human resources and organizational capabilities to implant a form of Western capitalism in Asia.

Therefore, in Japan, during the nineteenth and early twentieth centuries, the primary carriers of capitalist development were coalitions of political and economic elites.[5] Japanese capitalism was not a creation of a merchant class, although a few merchants participated in the elite coalition. Nor was Japanese capitalism a creation of the peasants, although peasants certainly changed their productive and labor outputs drastically. By comparison with the Chinese case, as we will see, Japanese capitalism is a creation of political economy, of a mutually reinforcing system of governmental controls and elite economic privileges. In a very short period, the Japanese were able to shift from small-scale production of handicraft goods to large-scale production of industrial products, from small factories to hierarchies of bureaucratically controlled corporations organized into conglomerate networks.

CHINESE ENTREPRENEURIAL CAPITALISM

The nineteenth-century institutional foundations of the Chinese forms of capital-ism—politically, economically, and socially—were nothing like those of Japan. In the period between 1850 and 1890, it is impossible to imagine the Qing court sending large groups of scholars to Europe and the United States to learn about Western ways. The small efforts that were made largely failed (Kuo and Liu 1987). It is impossible to imagine the court creating and then implementing detailed plans for economic development. Even the much vaunted "self-strengthening movement" in the 1860s and 1870s was confined largely to military reforms, and those were crushed in military defeats inflicted by France and Japan. It is even more difficult to imagine the court successfully enforcing a policy of borrowing organizational patterns from the West and implementing them successfully in local society. Listen to the words of Li Hung-chang, China's dominant modernizer in the nineteenth century.

> "Although I have never been in Europe, I have been inquiring and investigating West-ern political and cultural conditions for nearly 20 years, and I have formed some gen-eral ideas. I have stated in detail the necessity of opening coal and iron mines, of build-ing telegraph lines and railways, and of opening schools for pursuing Western knowl-edge and sciences in order to train men of ability... Prince Kung agreed with my sug-gestion, but said that nobody dared to promote such actions [at court.]....[In any event] the gentry class forbids the local people to use Western methods and machines, so that eventually the people will not be able to do anything. All these undertakings have been promoted by me alone; but it is as difficult to achieve a result as it is to catch the wind. Scholars and men of letters always criticize me for honoring strange knowledge and for being queer and unusual. It is really difficult to understand the minds of some Chinese." (Quoted in Li 1967: 108–109)

The Qing rulers could not establish a national capitalist-oriented political economy as the Meiji reformers were able to do. Although the Manchus ruled a great empire, their domination did not extend into their own local society. Below the administrative veneer of the imperial regime were politically elusive villages and marketing towns organized through kinship and status. Even had they so de-sired, the political elites could not mobilize China's vast human and material re-sources. To Chinese in local society, "Heaven is high and the emperor is far away."

Although China did not develop a state-based capitalism in the nineteenth cen-tury, there was a capitalist transformation among the Chinese nonetheless. The carriers of Chinese capitalism were not political elites, but rather the heads of households who wanted to achieve some wealth and local renown. These heads of household were peasants, merchants, artisans, and occasionally scholars; they were not organized as distinct classes of people, but rather they were family heads who moved into and out of ambiguously defined social and economic roles. The organizational medium for this Chinese economy rested largely on individual entrepreneurs and family firms embedded in extensive regional commercial networks, networks of fellow regionals.[6] This was an economy organized through institutions controlled by people embedded in local society. From the time of the Ming Dynasty (1368–1644), the Chinese economy has always been a triumph of local society, never of the state.

Family, kinship, and regionally based institutions shaped economic activity and nurtured distinctive forms of enterprise structure. Because the household, the *jia*, was the critical unit in both community and kinship organization, Chinese did not make a rigid separation between the household and the firm.[7] Accordingly, firms were like households, and like households, Chinese enterprises were usually small in size. If the family businesses were really successful, however, the firms, like the households of prominent scholars, grew larger as more relatives and friends were included in the expanding circles of household members. Huge businesses, however, were very rare, because most wealthy businessmen did not try to create larger and larger horizontally or vertically integrated firms, as occurred in Japan or the United States. If they remained economically active at all and did not retire to the countryside, as so many wealthy businessmen did, they invested in extensive networks of family members and friends running small and middle-sized firms, often covering several areas of business and in diverse locations.

The reasons for this strategy were several. The first reason is the effects of inheritance upon shaping business practices (Wong 1985). Japanese inheritance practices rest on the centrality of the stem family (*ie*) and upon the practice of primogeniture. A large firm could be passed on intact to one son, usually the eldest. By contrast, Chinese inheritance practices rest on the importance of maintaining the patrilineage and hence on partible inheritance, with each son receiving an equal share of his father's estate so that each son can establish an independent household. If the father worked to create a single large business, it would almost certainly be broken up and the assets divided (*fenjia*) after his death. A more reasonable strategy would be to start multiple small businesses that could be passed on intact to the sons after the father's death. This inheritance pattern is reinforced by an institutionalized system that creates economies of scope and scale, not from individual firms, but rather from networks of interconnected firms. Businesspeople use these networks, based on reciprocal relationships (*guanxi* networks), to raise investment capital, secure the necessary labor, manufacture products, and distribute commodities.[8] Building and rebuilding these networks creates an economy based on deal-making entrepreneurship.

This type of entrepreneurial economy, composed largely of small and medium-sized family firms linked together through various types of competitive as well as cooperative social relationships, is not conducive to developing heavy industries, certainly not in the nineteenth century. Instead, this household-based economy produced a type of petty commercial capitalism.[9]

You might ask what is capitalistic about the petty commercial practices of the Chinese in the nineteenth century. This would be a good question, because there is nothing essentially capitalistic, in the Western sense of the term, about these practices at all, except for the fact that the Chinese used them very successfully to make a lot of money. In fact, we can trace many of these commercial practices back to economic expansion that occurred during the Ming dynasty. But the fact is that these economic practices were very flexible, did not rely on state patronage, built communities of trust among close colleagues, and were readily adapted to seizing economic opportunities. Founded squarely on institutions of family and locale, these flexible economic practices offered the Chinese their opening, their passageway into a world economy that was just then in the process of becoming globally integrated.

On this score, the record is also absolutely clear. Less than 10 years after the opening of China and the founding of Hong Kong, Chinese peasants, merchants, and artisans began to migrate around the world in search of their fortunes. In absolute terms, this migration was extremely large in its day, probably the largest free migration in the world in the nineteenth century. The migration was widely dispersed throughout the world, although the majority of the migrants went to Southeast Asia. The migration was also, from a comparative perspective, quite extraordinary. It was a temporary migration and, like the economic activity itself, was well organized through fellow-regional relationships. The majority of the emigrants planned to and eventually did return to their hometowns.[10]

By contrast, in this same period, the Japanese hardly migrated at all. The only other country in Asia besides China that produced many migrants in these years was the British colony of India, whose people migrated to other spots in the British empire. The Chinese, however, migrated all over the world wherever money was to be made.

The Chinese searched for gold in California and in Australia in the 1850s and 1860s, and were very successful, but when the mines dried up, they turned to other pursuits, such as digging canals and building railways; they also founded and operated small businesses. However, the Chinese migrated mainly to Southeast Asia. Some Chinese had lived in Siam, Java, and the Philippines for a long time, serving the rulers of those countries as privileged merchants and tax farmers. In the last half of the nineteenth century, these Chinese were now joined by hundreds of thousands of newly emigrating Chinese, who poured into every corner of Southeast Asia. Most were wage laborers, but a sizable minority became very successful businessmen. These Chinese businessmen organized networks of interconnected small firms to collect and process primary products such as timber and rice and to distribute sundry goods throughout the countryside. By the second decade of the twentieth century, the Chinese dominated the service and manufacturing sectors of the local economies throughout the entire region and were major figures in trade between Asian countries and the West.[11]

By the turn of the century, Chinese merchants and small-scale manufacturers largely dominated the most modernized parts of the Chinese economy as well (MacPherson and Yearley 1987). In every sector, except in heavy industry, local Chinese were able to outdo Westerners in the production and sale of consumer products for the Chinese. The Chinese bought very few cars, tractors, or trains, but they did buy a lot of textiles, cigarettes, matches, and small household items. Moreover, with a few notable exceptions, the Chinese controlled banking, retailing, and wholesaling, and by the 1920s, when department stores became important, the Chinese controlled the department stores, too (Chan 1982).

Hong Kong was the center of this capitalist expansion. One observer (Remer 1933: x, cited by Hicks 1993: xxxiii) in the 1930s unambiguously said that Hong Kong was "the economic capital of the overseas Chinese." A small research team at the University of Washington, of which I am a part, is examining the business structure of Hong Kong in the period before and during World War II, in an effort to establish a baseline for Hong Kong's industrialization. We have found that most firms in the 1930s and 1940s were owned by people coming from or still living in districts in the Canton delta, such as Taishan, Nanhai, Zhongshan, and Xinhui. These people jointly owned sets of firms that often included hotels, restaurants, insurance companies, import/export companies, banks, and investment and loan companies—all designed to aid the flow of human and material resources from Guangdong, through Hong Kong, into the rest of the world and then back again.

In the years before World War II, Hong Kong served as a capitalist funnel. Hundreds of thousands of Chinese emigrants from the Guangdong and Fukien hinterlands left from and returned to Hong Kong every year (Hicks 1993: 18–20). Billions of Chinese dollars flowed through Hong Kong banks and remittance centers. Some money left China for investments in distant places, but the larger portion flowed into China in the form of remittances—wages and profits from work performed elsewhere. The money flowing into China fueled the commercialization of South China in the period before World War II.

What is frequently forgotten is the fact that Hong Kong played the same role in the economy of China as it did in the economies of Southeast Asia. In the early twentieth century, organizing their commercial activity largely through Hong Kong, the Cantonese were the largest group of businessmen in Shanghai, and they largely controlled the distribution of imported sundry items throughout China.

While Japan's more or less closed economy was gearing up for the war in Asia, the economies in which the Chinese predominated opened up to global trade. These economic advances occurred in China and in Southeast Asia without the support and coordination of a strong state. In Japan, the state legitimized capitalism, coordinated elite interests, and resolved conflicts among the elites. In the same period in China, the state collapsed. That, however, did not hinder as much as it freed Chinese entrepreneurs to create networks that spanned political boundaries and worked despite, not because of, politics. The weakening and ultimate defeat of the Chinese state opened commerce and industry on the China coast and connected the Chinese with capitalist developments elsewhere. Chinese migration resulted from these conditions. Moreover, with the decline, collapse, and disintegration of the Chinese political order, the real forces of Chinese capitalism, the household entrepreneurs, moved to where money could be made—to such safe havens on the coast as Shanghai, Canton, and other treaty ports, and overseas to Southeast Asia, Hawaii, and the American West Coast.

To summarize, then, in the century before World War II, Chinese had integrated themselves into the expanding global economy; they rode the waves of capitalism around the world—in Shanghai, California, Australia, England, the Caribbean, and Southeast Asia. Based upon their flexible networks and hard work, they monopolized selected economic niches in many countries throughout the world. In contemporary terminology, we would say that they monopolized segments of the service sector in the world economy in the late nineteenth and early twentieth centuries. They were retailers, wholesalers, and financiers; they were the world's most prominent capitalist merchant group. Though integrated in and dependent on the global economy, this household-based form of capitalism was independent from any one political order.

On the other hand, after a short period of embracing all things Western, the Japanese elite successfully resisted becoming dependent on international trade. Instead, they created their own internal markets and built their own version of a strong corporate-oriented political economy. They started as industrialists producing for local and regional markets and from there expanded into the service sectors by organizing their own banks and trading companies, and only then did they gradually begin to integrate themselves into the world economy. The Japanese and Chinese responses were separate reactions to the spread of Western imperialism; both were equally capitalistic and both have led historically to distinct trajectories of economic development.

ECONOMIC DEVELOPMENT IN THE SECOND HALF
OF THE TWENTIETH CENTURY

In a rather schematic way, I have described the patterns of capitalist development in Asia before World War II. Now I want to ask, did World War II end these trajectories? Or despite the interruption caused by the war, have these trajectories resumed in the last half of the twentieth century? I want to offer here an answer to these questions by listing five observations concerning post-war development that point to the resumption of the two trajectories of development.

First, if we think historically, it is clear that the Japanese pre-war capitalist trajectory quickly reasserted itself after the war. Japan was able to restore its form of capitalism because it was able to restore its political economy. The Japanese economy was rebuilt in the 1950s. The Cold War forced the United States to see Japan as its primary ally in East Asia and support its economic reconstruction. Shortly after the American occupation ended, the new Japanese government, centered on administrative agencies, began to refurbish Japanese-style capitalism by rebuilding a system of political economy in tune with the world as it existed in the post-war era.

One of the first steps of this administrative government was to create a new industrial structure. The American occupation forces had outlawed and disbanded the family-centered enterprise groups, the pre-war zaibatsu, by making each firm in the group independently owned and eliminating the family-owned holding company at the center of each group. But shortly after occupation ended, with the blessings of the Japanese bureaucracy, the firms in the former zaibatsu renewed their economic alliances and created a new system of business groups without family ownership. Capitalizing on opportunities presented by the Korean War and the Cold War, these enterprise groups, often referred to as the *keiretsu*, worked hand-in-hand with the government and quickly resumed their economic domination over the domestic economy.[12] The huge production networks that resulted from these alliances manufactured products that would sell both domestically and internationally. By the mid-1980s, the sales of the largest firms in these enterprise groups alone represented 81 percent of Japan's gross domestic product (Hamilton, Zeile, and Kim 1989). In the 1980s, sheltered by an umbrella provided by the state, the manufacturing *keiretsu* led the Japanese form of capitalism to a world prominence that it had never enjoyed before the war.

My second observation is that whereas the Japanese state easily rebuilt Japan's corporate capitalism, the entrepreneurial base of Chinese capitalism was much more difficult to restore quickly for very obvious reasons. The first 35–year period, from 1945 to 1980, was one of intense political change in Asia. With the exceptions of Hong Kong, Thailand, and a few Himalayan kingdoms, every location in Asia in the decade after World War II not only had new governments but also new forms of government. For most locations, direct colonial rule ended and independence was declared. China, of course, received its new government through revolution, and Japan through defeat and occupation. Whatever their forms, however, new governments never have an easy time. Civil wars occurred in Korea and Vietnam, and rebellions, coups d'état, repressions, and insurgencies were the rule elsewhere.

This political turmoil caused two major changes in the way Chinese entrepreneurs were able to do business. First, the greatest change in the immediate postwar period came as a consequence of the Chinese revolution. In pre-war days, the Chinese mainland, even more than Japan, had been the core of Asia's integration into the global economy. Hong Kong and Shanghai were at the center of this core. Suddenly, the Communist Revolution cut off the mainland, economically and politically, from the rest of the world.

A second and equally important change came with the dismantling of colonial rule in East and Southeast Asia. Throughout pre-war Asia, colonial connections had driven many lines of trade and manufacturing in which the Chinese were directly or indirectly involved. The war and its political aftermath destroyed these trade patterns. The leaders of new nations wanted new economies that were separated from colonial dependencies. Following the economic thinking of the time that recommended import substitution, most of these new leaders tried to create their own largely independent domestic economies. These leaders nationalized many industries and started numerous other state-owned or state-controlled enterprises. They also tried to create classes of domestic industrialists. They tried to regulate and organize the flow of economic activities within their own borders. Therefore, by the end of the 1950s, pre-war commercial connections had mostly been severed, and new ones had not yet formed.

The Japanese war, decolonialization in Southeast Asia, and the communist revolution on the mainland had essentially destroyed the commercial capitalism of the pre-war period. Therefore, with only one exception, the Chinese living outside the PRC in Asia between 1945 to the early 1960s came under intense pressure to nationalize their economic and political interests. Governments throughout the region watched the activities and questioned the loyalties of first-, second-, and sometimes third-and fourth-generation Chinese businessmen. In the first 30 years after the war, throughout almost the entire region, Chinese entrepreneurialism was directly challenged and channeled by changing political fortunes in the post-war period.

My third observation is that Hong Kong was the only exception to this rule during the immediate post-war period, and it is in Hong Kong that Chinese entrepreneurialism first reemerged as an independent force in world capitalism. The normal explanation for Hong Kong's post-war industrialization is its extraordinary post-war circumstances. Immediately after the war, the British colonial government tried to resume business as usual in a very unusual time. By 1950, virtually all economic exchanges with the mainland came to an end, and Hong Kong ceased to be an entrepôt. But, as if to compensate for this sudden end to trade, Hong Kong found itself awash in money, laborers, and entrepreneurs. In the 1950s, investment money, some fleeing from China before the revolution and some remittances from Southeast Asia that were cut off from entering China, arrived and stayed in Hong Kong. Refugees escaping communist domination built squatter settlements all over the colony, thus supplying a low-wage labor force. And some prominent entrepreneurs from Shanghai moved their factories there. Most people argue that this combination of factors allowed Hong Kong to quickly shift its economy from that of trading entrepôt to industrial enclave.

Although these resources certainly contributed to rapid growth, let me argue that the underlying reason for Hong Kong's industrialization was Chinese commercial entrepreneurialism, a resumption of Chinese involvement in the world economy. Chinese businessmen in Hong Kong had to find markets for products that were or could be produced in a small enclave cut off from normal trade patterns and with no natural resources other than its people. Unlike Japan, Hong Kong, even in the earliest stages of post-war growth, did not have sufficient local markets to consume the goods produced in its factories. As Wong Siu-lun (1988: 74) notes in his seminal study on the Shanghai industrialists in Hong Kong, marketing was always the biggest problem faced by textile manufacturers, so important in fact that factory owners themselves or their closest representatives "usually traveled in person to look for potential markets and to negotiate face-to-face with their clients."

The markets that Hong Kong entrepreneurs found were part of and integral to a rapidly changing global economy. Fueled by post-war consumerism in the United States and Europe, department stores and "dime stores" were springing up all over both regions and were offering "ready-to-wear" clothes, toys, simple electrical appliances, and other fairly inexpensive household items. Using their commercial know-how and a lot of hard work, Hong Kong entrepreneurs began to link up with what Gary Gereffi (1993) calls the "big buyers," purchase agents who represented large retail and wholesale firms in the West, such as Sears, Montgomery Ward, J.C. Penney, Marks and Spencer, and the Bon Marché.

This pattern of doing business began with rattan furniture, plastic flowers, and textiles, but was soon repeated with a broad range of household non-durable consumer goods—garments, watches, toys, transistor radios, you name it (Turner 1993,

1996). The firms manufacturing these items were modest in size, tiny compared to production networks in Japan, and they were not organized in huge industrial configurations. Rather, grouped often in small, loosely organized subcontracting networks that were reminiscent of pre-war commercial networks, Hong Kong firms became the manufacturing links in long commodity chains that began in the West with designs, orders, and specifications, and ended back in the West with marketing, retail, and consumption.

These buyer-driven commodity chains overwhelmingly originated in the United States, Great Britain, and Germany. The trade statistics show this pattern very clearly. Throughout the decade of the 1950s, export trade with the United States and Europe was at a very low level and was steady or declining slightly. The upward trajectory of export trade started in 1961 and has grown rapidly since that time. But until the early 1980s, the export trade of Hong Kong was overwhelmingly accounted for by trade with just three countries: the United States, Great Britain, and Germany. In 1975, for instance, the United States, Great Britain, and Germany alone accounted for nearly 60 percent of Hong Kong's total exports. In the same year, Hong Kong's exports to Japan accounted for only 4.2 percent, Singapore for 2.7 percent, and Taiwan for less than 1 percent (Cheng 1985: 177).

The old Southeast Asian-centered trading patterns had vanished, and a new set of trading patterns had appeared. But despite these changes, continuity in organization and control remained. Hong Kong entrepreneurs let the markets pull products. Networks of small firms hunted for and then responded to that market demand (Turner 1996). Such a system of commercial capitalism is very different than the Japanese form of capitalism in which large manufacturing corporations create products and push those products into markets. The Japanese system is demand-creating, and Chinese system is demand-responsive.

My fourth observation is that while Chinese entrepreneurs in Hong Kong began to reconnect with the global economy, Chinese entrepreneurs in Singapore and Taiwan were still embedded in nationalist regimes. In other words, Hong Kong was exceptional, but Singapore and Taiwan were not, at least not until about a decade later. It was not until Singapore declared independence in 1965 that there was any long-term security for Chinese economic interests anywhere in Southeast Asia. Remember that between 1959 and 1968, the anti-Chinese pogroms occurred in Indonesia, and as late as 1969, race riots occurred in Malaysia. The Chinese in Southeast Asia everywhere lived under the shadow of nationalist politics at least until the 1970s, and some still do today.

Perhaps for this reason, when political officials in Singapore initially formed their industrial policy, they elected not to encourage Singapore's own Chinese entrepreneurs. Instead, they decided to develop many state-owned enterprises and to encourage a broad range of multinational firms from the United States, Europe, and Japan to build manufacturing and service operations in Singapore.

On Taiwan, the great majority of the Chinese—the Taiwanese Chinese—also came under intense pressure to nationalize their interests, but since Taiwan was ruled by the Chinese, the ethnic dynamic in Taiwan was to be Chinese rather than something else. In the 1950s, however, Taiwan's import substitution policies blocked most attempts by local businesspeople to trade beyond state boundaries.[13] It was not until the early 1960s that this pattern began to change, and when it did, the initial entrepreneurial linkages were with Japanese trading groups and Japanese manufacturers.[14] For a time, Taiwanese manufacturing firms served as the subcontracting ends of the production networks of Japanese business groups, which is a very different position in the global economy from the one assumed by Hong Kong firms.

My fifth and final observation is that it was not until the early to mid-1980s that the entrepreneurial foundations of Chinese capitalism were fully reestablished outside the People's Republic of China. In the late 1970s, political stability came to the core countries of Southeast Asia—Thailand, Malaysia, Indonesia, and Singapore. All of them began to relax their economic nationalism. At the same time, mainland China started its economic reforms and opened its economy to outsiders. Soon thereafter, China and Southeast Asia began to attract huge amounts of direct foreign investment. Much of this investment came from firms in Japan, Taiwan, and Hong Kong, all of whom were looking for cheaper sources of labor and other economic advantages.

These crisscrossing investments were fueled by a new retail revolution that was occurring worldwide, fueled by the development of mall shopping, super discount stores, and brand name merchandisers such as the Gap, the Limited, Nike, Reebok, Dell Computers, and Mattel Toys, all of whom were manufacturers without factories. Computerized inventory systems, rapid sea and air transportation, and saturation advertising accompanied these trends in mass merchandising.

Chinese entrepreneurs quickly took advantage of these new opportunities. They manufactured the newest products, bought the choicest real estate, and made the best deals of anyone doing business in Asia. The new Chinese entrepreneurs from Taiwan, Hong Kong, and Southeast Asia were no longer petty capitalists and no longer bound by considerations of region and lineage.

Their success in Hong Kong, Taiwan, and Southeast Asia came quickly in part because they were economically the most agile and the most mobilized segments of the population. Often Western-educated, they recognized the opportunities presented by changing political and economic environments. Their success allowed them to assume positions of great economic power in their home economies. In Hong Kong, the deal-making Chinese entrepreneurs bought out most of the British hongs. In Taiwan, the private firms owned by ethnic Taiwanese eclipsed the state- and party-owned firms. Throughout Southeast Asia, the ethnic Chinese gained control of the most dynamic sectors of the economy. Chinese entrepreneurs became the super capitalists of Asia.

Hong Kong is again at the center of this capitalist development. Hong Kong's manufacturing base is now in Guangdong, and Hong Kong is again the capitalist funnel through which human and material resources move into and out of China. The largest investors in China are from the Chinese-dominated economies outside of China: Hong Kong, Taiwan, and Singapore. Until the Asian business crisis, the largest multinational firm in Thailand, the Chaeron Pokphand Group, an enterprise group owned and controlled by ethnic Chinese, was also the largest single investor in China and they may still be today, although the investment picture in China is less distinct than it was before the crisis began.

Unlike the pre–World War II period, the Chinese state is resurgent, but the Communist regime, for all its bravado, is quickly and surely losing control of the economic activities of Chinese local society. The tension, even the contradiction, exists between the regime at the center and the authority vested in local institutions (Wank 1998). If the accounts of Chinese development are correct, then it seems, once again, that the state continues to contribute much less, and local society much more, to capitalist expansion. Moreover, the commercialization and industrialization of China is being aided by money flowing in from Chinese living outside of China. In shape, if not in substance, the capitalist trajectories of Asia have returned to their pre–World War II forms.

Hong Kong is now a part of China and has begun the 50-year experiment of "one country, two systems." I, of course, do not know what is going to happen as a result of this protracted political experiment. But I will confidently predict that the change in Hong Kong's sovereignty will not bring an end to the trajectory of Chinese-led capitalism that I have described in this paper. Nor do I think it will mark a new beginning. The past is too much with us for that.

NOTES

An earlier version of this paper was presented in the "Hong Kong Lectures on Business and Culture" at the University of Hong Kong, 7 October 1995.

1. In this section, I draw freely from my earlier essay "Overseas Chinese Capitalism" (Hamilton 1996).

2. I should perhaps qualify this statement by noting that while China lost all its wars with outside powers, it continued to have some success in battles in inner Asia.

3. Taiwan's government has tried to create automobile exports but has had no success to date, even though there are a number of automobile-producing firms in

Taiwan. On Taiwan's automobile industry, see Noble (1987).

4. One of the first statements of this point was made by Alexander Gerschenkron (1962) and one of the most recent by Alice Amsden (1989).

5. For additional background on the formation of capitalism in Japan, see Garon (1987), Samuels (1987), Smith (1959), and Westney (1987).

6. A classic statement of the relationship between enterprise and family is found in Fei (1992: chap. 12); also see references in Gary G. Hamilton and Wang Zheng's, introduction to Fei's book (Fei 1992: 1–34).

7. This point needs further research. For useful beginnings in this direction, see Wong Siu-lun (1985) and Redding (1990).

8. For more on the importance of personal relationship in business, see relevant chapters in Hamilton (1991).

9. Yen-p'ing Hao (1986) characterizes the late imperial economy as "commercial capitalism." The term is adequate for the nineteenth century because a great deal of the economic expansion that occurred then in China was indeed commercial and not industrial. But the term "commercial capitalism" is inadequate now because although similar family principles and types of networks are still being used, employed in putting together small firms to manufacture industrial products, for instance garments in the hinterland of Hong Kong and bicycles and computer components in Taiwan.

10. For an excellent discussion of Chinese migration in the pre-war period, see Hicks (1993).

11. The literature on the Chinese in Southeast Asia is substantial. A basic text, though quite old, is still Purcell (1965). Also see Skinner (1957), Wickberg (1965); Lim and Gosling (1983), and most recently, Wang (1991).

12. For a discussion of the dissolution of the *zaibatsu* during the American occupation, see Hadley (1970). For a discussion of the state's role in restoring Japan's political economy, see Johnson (1982).

13. In the 1950s the Taiwanese state pursued a policy of import substitution, first by nationalizing Japanese-owned firms in agriculture and manufacturing and later by creating new firms for steel and petroleum production. The state also promoted private sector production, largely for local markets, in critical import-substitution industries, such as textile and chemical production. The state also controlled exports.

14. Before the war, Japan relied on agricultural products from Taiwan. In the 1950s, Japanese trading groups reestablished these ties with Taiwanese-owned firms. Serving buyers of Taiwan's products for the Japanese market, these groups soon expanded the range of goods that they traded. In the same period, a group of Taiwanese manufacturers began subcontract production for firms in Japanese enterprise groups, firms including Toshiba, Sony, Sharp, and Matsushita. Such Taiwanese firms as Tatung and Sampo began by assembling, or manufacturing parts for, household electronics products, primarily radios and TVs. Today one of Taiwan's largest producers of consumer electronics, Tatung, is under license from

Toshiba. Sampo, another of Taiwan's largest makers of consumer electronics, produced parts for Sony and Sharp. Matsushita, Japan's largest maker of household electronic products, started an independent firm and sponsored subcontracting and product assembly networks in Taiwan in the early 1960s. A look at Taiwan's export and import trade statistics demonstrates this link to Japan. In 1955, Japan received 59 percent and North American 4 percent of Taiwan's total exports. Ten years later, in 1965, Taiwan producers still sent 30 percent of all their total exports to Japan and only 21 percent to North America. It was not until 1967 that United States passed Japan as the leading buyer of Taiwan's products. The import statistics are equally revealing. Taiwan has run a very large trade deficit with Japan every year since 1960. In fact, since record keeping began in 1952, Japanese imports have always ranged between 20 and 40 percent of Taiwan's total imports. For a discussion of the Japanese role in Taiwan's early industrialization, see Gold (1986).

REFERENCES

Amsden, Alice. 1989. *South Korea and Late Industrialization.* New York: Oxford University Press.

Chan, Wellington K. K. 1982. "The Organizational Structure of the Traditional Chinese Firm and Its Modern Reform," *Business History Review* 56, no. 2 (Summer): 218–235.

Cheng Tong Yung. 1985. *The Economy of Hong Kong.* Rev. ed. Hong Kong: Far East Publications.

Fei Xiaotong. 1992. *From the Soil: The Foundations of Chinese Society.* Berkeley: University of California Press.

Feuerwerker, Albert. 1958. *China's Early Industrialization.* Cambridge, Mass.: Harvard University Press.

Garon, Sheldon. 1987. *The State and Labor in Modern Japan.* Berkeley: University of California Press.

Gereffi, Gary. 1993."The Organization of Buyer-Driven Global Commodity Chains: How U.S. Retail Networks Shape Overseas Production Networks," in *Commodity Chains and Global Capitalism*, edited by Gary Gereffi and Miguel Korzeniewicz, pp. 95–122. Westport, Conn.: Greenwood Press.

Gerschenkron, Alexander. 1962. *Economic Backwardness in Historical Perspective.* Cambridge, Mass.: Harvard University Press.

Gold, Thomas B. 1986. *State and Society in the Taiwan Miracle.* Armonk, N.Y.: M. E. Sharpe.

Hadley, Eleanor. 1970. *Anti-Trust in Japan.* Princeton: Princeton University Press.

Hamashita, Takeshi. 1988. "The Tribute Trade System and Modern Asia," *Memoirs of the Research Department at the Toyo Bunko* 46; 1–25.

Hamilton, Gary G. 1996. "Overseas Chinese Capitalism," pp. 328–342 in *The Confucian Dimensions of Industrial East Asia*, edited by Tu Wei-ming,

Cambridge, Mass.: Harvard University Press.

Hamilton, Gary G., William Zeile, and Wan-Jin Kim. 1989. "The Network Structures of East Asian Economies," in *Capitalism in Contrasting Cultures*, edited by Stewart Clegg and Gordon Redding, pp. 105–129. Berlin: Walter de Gruyter.

Hamilton, Gary, ed. 1991. *Business Networks and Economic Development in East and Southeast Asia*. Hong Kong: Centre of Asian Studies, University of Hong Kong.

Hao Yen-p'ing. 1986. *The Commercial Revolution in Nineteenth-Century China*. Berkeley: University of California Press.

Hicks, George L, ed. 1993. *Overseas Chinese Remittances from Southeast Asia, 1910–1940*. Singapore: Select Books.

Johnson, Chalmers. 1982. *MITI and the Japanese Miracle*. Stanford: Stanford University Press.

Kuo Ting-Yee, and Liu Kwang-Ching. 1978. "Self-Strengthening: the Pursuit of Western Technology," in *The Cambridge History of China, Late Ch'ing 1800–1911*, Part One, Volume 10, edited by John K. Fairbank, pp. 537–542. Cambridge: Cambridge University Press.

Li Chien-nung. 1967. *The Political History of China, 1840–1928*. Stanford, Calif.: Stanford University Press.

Lim, Linda, and L. A. Peter Gosling, eds. 1983. *The Chinese in Southeast Asia*. 2 volumes. Singapore: Maruzen Asia.

Liu Kwang-Ching. 1962. *Anglo-American Steamship Rivalry in China, 1862–1874*. Cambridge, Mass.: Harvard University Press.

MacPherson, Kerrie L, and Cliffon K. Yearley. 1987. "The 2-1/2 % Margin: Britain's Shanghai Traders and China's Resilience in the Face of Commercial Penetration," *Journal of Oriental Studies* 25, no.2: 202–234.

Morikawa, Hidemasa. 1992. *Zaibatsu, The Rise and Fall of Family Enterprise Groups in Japan*. Tokyo: University of Tokyo Press.

Noble, Gregory. 1987. "Contending Forces in Taiwan's Economic Policymaking," *Asian Survey* 27, no. 6 (June): 683–704.

Purcell, Victor. 1965. *The Chinese in Southeast Asia*. London: Oxford University Press.

Redding, S. Gordon. 1990. *The Spirit of Chinese Capitalism*. Berlin: Walter de Gryuter.

Remer, C. F. 1933. *Foreign Investments in China*. New York: Macmillan.

Samuels, Richard J. 1987. *The Business of the Japanese State*. Ithaca, N.Y.: Cornell University Press.

Skinner, G. William. 1957. *Chinese Society in Thailand*. Ithaca, N.Y.: Cornell University Press.

Smith, Thomas C. 1959. *The Agrarian Origins of Modern Japan*. Stanford: Stanford University Press.

Tu Weiming, Milan Hejtmanek, and Alan Wachman, eds. 1991. *The Confucian*

World Observed, A Contemporary Discussion of Confucian Humanism in East Asia. Honolulu, Hawaii: The East-West Center.

Turner, Matthew. 1993. "Ersatz Design: Interaction between Chinese and Western Design in Hong Kong 1950s–1960s." Unpublished Ph.D. dissertation, Royal College of Art, London.

Turner, Matthew. 1996. "Hong Kong Design and the Roots of Sino-American Trade Disputes," *The Annals of the American Academy* 547 (September): 37–53.

Wang Gungwu. 1991. *China and the Chinese Overseas*. Singapore: Times Academic Press.

Wank, David L. 1998. *Commodifying Communism: Markets, Trust, and Politics in a South China City*. Cambridge: Cambridge University Press.

2 / Localism and the Organization of Overseas Migration in the Nineteenth Century

EDGAR WICKBERG

By 1900 at least 3 million Chinese lived outside China, 90 percent of them in Southeast Asia. Overseas settlement was not a new story for the Chinese. Migration within Asia was centuries old. But nineteenth-century migration was much larger in volume than before, and it included several new destinations outside Asia. Between 1840 and 1900, an estimated 2.4 million Chinese traveled to Southeast Asia, the Western Hemisphere, and Australia/New Zealand. By century's end, the overwhelming number were still in Southeast Asia, but over 250,000 lived elsewhere: perhaps 30,000 in Australia/New Zealand, 90,000 in the United States, 15,000 in Canada, substantial numbers in Peru and Cuba, and smaller numbers in South Africa and parts of Europe.[1] The other new development in Chinese overseas migration in the decades after 1850 was its jumping-off and return point, which increasingly came to be Hong Kong.

Why this great emigration push and why these destinations? In China by the nineteenth century a combination of internal and external pressures had become severe. Internally, three centuries of rapid and sustained population growth had put increasing pressure on the cultivable land stock of this basically agricultural country. Commerce had grown apace, but there was no breakthrough: An industrial revolution that might have given employment to displaced peasants did not happen. Added to this was a new external force: the Opium Wars of the mid-nineteenth century brought an unwilling China into the capitalist world system. The combination of these internal and external pressures, and the growing inability of the Chinese government to handle them, led to severe dislocation, especially in coastal China. The Taiping Rebellion and other massive sociopolitical upheavals cost millions of lives and devastated large areas of East and Southeast China. Those who survived sought opportunity by migrating overseas.

Overseas opportunities—the new ones, at least—took the form of demand for large numbers of laborers to work in mines and plantations and to build railroads. In Southeast Asia, colonial rulers responded to the demands of industrialized economies elsewhere by attempting to become more systematic producers of goods for export—whether agricultural or mineral. In the Western Hemisphere, territorial expansion over continental land masses engendered huge railroad-building projects.

Two migration systems were designed to meet these demands (Sing-wu Wang 1978). One was the contract, or so-called "coolie labor," system, which supplied labor to plantations and mines, principally in Southeast Asia and Latin America. The other was the "credit ticket" system, used for most other kinds of migrants. In the first, laborers were recruited on contract to work for specific time periods; their passage to and from the work-site country was paid by the contractor. Non-Chinese were usually the ultimate contractors in the country of destination, but Chinese usually served as the immigration brokers and recruiters on the China coast. This trade, which flourished from 1840 to 1870, led to shameful abuses: recruitment by deception, high mortality rates aboard overcrowded ships, and ill treatment in the country of destination. The Chinese themselves contemptuously called it a "pig trade." Eventually, through international negotiation, the trade came to an end. Although this form of migration carried a large portion of the migrants for a time, it served only certain areas of the Diaspora, and, over the whole nineteenth century, more migrants went via the credit ticket system. In this system a prospective employer or relative—the latter frequently already overseas—paid for ship passage, which was to be worked off after arrival at the new destination. In addition to these two major migration systems, a third method, chain migration, is often mentioned. In this version, a single male member of a family who had established himself abroad sent for a teenaged son or nephew or took one back with him after one of his own periodic visits to China; or, alternatively, an old emigrant returned to his native village to recruit new migrants (Chan 1986: 11–12; Wickberg 1965: 172).

Mention of the family recalls how important kinship—and home locality—were to the overseas migration of Chinese. Migration—even within China itself (and there was a long history of that)—was a common strategy used by families to cope with hard times or improve family fortunes. Within China, single males migrated and sojourned elsewhere, then commonly sent back remittances. Migration might be to nearby towns or to near or distant cities. Thus, within China, a basic pattern was set—one of single-male rural-to-urban movement, sojourning, and remittance sending. Moreover, once in an alien environment, it was localism, or common native-place ties, that drew together sojourners from the same place into mutual aid organizations (Honig 1992: 7; Rowe 1984: chap. 7). These two patterns were repeated for most migrants overseas right up to the post–World War II era. overseas migration usually occurred from rural China to an urban site overseas.

Most Chinese overseas migrants of the nineteenth century were rural peasants from the provinces of Fujian and Guangdong on the southeast coast of China. These people had a long history of migration within China and especially overseas. The latter was an outgrowth of their local economies. Arable land was in short supply and population was crowded on it. Hence, overseas trade went back many centuries. As a Fujian gazetteer put it, "The fields are few but the sea is vast; so men have made fields from the sea" (Cushman 1993; frontispiece). Asian and non-Asian traders had long visited Fujian and Guangdong ports; and seagoing junks from these provinces ranged up the coast of China, east to Japan, and south and west to the Malay Peninsula and beyond. By the sixteenth century, about 10 counties in Fujian had developed a regular practice of overseas migration as a family and locality strategy. By the nineteenth century many localities had economies that were dependent on fishing, overseas trading, and remittances from family members overseas (Lin et al. 1993: 228; Ng 1983, 1990; Skinner 1957: 123–24; Wickberg 1965: 71 n., 172, 226–27; Zhuang 1958).

Families were not the only beneficiaries of overseas migration. In Fujian and Guangdong families were almost always a part of localized kinship organizations or lineages (zu). These were bodies of anywhere from a few hundred to several thousand members who shared descent from a common male ancestor. This ancestral principle was the basis of their corporate ownership of property, sponsorship of education and welfare for members, and ritual and other collective activities. By the nineteenth century, local lineages competed with one another for local prestige, wealth, and power (Freedman 1979: 341). Thus, though lineages did not necessarily finance overseas migration, the earnings of overseas members were of interest to them.[2] A migrant overseas, having satisfied his obligations to his own family, might send additional surplus to be used for local amenities or assets that would benefit the lineage. Contributions to the construction of a new lineage ancestral hall might come from that source, as indeed they do in the 1990s.

In short, then, nineteenth-century overseas migration was not merely a short-term response to current demands; it was also an expansion of long-established practices for the families of coastal Fujian and Guangdong, the lineages to which they belonged, and the localities in which they lived. By the nineteenth century, many such localities had become "emigrant communities" (Chen 1940), heavily dependent upon remittances from members overseas. They were also centers of outward orientation and familiarity with the outside world. The peasants of these regions had, in effect, received preparation for life overseas through information brought back by family members or others from their locality.

A migrant left his village for a nearby port city. In earlier centuries, when emigrants traveled only on Chinese junks, ports of embarkation were numerous (Cushman 1993: chap. 2; Ng 1983, Ng 1990: chap 2; Skinner 1957: 41–42). But a new system came into being as a result of the Opium War. China's defeat in that war opened up the coast to Western trade and residence on terms essentially dictated by the victorious British. Five ports were to be opened by treaty (hence, the "Treaty Ports") to Western trade and residence. These now became centers of business development. Western square-rigged vessels—and later, by the 1870s, steamships—ran passenger lines from the Treaty Ports to Southeast Asia, which Chinese migrants now began to use. The Treaty Port cities were also a cultural twilight zone between the outside world and the Chinese interior. Their business methods and way of life were a mixture of Chinese and Western (Hao 1970; Hao 1986; Murphey 1974). As colonial cities simultaneously developed in Southeast Asia, along partly Western and partly Asian lines, there was a kind of commonality between them and China's Treaty Ports. Migrating Chinese who had been to a Treaty Port already had an idea of what they would encounter in a port city in Southeast Asia. Of the five original Treaty Ports—Shanghai, Ningbo (Ningpo), Fuzhou (Foochow), Xiamen (Amoy), and Guangzhou (Canton)—two (Fuzhou and Xiamen) became major ports for overseas migration. Fuzhou took the smaller number of emigrants who left from counties in Northern Fujian. Xiamen took the major flow of South Fujianese, or Hokkiens. Guangzhou's possible role was largely preempted by the establishment of Hong Kong.

HONG KONG: THE CENTER OF DEMARCATION

Added to the Treaty Ports was the new port of Hong Kong. The island of Hong Kong became a British possession in 1842 as a result of the Opium War. In subsequent years, the Kowloon Peninsula was added and, in 1898, and only by 99-year lease, the then rural New Territories were added. Hong Kong, now a free port, became both the major port on the South China coast and the transshipment and distribution point between Southeast Asian and East Asian trade. It was in this entrepôt role that Hong Kong flourished. So important did it become that ships carrying passengers and goods to one or another of the Treaty Ports almost invariably stopped at Hong Kong. Hong Kong was like a Treaty Port on a grander scale. It became a kind of home base and communications center for Chinese who had gone abroad. In Hong Kong the leading Chinese merchants set up a number of charitable institutions for the Chinese population. One of these, the Tung Wah Hospital, also took on the job of being the informal communications conduit between the Chinese Diaspora of the day and officials in China. When Chinese overseas donated money for famine relief and other causes in China, the Tung Wah collected the funds. When overseas Chinese leaders sought independent and informed Chinese advice on their affairs and China's, they found it at the Tung Wah.

Elderly Chinese overseas who hoped to be buried in their native locality could be assured that the Tung Wah would handle it (Sinn 1989; Wickberg 1965: 216).

When a non-contract migrant went abroad, he typically began by working for someone else—either someone to whom he was indentured or else a relative. If all went well, this could be a kind of apprenticeship. After learning a trade, he might then be able to go out on his own. Working for oneself—not for others—was a characteristic desire of Chinese migrants. A job with less income might be preferable if it meant being one's own boss. If the employer were the owner of a large shop or other business in Southeast Asia (a *towkay*), he might give a line of credit and the opportunity to run a branch operation to the erstwhile apprentice.(Wickberg 1965: 72–74, 176). Whatever the case, much depended upon hard work, frugality, and good fortune. Though actually derived from their Southeast Asian experience, these virtues of hard work, frugality, and the associated dream of "rags to riches" became inscribed in the thinking of migrants as basic Chinese values (Abraham 1986; 13–14 especially). Few lived the story, but most dreamed it.

Whatever the outcome, a young migrant would at some point return to his home locality to find a bride. Leaving her to care for his parents, he would return to the "field," making periodic trips back to father children, some of whom (sons) would be brought overseas as teenagers. If his business prospered, he might at some point bring his wife and female children as well. But that rarely happened in the nineteenth century, partly because it was not the custom for women to emigrate. In fact, the few women in overseas Chinese societies were usually prostitutes.

In short, overseas Chinese societies of the nineteenth century were, in appearance if not in law, "bachelor societies." Remittances were sent to support families—wives, small children, and elderly dependents waiting in the "emigrant communities." But retirement to one's native locality in China was an ideal. If that could not be achieved in life, then, as indicated above, one's bones should be buried in home ground if financially possible. Chinese are a great migrating people but, paradoxically, also one with a strong sense of home place and a desire for rootedness.

DESIGNATION: SOUTHEAST ASIA

Southeast Asia, or the Nanyang (South Seas), was always the major destination for overseas migrants from China. Routes of migration in the nineteenth century were partly traditional but partly the result of modifications caused by economic and technological changes. Five regional and dialect-based groups of Chinese migrated to the Nanyang. The Hokkiens, from southern Fujian, were the earliest, settling in substantial numbers in Manila and Batavia (Jakarta) by the early seventeenth century. By the eighteenth century, members of the other four groups were also migrating. These were the Teochiu (Chaozhou) from eastern coastal Guangdong, the Hakka from highland regions in eastern Guangdong, the Cantonese from a dozen counties around and to the west of the Pearl River delta, and the Hailam, or Hainanese, from the island of Hainan off the Guangdong coast. Teochiu and Hakka exited via Swatow (Shantou) at the mouth of the Han River Delta, and Hainanese from ports on that island. Cantonese usually did not embark from Guangzhou; Macau had been the emigration port for some time before the nineteenth century. It continued for a time as a coolie trade port, but increasingly, general emigration business was taken over by Hong Kong.

In the countries of destination, the mix of Chinese regional groups varied from one place to another and changed with immigration flows. In 1800, the Chinese population in the Philippines was entirely Hokkien; by the end of the nineteenth century, there was a Cantonese minority of 5–15 percent (Wickberg 1965: 22, 177, 179). In the nineteenth century, the Teochiu attained a majority position in Thailand, much ahead of the other four groups. Cantonese were the leaders in Cambodia (though overwhelmed by Teochius in the twentieth century) and dominated in Vietnam, despite a strong Teochiu presence (Willmott 1967: 17; Skinner 1957: 35-52). Farther west and south, leadership was less discernable. Hokkien continued to enjoy certain linguistic and occupational advantages since they had arrived first. But all five groups were strongly represented in Malaya, Singapore, and Indonesia. Burma's Chinese were Hokkien, Cantonese, and Yunnanese, the last of whom had immigrated across a land border. Everywhere, occupations tended to become monopolies, or a least areas of advantage for one group or another, though which groups dominated which occupations varied among countries. But these classifications were hardly static. Overseas, as in China, dialect-based and more localized groups competed, and sometimes fought, over economic opportunities and advantages.

The range of occupations and economic activities of the Southeast Asian Chinese was extremely broad, as was their contribution to the economies of the area. Besides working as laborers in the nineteenth century, the Chinese were engaged in the China–Southeast Asia trade at both ends. Within their countries of residence they were wholesalers and retailers. They imported and distributed goods from China and elsewhere, and they collected local produce for export abroad. They were a major force in retail trade at all levels. The leaders of local Chinese populations were also the most important merchants, whose activities might include coolie brokerage and revenue farming. This last meant contracting with colonial governments for the lucrative monopoly distribution of opium and alcohol products (Skinner 1996: 80–85; Trocki 1990). Besides these leaders, there were other merchants of descending size and importance. Chinese were also artisans and service providers. The business section of a Southeast Asian city looked very "Chinese."

And guidebooks to Western trade in Southeast Asian ports generally listed the major merchants of the locale with whom the foreigner would be doing business—all Chinese (*Chronicle and Directory* 1873, 1891). In short, Chinese occupied a leading position in the urban economies and their urban-rural networks in Southeast Asian countries.

Although most Chinese were urban, there was an important rural element (Heidhues 1996). Mining and plantation work was, of course, non-urban. But Chinese were also independent farmers—from market gardeners around Manila, Jakarta, and Bangkok to reclaimers of vast tracts of land in parts of Indonesia. Sometimes they worked together in large groups bound by brotherhood-type organizational ties. At other times they farmed as individual small freeholders. In the nineteenth century, Southeast Asia stressed crops for international markets. It was the Chinese who were often the innovators of cash-crop farming, developing such goods as sugar, pepper, gambier, and rubber. This aspect of Chinese enterprise appeared not only in Southeast Asia but was found also in the Sacramento-San Joaquin Valley region of California (Chan 1986). In Southeast Asia, urban and rural came together when urban merchants, most often Hokkien or Teochiu, financed and collected the crops that other Chinese farmers, often Hakkas, produced.

In the colonial parts of Southeast Asia, governments viewed the Chinese with some ambivalence. Governments made use of the Chinese at several levels: at the top, as revenue farmers and trading agents for governments, or at the bottom, as gang labor to develop mines and plantations. The entrepreneurial and general economic value of the Chinese was much appreciated, but at the same time, there was apprehension that the Chinese, if allowed their way beyond a certain point, would simply overwhelm, exploit, and marginalize the less aggressive and economically less sophisticated indigenous people. In some colonies, such as the Philippines and Dutch East Indies (Indonesia), colonial governments applied elaborate rules to restrict certain Chinese activities and limit their contact with non-Chinese. This did not always work as planned. The Dutch limited travel for Chinese in nineteenth-century Indonesia. But in the interests of state revenue, Chinese opium contractors were exempt, thus allowing them to establish long-distance opium distribution networks that became general trading networks (Rush 1990). The Spanish in the Philippines formally organized Chinese and non-Chinese into separate self-regulating bodies. But these broke down in the course of economic growth in the nineteenth century (Wickberg 1965: 30, 135). Beyond a certain point, too, self-governing Chinese were a threat to the late-nineteenth-century colonial goals of greater, more efficient territorial and administrative control. The Dutch fought a war to end the independence of Chinese settlers in West Kalimantan (Borneo). The Spanish allowed the rule of Chinese headmen (*capitanes*) over their fellows, but only with the intervention of a Spanish parish priest. In British Malaya and Singapore, brotherhoods ("secret societies") were brought under control and outlawed, and the independent power of the headman reduced thereby (Skinner 1996: 80–86; Trocki 1990: 161-182).

Local non-Chinese also viewed the Chinese with some ambivalence. They appreciated the innovative contributions of the Chinese in such areas as sugar-processing technology and double-cropping techniques for growing rice. In many regions Chinese were addressed by natives as "uncle," implying respect and perhaps even acceptance of a kind of tutorial relationship.[3] In Vietnam, Chinese immigrants benefited by popular association with the Chinese culture, which was the model for Vietnamese government, and the Chinese language, the written language used by educated Vietnamese. Chinese theater was performed and appreciated by non-Chinese in Vietnam, Cambodia, and Thailand. Farther south, by the last years of the nineteenth century, Chinese historical romances and novels were being translated for non-Chinese readers into Malay and Indonesian (Salmon 1987). But there was also resentment of Chinese economic preeminence and, as nationalism began to develop in Southeast Asia, a growing awareness of Chinese dependence upon colonial rulers for their advantageous economic position. In the Philippines, *intsik*, originally a form of respect when addressing Chinese, became a term of opprobrium. In anti-colonial risings, Chinese sometimes sided with the native peoples. But the feeling grew among the latter that Chinese could not be relied upon because their commitments were seen as strictly family and business related.

For their part, the Chinese brought to Southeast Asia not only their skills and experiences but also a set of Chinese cultural values as had developed in Southeast China by the nineteenth century. These centered on ancestral locality versions of Chinese familism, with emphasis on both ancestry by genealogy and by place. Family prosperity was a major goal and the means were family discipline and mutual support. But along with economic goals were cultural considerations, sharpened by contact with non-Chinese, whose apparent values could easily be contrasted, often negatively, with those the Chinese ascribed to themselves. Chinese brought their religions: Chinese Buddhism in the form of exclusively Buddhist temples and Chinese Popular Religion—a mixture of Buddhism and Popular Taoism—in the form of temples of syncretic religion. Local tutelary deities that protected specific "home" regions in Fujian or Guangdong were imported and given new mandates. But Chinese, in this as in so many other ways, were amazingly adaptable. In the Philippines, many Chinese converted to Catholicism, often identifying Catholic saints or manifestations of the Virgin with Chinese popular deities. Saints' feast days were celebrated with fireworks and Chinese musical groups on parade (Wickberg 1965: 193). In mainland Southeast Asia, where Theravada

Buddhism was strong, Chinese easily adjusted their Mahayana version to fit or simply switched from one to the other. Islam, in Malaya and Indonesia, was more difficult. But some Chinese converted, at least nominally (Reid 1996: 45; Skinner 1996).

Most interesting of all, the Chinese in Southeast Asia, whatever their original intentions, were both sojourners and settlers (Reid 1996). Business was often too successful to abandon for a return to China. But there were also family considerations. Single, Chinese males and indigenous women regularly formed alliances, whether legitimized or not. This was a phenomenon dating back to at least the seventeenth century. By the nineteenth century important and distinct societies of local-born Chinese had developed, intermediate between the Chinese from China and the indigenes. These were locally adapted or creolized groups, and they were found in the Philippines, Indonesia, and British Malaya. The Mestizos of the Philippines, the Peranakans of Indonesia, and the Babas of Malaya had varying historical trajectories. The Mestizos, descendants of Chinese and Filipinas, acquired business skills and opportunities from their fathers but took their religion and much else, culturally, from their mothers. They were Catholic and attracted to Spanish culture, but identified themselves completely with the Philippines. During the nineteenth century they joined the rising Filipino middle class to form the new elite of the Philippines. They thus disappeared as a special class. Peranakans, whose culture was a mix of Indonesian and Chinese with Dutch overtones, remain as a separate, formally defined group down to the present. Babas blended Malay and Chinese with English overtones. They were a much smaller group than the Mestizos and Peranakans, and by the middle years of the twentieth century, they were disappearing. Classified as Chinese by governments, they were being reabsorbed into the Chinese community of Malaysia (Skinner 1996).

Thailand was a different case from those just related. The Chinese there were never part of a colonial society, and until the early years of the twentieth century, they enjoyed great freedom of movement and opportunity. The more successful Chinese were part of the Thai monarchy's business operations and its extensive trade and diplomatic relations with China. Successful Chinese in Thailand intermarried, assumed Thai names, and moved with and into the highest levels of Thai society. The Thai royal dynasty, established late in the eighteenth century, was itself of part-Chinese origin (Skinner 1957).

Of the Chinese in nineteenth-century Southeast Asia, then, we can say that they were deeply and creatively involved everywhere in local economy, society, and culture. They were economically salient as well as socially and culturally influential. But they were politically vulnerable, dependent on their usefulness to governments. Late in the century, as China began to show interest in the Chinese abroad, a way out of that problem seemed to appear. Chinese in Southeast Asia negotiated with China for the establishment of consulates to protect their lives and property in the face of rising anti-Chinese incidents. The Singapore consulate, established in 1877, soon became a consulate-general for all of Southeast Asia. Other consulates would follow in the twentieth century.

DESTINATION: NORTH AMERICA

The second great destination of the nineteenth century was North America, specifically, the United States and Canada. Here the historic, ethnic, and economic situations were totally different from those in Southeast Asia. In both locations, Europeans were taking over new territories and strengthening their control over them. But in the Southeast Asian case that had developed slowly over 200 years or more, the Chinese had acquired a strong position in regional and local economies. When Europeans introduced industrialism in the nineteenth century, the Chinese there were already in an entrenched position, with bases and networks in place to benefit from the new opportunities.

By contrast, in North America, the European frontier met the Chinese frontier on the West Coast of the continent in the 1850s. For a brief interval there were several places on that coast where Chinese were 20 percent or more of the population and an even larger proportion of the labor force (Chan 1986: 42–51; Saxton 1971 3–18, 258; Wickberg et al. 1982: 49; tables 1, 5; Wynne 1964: appendices I, III, V, VIII). But that soon ended. As in Southeast Asia, the Chinese wished only to govern themselves and had no interest in governing non-Chinese. The Europeans, however, wished to control territory and all those in it, and so established European-style governments and laws, to which the Chinese became subject. Some of those laws limited Chinese immigration by excluding Chinese laborers (the American version); others established a head tax to achieve the same end (one Canadian version); and most governments also denied the franchise to all ethnic Chinese, thereby making it difficult for any changes in their favor to occur (Wickberg et al. 1982: chaps. 4–5). Clearly, from the viewpoint of the descendants of immigrants from European shores, Europeans were meant to control western North America, deciding whether or not and on what terms these useful but troublesome "strangers from a different shore" (Takaki 1989) could remain. In British Columbia, the denial of the franchise was shortly followed by rulings of professional societies: persons who could not vote could not qualify to practice dentistry, accountancy, or law in that province (Wickberg et al. 1982: 83). All across western North America, the Chinese were viewed as physically and culturally alien and economically threatening. European labor saw Chinese labor as undercutting them and pointed out the willingness of Chinese to act as strike-breakers in some cases. (There is, however, abundant evidence of Chinese forming their own labor organizations and going on strike because of unfair treatment [Lai 1980: 220; Saxton

1971: 9–10, 104, 215–18; Wickberg et al. 1982: 47, 50, 130–311.) Chinese were treated as a despised minority that could be ridiculed and mistreated without fear of reprisals from mainstream society.

The European frontier, which carried with it industrialism and Western legalism, thus nipped Chinese in the bud, limiting their numbers and making it impossible for them to secure toeholds in most sectors of the new order except for the lowest. As in Southeast Asia, the Chinese were imported because they were considered industrious. But in North America, their willingness to work cheaply came up against militant white labor, a situation for which there was no analogy in Southeast Asia. Southeast Asia was a more attractive frontier for Chinese. It was clearer and easier to get to, Chinese already had established a strong position there, and there was some hope that China's nearness might provide some protection for Southeast Asian Chinese. In the 1880s and 1890s, the new Chinese navy sent out warships to cruise that area (Wickberg 1965: 218–26). Nothing like that could have occurred along the west coast of North America. There, the Europeans could readily bring their economic and military power to bear once the railroads were built (Chan 1986: 39–42).

Ironically, it was Chinese who built much of the railroads that linked the United States and Canada and made it possible for European-derived economic and political power to prevent major Chinese influence on the economy. Railroad building was a second-stage activity of the Chinese immigrant tide. The first-wave members were gold seekers, who arrived in response to the strikes in California and British Columbia and the expectation of additional finds elsewhere in the American West. By the 1860s in the United States and the 1880s in Canada, industrialists recruited Chinese for railroad and other types of manual labor. This recruitment made use of the networks of Chinese already living in North America. Cantonese, who had come from the same dozen counties of Guangdong that had fed Southeast Asian emigration, now recruited other Cantonese, who departed, as had the previous emigrants, via Hong Kong or Macau. Although some came on contracts, the abuses were not comparable to those in Latin America.

But at the end of their contracts, the Chinese often were not sent back, thereby becoming a floating population that drifted to towns, cities, and farmlands, or areas of resource industries, looking for work. Chinese now became active in many stages of the farming, fishing, mining, and forest industries. Like many non-Chinese immigrants to the United States and Canada, they were sojourners at first, moving about from one region and one occupation to another. By the 1880s, they were moving east across the continent, establishing Chinatowns in places like Chicago, Toronto, Montreal, New York, and Boston, to join those already founded in San Francisco, Portland, Victoria, and Vancouver. Chinese occupations were myriad: market gardeners around towns and cities; restaurateurs; factory workers;

miners; cowboys (and cooks for miners and cowboys); and the classic domestic occupations (laundryman and houseboy), all pursuits that neither competed with nor threatened white males. In the American South, the end of slavery brought a brief demand for Chinese plantation labor and led to a scattering of Chinese in that region. These Chinese, like those on the Canadian prairies, often became operators of general stores serving a diverse clientele. Wherever there were concentrations of Chinese, there were Chinatowns, and wherever there were Chinatowns, there were stores established to serve other Chinese, as well as laundries and tailoring shops that might serve non-Chinese (Chan 1986: 51–78; Lai 1980: 219; Royal Commission on Chinese Immigration 1885). The "rags to riches" dream was present, but unrealized—again, quite unlike Southeast Asia, where wealthy Chinese were beginning to appear by 1900. In North America the major merchants were major only in the small and mostly unimportant (California agriculture aside) "ethnic" economy of the Chinese. Leading merchants of Chinatowns imported goods from China only for other Chinese, not for the general public. They were not involved in the export trade to Asia.

The trend of Chinese settlement by 1900 was increasingly from rural to urban. Chinese who worked in the forests, on mining frontiers, or in fishing areas sometimes formed brotherhood organizations ("secret societies"), such as the Zhigongtong (Cheekongtong) in the gold rush settlement of Barkerville in British Columbia. The Zhigongtong organizations, related to the Hongmen tradition from which a variety of "secret societies" or "tongs" sprang up, attempted to control certain kinds of gang labor opportunities, as had similar societies in Malaya (Ownby and Heidhues 1993; Wickberg et al. 1982: 30–35, 92–93). But these societies moved to towns and cities in keeping with the rural-to-urban trend. In Hawaii, contract laborers from one county of Guangdong, brought to work on sugar plantations, completed their contracts and headed for Honolulu (Lai and Ueda 1990: 232). Similarly, Chinese in Peru headed for Lima as soon as they had fulfilled their plantation labor commitments (Wong 1978). Only the Chinese of the Sacramento and San Joaquin valleys remained in agriculture on a large scale, making major contributions to California's agriculture. Unlike Southeast Asia, where Chinese technological and organizational innovations were usually recognized, there is little evidence of such in North America.[4]

The Chinatowns that developed in the cities were quite unlike those in Southeast Asia. In Southeast Asia, Chinatown was the place where everyone shopped. In North America, it was where everyone gambled and sought opium (legal in North America until the early twentieth century). Until 1900, there were almost no Chinese women in North American Chinatowns. But unlike Southeast Asia, that did not result in a large number of intermarriages. By the 1880s, the trend was for Chinese to move from rural to urban sites. The more the Chinese retreated into

Chinatowns from rural areas and small towns, the less contact they had with non-Chinese (Chan 1986: 404–07), and hence the less likelihood of intermarriage. In Southeast Asia, the indigenes were the majority of the population and they were constantly in touch with the Chinese. In North America, aboriginal people were a minority and rarely played an important role in Chinese lives. Given attitudes in the European majority, there was little intermarrying in that direction and no geographical concentration of those who did. The few "creolized" second-generation Chinese in North America who appeared in the twentieth century were the offspring of all-Chinese families and did not form a separate cultural group.

Chinatowns were the focal point of Chinese culture. North America was strictly a Cantonese frontier, so there were no dialect-based regional groups, although there were sub-dialect locality organizations. Language and culture were those of the *seiyap* (Four Counties) region of Guangdong. Chinese religion was expressed more often by shrines in homes and shops than by freestanding temples as in Southeast Asia. Christian churches directed some of their mission work toward local Chinese, who often responded positively. The English lessons taught by churches were often the initial attraction, but the social and religious dimensions of Christianity were also valued (Wickberg et al. 1982: 94–97, 122–28). In the late nineteenth century, anti-Chinese movements and incidents became common in western North America. Europeans tended to view the Chinese as acceptable only for jobs Europeans did not want. Otherwise, they were treated with scorn and ridicule. An abundance of stories documented supposed European superiority. Chinese were labeled "Chink" and "John Chinaman," with accompanying negative stereotypes. Racial and cultural stereotypes and economic and political history combined to produce a multitude of anti-Chinese incidents, many of them violent. These took place in cities, towns, and rural areas, from San Francisco, Los Angeles, Seattle, and Vancouver to Chico (California), Ashland (Oregon) and Rock Springs (Wyoming) (Chan 1986: 39–40, 58, 88; Lai 1980: 220; Saxton 1971: 6–10; Wickberg et al. 1982: 62–63; Wynne 1964: 72, 97–98, and chap. 6).

There was little the Chinese could do to fight against this. North American governments, unlike those in Southeast Asia, derived little revenue or other direct economic benefit from the Chinese. Once major labor needs had been met in the 1880s, governments had little vested interest in protecting the Chinese. China established an embassy in Washington, D.C., in 1875 and a consulate in San Francisco, the latter's mandate informally including western Canada as well as the western United States. The Chinese ambassador to the United States had to deal mostly with Chinese labor and protection issues. Hence he was also put in charge of representing China in Peru and Spain (with reference to Cuba), where similar problems existed. Despite China's weakness and its distance from North America, Chinese diplomats achieved some successes in negotiation, notably indemnities to Chinese for the Rock Springs incident (Yen 1985: 224–234).

SETTLEMENT PATTERNS IN THE EARLY
TWENTIETH CENTURY

In the first half of the twentieth century, Chinese overseas continued to settle increasingly in urban areas. Chinese women began to migrate and family reunions overseas had become common everywhere by the 1930s. In Southeast Asia, intermarriage declined somewhat but continued to be important. The children of all-Chinese families, and often mixed families, too (Indonesian Peranakans excepted), now underwent an experience of re-sinification. The larger number of families—and thereby children—in overseas Chinese societies and China's growing political interest in overseas Chinese led to the establishment of Chinese schools, in which the governments of China took a keen interest. Children of all-Chinese families and those of mixed background attended. The Southeast Asian schools were comprehensive, all-day affairs, teaching academic courses and occupational skills as well as Chinese language and culture. Increasingly they oriented the students toward a presumed future as citizens of a modernizing Chinese nation. By the 1930s, as Japan invaded China, China's leadership urged Chinese schools overseas to put the salvation of China ahead of their local concerns (Akashi 1970; Purcell 1965; Wang 1991: 198–200). Meanwhile, nationalist and independence movements were growing among the indigenous people of colonial Southeast Asia—movements with little room for the Chinese. Even in Thailand, where Chinese could elect to become Thai citizens, as was generally impossible elsewhere, Chinese and non-Chinese were growing apart.

In North America, as Chinese family life developed, much of it was centered on Christian churches. In the United States, the second generation, locally born, were thereby citizens who could claim rights as Americans, whether successfully or not, and could go to court to seek them. In Canada, citizenship (British Subject status) was more complex as to rights possessed and did not become clear-cut until the Canadian Citizenship Act of 1947 (Wickberg et al. 1982: 119, 181, 208–209). In any case, the relevant discriminatory laws were based on race, not nationality. Discrimination continued for both of these second-generation groups.

Theirs was a dual educational experience unlike anything in Southeast Asia. North America's Chinese schools were supplementary, not comprehensive. The after-school Chinese school taught only language and culture. During the normal school day, Chinese children interacted with non-Chinese peers, when they were not segregated. They learned the lessons appropriate to full status in North American society. In the after-school hours they learned, with other Chinese children, the lessons appropriate to their economic and social marginality. One had to learn Chinese language and cultural skills in order to fit into the jobs available to young ethnic Chinese, which were all in Chinatown. Their schooling thus provided lessons in the ideal by day and in reality by night.

Meanwhile, China pulled at the Chinese of North America as it did those of Southeast Asia. For many, a strong, modern China was seen as the only hope of improving opportunities for themselves abroad and for their families in South China. From the last years of the nineteenth century, governments in China increasingly sought to involve the Chinese abroad in the strengthening and modernizing of China. China's Citizenship Law of 1909 claimed ethnic Chinese everywhere as citizens of China. The term "overseas Chinese" entered official usage, implying ultimate political and other commitments to China. After 1912, the republican governments of China encouraged Chinese abroad to invest economically and participate politically in China. Some of China's political parties established branches abroad. Especially effective was the Kuomintang (KMT) of Sun Yat-sen, who was himself a Cantonese with an overseas Chinese background. Much money was raised in overseas Chinese societies in support of Sun's revolutionary movement and subsequent campaigns and causes. The KMT government of post-1928 China paid especial attention to overseas Chinese affairs, including support for overseas Chinese schools. By the 1920s and 1930s Chinese societies abroad were commonly divided into "left" and "right" factions, reflecting the politics of China itself (Wickberg et al. 1982: 74–77, and chaps. 8, 12, 14).

For many Chinese overseas, China's politics were a preoccupation and a kind of distraction. But they also made up one dimension of the reality of Chinese life abroad: uncertain political status wherever they were, which left them in a kind of limbo, caught for a prolonged period between China and their countries of residence. In some ways this problem was more acute for the Chinese of North America. Southeast Asian Chinese were educated in Chinese for a life in which Chinese was the key language of business and signs of Chinese economic salience and business success were everywhere. Discrimination and political marginality were at least partly offset by the fact of economic centrality. North American Chinese youth had the stark contradiction between the ideal and reality thrust in their faces. The language and culture they learned fitted them for a life in a small, marginal part of the economy. And they were just as marginal in every other way: socially, culturally, and politically. Small wonder, then, that when Chinese-American writers emerged after World War II, the historical question they had to address was one of marginality and its causes.

CONCLUSION: CHINESE MIGRATION TODAY

With this historical background, let us now "fast-forward" to the present. As the later chapters in this book will show in more detail, the overseas Chinese we see today are in sharp contrast to those just discussed. Although some are poor, a large number come with substantial assets, which include both money and skills. They arrive on jets from Hong Kong or some other jumping-off place. Although some seek merely reunion with families and have modest hopes of life-success, many come in order to advance careers that are already well begun. Such people need never be restricted to Chinatown and ethnic job–patronage methods of the old sort. Their business and professional skills allow them to participate in the general, cosmopolitan economy. They are not limited to any marginal, ethnic enclave economy. In fact, in some cities, they play a major role in the local economy. Indeed, since the 1970s and 1980s, countries around the world are once again recruiting Chinese, but this time Chinese with the skills and entrepreneurship needed for national success in a technological age.

Chinese now come as families. If a single male goes ahead, he may be a university student who will soon be followed by the rest of the family. Or, more often, wives and children come and are settled abroad first, while the father commutes between their residence and his business interests in Asia. Sojourning still occurs, but now that Chinese communities are made up of families, it is family sojourning. Hopes are not fixed on retirement to native villages in south China. Sojourners are those who are looking ahead to the next country of possible residence if things fail to work out at the present site. Indeed, there are now many Chinese who have lived for a time in more than one locale outside of China. Thus, favored destinations like San Francisco, New York, Sydney, Vancouver, Toronto, and London receive immigrants of this kind. These sojourns offer a rich experience. Rather than being, say, Cantonese who are coming direct from China, these immigrants may be Cantonese who have lived for long stretches in Hong Kong, Johannesburg, and Manila. Where, then, is a "home" to go back to? Even those whose experience has merely been of travelling from Guangdong to Hong Kong and spending several years there are very different from earlier Cantonese migrants. They, or their parents, may have been rural people from Guangdong, but they have spent their lives in urban Hong Kong at a time when it was undergoing tremendous economic growth and cultural changes. Thus, most of the immigration of the past few years is not from rural China to urban overseas city, but from urban (inside or outside of China) to urban.

Because the Chinese who migrate now come not only from China but from all over, with all kinds of experiences, the diversity of overseas Chinese communities has greatly increased. A Hokkien migrating directly from Fujian to Vancouver is very different from a Hokkien Taiwanese migrating to the same place. Both are different again from a Hokkien from the Philippines who has settled in Vancouver, or a Hokkien from Singapore who has reached Vancouver after living in Hong Kong and Taiwan. The Chinese, in short, are a global Diaspora. They are now "from" everywhere, have been everywhere, and have done everything. They still look back to China and send money to aid lineage halls and schools in ancestral districts. But in family terms, they are less likely to send remittances than to bring presents upon visiting ancestral villages, or to try to bring some family members overseas to be with them.

But not all Chinese are in constant motion. On the whole, Southeast Asian Chinese are not. In the post-war era, newly independent ex-colonial states cut off immigration from China. At the same time, the People's Republic restricted emigration and pursued ambivalent and inconsistent policies regarding overseas Chinese. Feeling cut off from China, the Southeast Asian Chinese became true settlers. Though subject to various economic and cultural restrictions, they generally prospered and their younger generations acquired university educations and moved into new professional and business fields, banking and property development in particular. These developments brought on the emergence of a new Chinese middle class able to communicate readily with non-Chinese and increasingly committed to the country of residence. In some places in Southeast Asia, the anti-Chinese laws and practices of the 1950s and 1960s were softened in the 1970s, and everywhere the opening of China to trade and travel brought new opportunities by the 1980s. Thus, Southeast Asia, once the favored destination of emigrants, could not be so in the 1950s-1970s, and by the time it was slightly opened again the changing immigration policies and economies of the major Anglo-Saxon countries were more attractive. It is these countries—Canada, the United States, Australia, New Zealand, and the United Kingdom—that are the most important attractions. Southeast Asia, however, continues to grow in population, due almost entirely to natural increase. It remains the home of over 80 percent of the world's overseas Chinese.

Those 30 million global Chinese represent a tenfold increase in number since 1900. Most of that growth has occurred in the past 25 years, as China has loosened its polices on emigration and return, as well as on investment by overseas Chinese and others. North America is second to Southeast Asia, with perhaps 3 million ethnic Chinese. At the end of World War II, as Euro-American attitudes toward Asians began to soften and grow more positive, Chinese in North America were given new opportunities. That and the growing economy produced, as in Asia, a local-born Chinese middle class. But just at that point, changes in immigration policy brought a flood of new immigrants from Hong Kong and Taiwan who revived the old Chinatowns with their money and attempted to redefine "Chineseness" in North America. Chinese schools had declined, because after 1945 Chinese youth had access to a wide range of "non-Chinese" jobs. But now new language and culture schools are being set up partly for heritage purposes but also to encourage the study of Chinese as a business language.

Hong Kong remains the door into and out of China, as well as a diversified manufacturing, trading, and banking center of global proportions. But more than that, it is the home of a self-created version of modern Chinese popular culture to which Chinese everywhere are attracted. Whatever other values Chinese carry with them as they go abroad or travel from one destination to another, we can be sure that they all look to Hong Kong as an example and model of modern Chinese economic success and as the capital city of modern Chinese culture.

NOTES

1. Estimates are based upon Chan 1986: 43; Lai 1980: 218–23; Lin et al. 1993: 78; Mackie 1996: xxiiii; Price 1974: 277; Wang Sing-wu 1978: 311–14; Wickberg 1965: 61, 169–70, and especially 148 n. 5; Wickberg et al. 1982: 296, 300.

2. Hokkien lineages did often finance overseas trade (Ng 1983: 216).

3. In Vietnam, "uncle" (Purcell 1965: 202, quoting Dennery 1933); in Java, *encik* (Nagtegaal 1996: 233); in the Philippines, *intsik* (Wickberg, personal knowledge).

4. Two exceptions are mentioned in Lai 1980: 219, the most familiar being Ah Bing of Milwaukie, Oregon, developer of the cherry variety that bears his name.

REFERENCES

Abraham, Collin. 1986. "Manipulation and Management of Racial and Ethnic Groups in Colonial Malaysia: A Case Study of Ideological Domination and Control," in *Ethnicity and Ethnic Relations in Malaysia*, edited by Raymond Lee, pp. 1–27. DeKalb, Ill.: Northern Illinois University Center for Southeast Asian Studies, Monograph Series, Occasional Paper No. 12.

Akashi, Yoji. 1970. *The Nanyang Chinese National Salvation Movement, 1937–1941*. Lawrence: University of Kansas Center for East Asian Studies.

Chan Sucheng. 1986. *This Bitter-Sweet Soil. The Chinese in California Agriculture, 1860–1910*. Berkeley: University of California Press.

Chen Ta. 1940. *Emigrant Communities in South China*. New York: Institute of Pacific Relations.

[The] Chronicle and Directory for China, Japan, and.... [title varies] 1873, 1891. Hong Kong: "Daily Press".

Cushman, Jennifer Wayne. 1993. *Fields from the Sea. Chinese Junk Trade with Siam during the Late Eighteenth and Early Nineteenth Centuries*. Ithaca, N.Y.: Cornell University Southeast Asia Program, Studies on Southeast Asia No. 12.

Freedman, Maurice. 1979. *The Study of Chinese Society. Essays by Maurice Freedman*. Stanford: Stanford University Press.

Hao Yen-ping. 1970. *The Comprador in Nineteenth-Century China. Bridge between East and West.* Cambridge, Mass.: Harvard University Press.

Hao Yen-ping. 1986. *The Commercial Revolution in Nineteenth-Century China: The Rise of Sino-Western Mercantile Capitalism.* Berkeley: University of California Press.

Heidhues, Mary Somers. 1996. "Chinese Settlements in Rural Southeast Asia: Unwritten Histories." in *Sojourners and Settlers. Histories of Southeast Asia and the Chinese,* edited by Anthony Reid, pp. 164–182.St. Leonards, NSW, Australia: Allen and Unwin for Asian Studies Association of Australia.

Honig, Emily. 1992. *Creating Chinese Ethnicity. Subei People in Shanghai, 1850–1980.* New Haven: Yale University Press.

Lai Him Mark. 1980. "Chinese," in *The Harvard Encyclopedia of American Ethnic Groups,* edited by Stephan Thernstrom, pp. 217–234. Cambridge, Mass.: Belknap Press of Harvard University Press.

Lai Him Mark and Reed Ueda. 1980. "The Chinese in Hawaii," in *The Harvard Encyclopedia of American Ethnic Groups,* edited by Stephan Thernstrom, pp. 231–234. Cambridge, Mass.: Belknap Press of Harvard University Press.

Lin Jinzhi et al.1993. *Huaqiao Huaren yu Zhongguo Geming he Jianshe* (Overseas Chinese and Ethnic Chinese and China's Revolution and Reconstruction). Fuzhou: Fujian Renmin Chubanshe.

Mackie, Jamie A. C. 1996. Introduction to *Sojourners and Settlers. Histories of Southeast Asia and the Chinese,* pp. xii–xxx. St. Leonards, NSW, Australia: Allen and Unwin for Asian Studies Association of Australia.

Murphcy, Rhoads. 1974. "The Treaty Ports and China's Modernization" in *The Chinese City between Two Worlds,* edited by Mark Elvin and G. William Skinner, pp. 17–71. Stanford, Cali.: Stanford University Press.

Nagtegaal, Luc. 1996. *Riding the Dutch Tiger: The Dutch East Indies Company and the Northeast Coast of Java, 1680–1743.* Leiden: KITLV Press.

Ng Chin-keong. 1983. *Trade and Society. The Amoy Network on the China Coast, 1683–1735.* Singapore: Singapore University Press, National University of Singapore.

———. 1990. "The South Fukienese Junk Trade at Amoy from the Seventeenth to Early Nineteenth Centuries," in *Development and Decline of Fukien Province in the 17th and 18th Centuries,* edited by E. B. Vermeer, pp. 297–316. Leiden: E. J. Brill (Sinica Leidensia XXII).

Ownby, David, and Mary Somers Heidhues, eds. 1993. *"Secret Societies" Reconsidered. Perspectives on the Social History of Early Modern South China and Southeast Asia.* Armonk, N.Y.: M. E. Sharpe.

Price, Charles A. 1974. *The Great White Walls Are Built. Restrictive Immigration to North America and Australasia, 1836–1888.* Canberra: Australian National University Press.

Purcell, Victor. 1965. *The Chinese in Southeast Asia.* 2nd ed. London: Oxford University Press.

Reid, Anthony. 1996. "Flows and Seepages in the Long-Term Chinese

Interaction with Southeast Asia," in *Sojourners and Settlers. Histories of Southeast Asia and the Chinese*, edited by Anthony Reid, pp. 15–49. St. Leonards, NSW, Australia: Allen and Unwin for Asian Studies Association of Australia.

———— ed. *Sojourners and Settlers. Histories of Southeast Asia and the Chinese.* St. Leonards, NSW, Australia: Allen and Unwin for Asian Studies Association of Australia.

Rowe, William T. 1984. *Hankow. Commerce and Society in a Chinese City, 1796–1889.* Stanford, Cali.: Stanford University Press.

[Report of The] Royal Commission on Chinese Immigration. 1885. Ottawa: Printed by order of the Commission.

Rush, James R. 1990. *Opium to Java: Revenue Farming and Chinese Enterprise in Colonial Indonesia, 1860–1910.* Ithaca, N.Y.: Cornell University Press.

Salmon, Claudine, ed. 1987. *Literary Migrations. Traditional Chinese Fiction in Asia (17th–20th Centuries).* Beijing: International Culture Publishing Corporation.

Saxton, Alexander. 1971. *The Indispensable Enemy. Labor and the Anti-Chinese Movement in California.* Berkeley: University of California Press.

Sinn, Elizabeth. 1989. *Power and Charity: The Early History of the Tung Hua Hospital, Hong Kong.* Hong Kong: Oxford University Press.

Skinner, G. William. 1957. *Chinese Society in Thailand: An Analytical History.* Ithaca, N.Y.: Cornell University Press.

———— 1996. "Creolized Chinese Societies in Southeast Asia." in *Sojourners and Settlers. Histories of Southeast Asia and the Chinese*, edited by Anthony Reid, pp. 51–93. St. Leonards, NSW, Australia: Allen and Unwin for Asian Studies Association of Australia.

Takaki, Ronald. 1989. *Strangers from a Different Shore.* New York: Penguin.

Trocki, Carl A. 1990. *Opium and Empire. Chinese Society in Colonial Singapore, 1800–1910.* Ithaca, N.Y.: Cornell University Press.

Wang Gungwu. 1991. "The Study of Chinese Identities in Southeast Asia." in *China and the Chinese Overseas* Essays by Wang Gungwu, pp. 198–221.Singapore: Times Academic Press.

Wang Sing-wu. 1978. *The Organization of Chinese Emigration, 1848–1888. With Special Reference to Chinese Emigration to Australia.* San Francisco: Chinese Materials Center, Inc.

Wickberg, Edgar B. 1965. *The Chinese in Philippine Life, 1850-1898.* New Haven, Conn.: Yale University Press.

Wickberg, Edgar B., et al. 1982. *From China to Canada. A History of the Chinese Communities in Canada.* Toronto: McClelland and Stewart Ltd.

Willmott, William E. 1967. *The Chinese in Cambodia.* Vancouver: Publications Centre, University of British Columbia.

Wong, Bernard. 1978. "A Comparative Study of the Assimilation of the Chinese in New York City and Lima, Peru, "*Comparative Studies in Society and*

History 20, no. 3: 335–358.

Wynne, Robert Edward. 1964. "Reaction to the Chinese in the Pacific Northwest and British Columbia, 1850 to 1910." PhD. dissertation, Department of History, University of Washington, Seattle.

Yen Ching-hwang. 1985. *Coolies and Mandarins: China's Protection of overseas Chinese During the Late Ch'ing Period (1851–1911)*. Singapore: Singapore University Press.

Zhuang Weiji. 1958. "Fujian Jinjiang Juanqu Huaqiao Shi Diaocha Baogao" (Report of an Investigation into the History of the overseas Chinese of Jinjiang Special District, Fujian), *Xiamen Daxue Xuebao. Shehui Kexue ban* Social Science Edition, Journal of Xiamen University 1: 93–127.

3 / Chinese Cities

The Difference a Century Makes

G. WILLIAM SKINNER

What difference does a century make? In this chapter I ask this question about China's cities and systems of cities. I pose the question in terms of a century not because a hundred-year span has any intrinsic significance, but simply because my own research career has inadvertently provided a setup. Twenty years ago I completed a study of Chinese cities as of the 1890s, the latest possible date for analyzing them prior to any significant modern transformation. The Treaty of Shimonoseki, which ended the Sino-Japanese War, triggered the onset of urban industrialization in China, so I took 1895 as my year of reference. In 1995 I was engrossed in a project designed to take advantage of excellent disaggregated data that have become available only in the 1990s, and today I'm nearing completion of a regional analysis of contemporary China. So, as it happens, I have something to go on in comparing China's cities today with those of a century ago. Such a comparison can serve to dramatize the magnitude and significance of urban change, while pointing up certain continuities. It can also provide context for an assessment of Hong Kong's changing role in China's urban system.

Let's start with the big picture. In the 1890s China's urbanization index was between 6 and 7 percent; as of 1990 it was about 20 percent. The urbanization index is the proportion of the total population residing in urban centers and, as such, is a function of the criteria used in classifying settlements as urban; so let me say that no matter how urban is defined—whether in terms of function, centrality, or population size—the magnitude of the change comes out about the same: The level of urbanization has increased threefold in the course of the last century. It will help us appreciate the significance of that change to look at some absolute figures. Focusing on the total row of Table 1, you will note that during the century, the population of China Proper (that is, excluding the Inner Asian territories) grew from approximately 375 million[1] to over 1.1 billion—almost exactly a threefold

Table 1. Urbanization by macroregion, China proper,
1890's and 1990+.

1890's

Macroregion	*No. of places	Urban pop. (000)	Total pop. (000)	% Urban
Lower Yangzi	270	4,750	40,000	11.9
Lingman**	193	3,093	34,000	9.1
Southeast Coast	138	1,668	24,000	7
Middle Yangzi	294	3,905	69,000	5.7
Upper Yangzi	202	2,503	44,000	5.7
Northwest China	114	1,301	24,000	5.4
North China	488	5,809	112,000	5.2
Yungui	81	714	16,000	4.5
Manchuria	? 60	? 500	?12,000	? 4.2
TOTAL	1,840	24,243	375,000	6.5

1990 +

Macroregion	*No. of places	Urban pop. (000)	Total pop. (000)	% Urban
Lower Yangzi	780	35,118	163,679	21.5
Lingman**	759	25,490	112,392	22.7
Southeast Coast	334	9,312	53,769	17.3
Middle Yangzi	824	29,521	179,247	16.5
Upper Yangzi	502	14,736	122,764	12
Northwest China	426	14,746	81,866	18
North China	875	49,865	289,729	17.2
Yungui	329	9,387	65,347	14.4
Manchuria	801	42,170	110,347	38.2
TOTAL	5,630	230,345	1,179,140	19.5

+ The territorial extent of macroregional systems varies
   somewhat between The two dates
* Number of central places with a population of 200,000 or more
** Includes Hong Kong in both years

increase. We may note that the total number of cities and towns with a population of 2,000 or more also increased about three times, from 1,840 to 5,630.[2] It follows that the total urban population must have grown about ninefold during the century and that the growth rate has been higher in large cities than in small cities and towns. Note the magnitudes involved. China's urban population was 24 million in the 1890s, and over 230 million in 1990.[3] That's more urbanites than we find in any other country of the world, regardless of urbanization level.

You might well ask how important cities and towns could have been for Chinese society and political economy in the 1890s, when the urban population accounted for less than 7 percent of the total. In fact, as in most agrarian civilizations, the urban hierarchy was all-important in shaping rural life. On the one hand, the entire governmental apparatus was urban, with lines of authority and control emanating from the imperial capital in Beijing, to provincial capitals, and on down to the capitals of prefectures and counties. On the other hand, all cities and towns, not just those that served as administrative capitals, provided economic and other central functions for their hinterlands and, in so doing, differentiated those hinterlands in significant ways. The general economic importance of an urban center in late imperial times was in large part a function of three factors: (1) its role in providing retail goods and services for a surrounding tributary area or hinterland, (2) its position in the structure of distribution channels connecting economic centers, and (3) its place in the transport network. In an analysis of 1890s data that systematically investigated these functions of cities and towns, I found that China's great metropolises were but the highest level of a seven-level hierarchy that extended down to rural market towns (Skinner 1977b). The marketing systems centered on these bottom-level towns, each typically encompassing 15–20 villages, constituted the basic building blocks of the economic hierarchy. Central places at each ascending level served as the nodes of ever more extensive and complex socioeconomic systems. At each level, the town or city at the system's center served to articulate and integrate activity in space and time. Just where a village was situated within this hierarchy of local and regional systems and, in particular, how it was related to the cities and towns at their centers overwhelmingly determined social and economic opportunity, living standards, and quality of life.

When considering *systems* of cities, we must recognize that China is on quite a different scale from Japan, Thailand, Iran or France. Throughout the last century, it has been more or less 10 times as populous as these standard-sized countries, and its internal differentiation has been and is correspondingly sharper. By the end of the nineteenth century, Tokyo, Bangkok, Teheran, and Paris each served as the central metropolis of a single, integrated urban hierarchy. The same could not be said of China. Based on my analysis, in the 1890s there were seven distinct regional urban systems, plus two emergent systems in the process of cohering into a

hierarchical urban system. Rather more surprising—and this is the most significant of the continuities I'll touch on here—the same nine systems emerge from
my analysis of 1990 data. The two regional systems that were poorly developed in
the 1890s have fully integrated urban hierarchies today.

We may pin the discussion to Map 1, which depicts the geographic extent of
these nine macroregional economies as of 1990 and plots the cities at the top of
each regional urban system. A detailed comparison of macroregional geography
reveals many shifts of boundaries along the peripheral macroregional frontiers
between 1890 and 1990, but only one of these is of major significance. The Lower
Yangzi region has expanded both to the north, incorporating a portion of the Huai
River valley, and to the south, capturing, as it were, the Ou-Ling subregion from
the Southeast coast. This territorial expansion of the Lower Yangzi reflects the
continued vitality of its regional economy and the growing centrality of its central
metropolis, Shanghai. Despite these shifts in the limits of macroregional economies, their core areas have changed little since the 1890s. And there has been
remarkable continuity in the central metropolises integrating the urban system of
each macroregion. Of the two macroregional economies that were merely emergent in the 1890s, Manchuria and Yungui, the present-day central metropolises,
Shenyang and Kunming respectively, were already dominant a century earlier.
For the rest, then and now, we find Chengdu and Chongqing the twin metropolises
of the Upper Yangzi, Wuhan the central metropolis of the Middle Yangzi, Shanghai the central metropolis of the Lower Yangzi, Fuzhou the metropolis of the Southeast coast macroregion, Xi'an and Taiyuan the twin metropolises of Northwest
China, and Beijing and Tianjin the twin central metropolises of North China. The
most important exceptions to this overall continuity are four cities that rose to
metropolitan rank in the course of the century. Two of these, Shijiazhuang and
Zhengzhou in North China, are sited at the junction of major north-south and east-
west railroads that were completed shortly after the turn of the century, and the
other two, Qingdao and Hong Kong, are outports established in the nineteenth
century by Western metropolitan powers. Another major category of urban centers that have moved up the hierarchy during the past century are industrial cities
that exploit nearby mineral resources, for example, Anshan in Manchuria, Tangshan
in North China, and Zigong in the Upper Yangzi.

In emphasizing the salience of regional systems of cities in China, I do not
mean to deny their interdependence; they are far from closed systems. But just as
France, Germany, and Italy each boasts a semi-autonomous, hierarchical system
of cities, even though they are intricately interrelated within a more inclusive Western European system, so the Lower Yangzi, Northwest China, Yungui, and the
other regional urban systems of China must be recognized as semi-autonomous
despite their partial integration into a national Chinese economy. In the sense that

China's macroregional systems, showing metropolitan cities, 1990

**Map. 1. China's macroregional systems, showing metropolitan cities
1990.**

Paris is *the* metropolis of France, Shanghai is *the* metropolis of the Lower Yangzi. But at the next level up, no city or pair of cities predominates. China's urban system, like Europe's, is decentralized.

It is, of course, true that interregional trade has grown enormously during the past century, facilitated by the expansion of mechanized transport, and it might be thought that this would inevitably strengthen the national economy at the expense of regional economies. But that argument overlooks the fact that transport modernization and trade growth have proceeded within as well as between regions. Macroregional systems of cities are far more tightly integrated today than they were a century ago, and in at least some macroregions the internal transport net has been greatly expanded and upgraded, whereas interregional routes, despite mechanization and upgrading, have not been appreciably intensified. That we find remarkable continuity and only very gradual change in the structure of China's urban systems attests the inertia induced by such factors as the largely unchanged structure of navigable waterways, sunk costs in cities and overland transport routes, the pervasive constraints of cost-distance in relation to topography, and the inexorable logic of increasing returns. In short, path-dependent development and historical contingency.

A closer look at Table 1 shows that the level of urbanization varied sharply from one macroregion to another—in 1990 as in the 1890s. The macroregions are listed in order of urbanization in the 1890s. Above all, the order reflects position with respect to the major waterborne trade routes. The Lower Yangzi, the most urbanized region, encompasses the mouth of the Yangzi, i.e., where the major internal waterway links to coastal trade routes. Next most urbanized were the coastal regions to the south, and after them the Yangzi regions farther upstream. By far the most dramatic change in urban systems during the past century took place in Manchuria. From 1668 until the last decades of the nineteenth century, the Manchu court banned the migration of Chinese peasants into the region. But this exclusion policy was eventually abandoned in the face of foreign threat and population pressure in North China, and by 1904 the entire region was open to peasant in-migration (Lee 1970). Russian and Japanese rivalry stimulated precocious development of an extensive rail network, which in turn facilitated the influx of land-hungry peasants from the North China macroregion. Then, early in the 1930s, the Japanese occupied the region and converted it into an industrial base. The PRC regime systematically built on this legacy. So it was that in the course of a century flat, Manchuria went from the weakest of China's macroregional economies with an urbanization index of under 5 percent to the country's most urbanized economy. More generally, it will be noted in Table 1 that differential rates of change during the past century have had the effect of reducing urbanization differences among the various macroregional systems. After Manchuria, the three regions that were least urbanized in the 1890s—Yungui, and North and Northwest China—saw higher than average levels of urban growth during the past century, whereas the most urbanized of the macroregions in the 1890s, the Lower Yangzi, exhibited a relatively low rate of urban growth during the century.[4]

Let us pause here to take a closer look at Lingnan's urban system at the close of the nineteenth century, with special attention to the role of Hong Kong. Then as now, the inner core of the Lingnan macroregion was very nearly coterminous with the Pearl River delta. The delta was, of course, dominated by Guangzhou (Canton), the central metropolis of the entire macroregion, but at the next level down it also supported two regional cities: Foshan and Jiangmen. Hong Kong's population, over 250,000 in 1898, placed it on a par with these two delta cities, but its central functions were anomalous: more limited that those of a regional city in certain ways, more extensive in others. On the one hand, Hong Kong lacked a "proper" hinterland, that is, an extensive dependent territory for which it provided the full range of urban functions. Foshan and Jiangmen were at once cultural and economic centers for their respective subregions, funneling goods, services, and credit into local distribution channels and housing religious, cultural, and welfare institutions that served, inspired, or interfaced with local systems. In these respects, Hong Kong's centrality did not extend beyond the New Territories, which it annexed in 1899. On the other hand, with respect to shipping, trade, and migration, Hong Kong played a role that was critical for the entire macroregional economy. As of the 1890s, Hong Kong had already become the major transshipment center for most of Lingnan (Endacott 1973; M. Chan 1995). To be sure, Guangzhou continued to dominate inland transport and trade within the macroregion, serving as the central collection point for exports and the distribution center for imports. But most of these imports and exports were transshipped in Hong Kong, which, in addition to its superior harbor facilities, offered banking, accounting, and insurance services geared to international trade. Hong Kong was also the usual port of embarkation for emigrants originating in central Lingnan (Endacott 1973). Often recruited by and through agents in Guangzhou, prospective emigrants usually proceeded by riverboat to Hong Kong, where over a hundred boarding houses served the "coolie traffic." Around the turn of the century, Hong Kong shipped out some 100,000 emigrants every year, almost entirely Cantonese and Lingnan Hakkas, to destinations in Southeast Asia, the Americas, and Australia/New Zealand (M. Chan 1975: 37). As of the 1890s, then, Hong Kong had usurped some of Guangzhou's metropolitan functions and served as Lingnan's major link to the world system.

To this point, I have emphasized continuities in the regionalization of China's urban system and in the dominant position of its major cities. But when we shift our focus from systems of cities to the cities themselves, we find that the twentieth century has brought about dramatic transformations. In their very physical appearance, Chinese cities today bear little resemblance to those of a century ago. We are fortunate to have access to a splendid corpus of photographs from the late nineteenth century that document the appearance of Chinese cities and their residents (e.g., Thomson 1982; Boerschmann 1982; Beers 1978). The architecture, especially the roof lines, the attire of the people on the streets, the iconography of arches and shopsigns—indeed, virtually every manifestation of culture that can be gleaned from such visual records—are unmistakably Chinese. And the absence of telephone poles, electric transmission wires, streetcars, buses, or even bicycles in these photographs of street scenes mark these cities as unmistakably pre-modern. Sad to say, the modernization of Chinese cities has entailed systematic desinification. Unreconstructed pockets are still to be found in some cities, but it is precisely these recognizably Chinese neighborhoods that lack sewers and other modern amenities. For the most part, the advent of mechanized transport—streetcars and buses and more recently motorbikes and automobiles—and a century of urban reconstruction and expansion have yielded cityscapes that are sprawling, rectangularly drab, and virtually culture free. In late imperial times, all cities that served as capitals, over 1,500 of them, were walled, and boasted both a bell tower and a drum tower near the center of the city. The state cult prescribed particular altars for sacrificial rites outside the walls and Confucian and military temples within. With few exceptions, these glorious artifacts of Chinese civilization are gone, if not torn down by mindless modernizers then destroyed by Maoist radicals in their zeal to discard the old, combat religious superstition, and free the socialist present from its feudal past.

Despite the antiquarian bias just revealed, I hold no particular belief for late-imperial administrative arrangements as they affected cities or for the prevailing modes of governance. These arrangements were in fact rather anomalous. In general, cities were not administered or governed separately from the county to which each belonged. Most—but not all—important cities were capitals in the sense that the magistrate's yamen was situated within the walled city, but the magistrate's responsibilities were not formally differentiated between city and countryside. In some of the highest-order capitals, the local administrative arrangement was even odder. Such metropolises as Beijing, Xi'an, Chengdu, Changsha, Nanchang, Nanjing, Hangzhou, Fuzhou, and Guangzhou each served as the capital of two counties. In these cases, the county boundary ran through the city, and the yamen of each county was located in the appropriate sector (Skinner 1977b). To be sure, the city as a whole was under the jurisdiction of the prefectural yamen, but once again only as an undifferentiated part of a much larger, primarily rural administrative unit. Quite apart from bureaucratic arrangements, in most cities of any appreciable size the population had organized itself into neighborhoods, normally defined in terms of streets rather than blocks, and these neighborhood associations, usually in the form of religious *hui*, took responsibility not only for the ritual purity of the area but also for its general order, harmony, and cleanliness (Schipper 1977; Skinner 1977c). In addition, major urban temples often became the foci of territorial units uniting several neighborhoods. By the late nineteenth century, many urban services were provided by non-governmental corporate groups financed through assessments and dues or the income from corporate property. The trend was toward cooperation, if not federation, among guilds, native-place associations, and/or gentry-dominated boards to provide a number of citywide services, including firefighting, policing, garbage collection, and charity (Rowe 1984; Elvin 1974; Skinner 1977c).

During the first half of the twentieth century, these ad hoc arrangements were superseded in many cities by the creation of true municipalities: formal administrative units limited to the city and detached from the surrounding county. This administrative practice was extended to lower-order cities by the Communist regime, and there are now some 500 municipalities Chinawide, though, to the confusion of not a few urban analysts, many county-level municipalities differ from counties only in name. In any case, the urban population today is formally organized under neighborhood committees, which, in the case of larger cities, are subordinate to government offices at the urban district or ward level. The rural administrative hierarchy of county–township–village is thus paralleled by an urban hierarchy of municipality–ward–urban neighborhood. State control is exerted not only via this territorial hierarchy but also through the *danwei*, or work unit, to which most urbanites are formally attached.

How do urban populations today differ from those of the 1890s? The most significant change has to do with gender composition or sex ratio. If one scrutinizes century-old photographs of Chinese street scenes, it becomes apparent that virtually all of the passersby were men. This reflects not only the fact that respectable women did not venture into the streets but also the strongly skewed sex ratio of rural-to-urban migration. In societies with patrilineal joint family systems such as that of traditional China, young women were kept close to home (if not at home) under the watchful eyes of parents before marriage and of parents-in-law after marriage. Only men were sufficiently mobile to take advantage of economic opportunities away from home. Those opportunities were concentrated in cities, and the sojourning strategies that were a characteristic feature of the premodern Chinese economy were largely limited to men. Women played virtually no role in the larger political economy prior to the Revolution. Urban merchants were almost exclusively male, and the bureaucratic state apparatus, wholly urban as noted earlier, was literally manned, that is, staffed entirely by men. Even clerical workers in the yamens were men, as were the jail wardens guarding female prisoners. As a consequence, prosperous cities that attracted large numbers of sojourners were very disproportionately male; city-wide sex ratios of over 200 were not uncommon.

In fact, to characterize family and gender patterns in late-nineteenth-century Chinese cities adequately, one must draw a critical distinction within the urban ecology. Most cities were characterized by two nuclei: one the center of merchant activity, the other the center of gentry and official activity (Skinner 1977c). The business district was dominated by shop-houses in which the salesrooms of stores and the workrooms of craft shops doubled as dining rooms and sleeping rooms for the largely male employees. Quarters were cramped because of high land values, the normal desire of businessmen to keep non-essential overhead down, and the frugality of sojourners. The sex ratio was sharply skewed because of the high proportion of sojourners who had left their families behind in their native places and the large number of unmarried apprentices. Men with families in the business districts were mostly shopowners, and their wives cooked meals for the entire workforce; their families were usually simple conjugal units: the married couple and their children. Apart from shopkeepers' wives, the only other women in the business districts were actresses, entertainers, and prostitutes. Certainly some of the men were functionally literate, but virtually all women in the business districts were illiterate. The location of the business nucleus appears to have been determined more by the merchants' transport costs than by convenience of access for consumers, and it was typically displaced from the geographic center of the walled city toward (or up to or even beyond) the gate or gates affording direct access to the major interurban transport route.

Not surprisingly, residents of the urban gentry tended to cluster near the official institutions of greatest interest to them. Academies, bookstores, stationery shops, and used-book stands favored locations near the Confucian school-temple and examination hall, and in general the gentry nucleus of the city tended to be on the school-temple side of the yamen. The gentry district was characterized by a high proportion of residences with spacious compounds, by relatively large and complex families containing more than one conjugal unit, and by a female population swelled by the concubines and maidservants of gentry households. Sex ratios, though far less extreme than in the business nucleus, were still unbalanced because of the concentration in these districts of sojourning male students and, in high-level capitals, of expectant officials. Sex ratios in gentry-dominated urban wards were typically 150:175, as against 225:300 in the business districts. In sharp contrast to the business districts, the men in gentry-dominated wards were normally classically educated and some of their wives and daughters were literate.

Changes in the gender system over the past century have been truly revolutionary in the cities, with major progress in the direction of greater equality occurring during the Maoist era. Even before the 1911 Revolution, urbanites were leading the way in establishing girls' schools and ending footbinding. The development of urban industry after 1895, especially the expansion of textile mills, meant that women could seek urban employment not only as sex workers and domestic servants but also as factory workers. The modest advances in female education and urban employment opportunities for women during the Republican period were followed during the Maoist era by dramatic educational advances and all-out efforts to bring women into the extra-domestic labor force. The Maoist programs to foster gender equality were particularly successful in the cities, and their legacy has not been appreciably undone by the more gender-differentiating policies of the Reform era. Today, the gender balance in cities is much less skewed than it was in the 1890s. The mean sex ratio of high-order cities as of 1990 varies from 103 in Manchuria and 106 in the Lower Yangzi to 112 and 113 in the Upper Yangzi and Yungui, respectively. As these extremes suggest, the sex ratio of cities is inversely related to the regional level of urbanization—relatively balanced in highly urbanized macroregions, relatively male-heavy in regions with low levels of urbanization. In addition, the sex ratio of city populations tends to increase as one moves down the urban hierarchy. The progression happens to be perfectly regular in the Northwest China macroregion, as shown in Table 2, but a similar albeit less monotonic trend obtains everywhere. In sum, the proportion of females in urban populations today is highest in the metropolitan cities of the most urbanized macroregions, with the proportion of females declining with regional urbanization and down the urban hierarchy.

That gender equality is more closely approximated in cities than in the countryside is apparent across a wide range of variables as of 1990. For instance, in the Upper Yangzi (my main case in point in the remainder of this paper), 74.5 percent of urban women over age 15 have been educated to the junior middle-school level, as against only 24.6 percent of rural women. Dichotomous contrasts of this kind, however, miss out on significant differentiation within the urban hierarchy. In fact, women's educational attainment and the opportunities for female employment both vary by level in the urban hierarchy. The closest approach to parity with men is seen in metropolises, with female disadvantage increasing steadily down the urban hierarchy and with distance away from the regional metropolis. Let me illustrate this point with data for the Upper Yangzi macroregion in 1990. Figure 1 displays the sex ratio by position in the internal structure of the macroregion of those educated to the level of senior middle school or higher. In this chart, counties are arrayed in rows according to a fancy urbanization index and in columns according to their zone in the core-periphery structure of the macroregion.[5] In comprehending the latter, it will help to refer to Map 2, which delineates the seven zones of the Upper Yangzi's core-periphery structure. The overall argument, borne out by the data in every case, is that the macroregional economy is internally differentiated such that the lowland areas near the metropolis are most "advanced" or "developed" and "modern," with a steady gradation through regional space to the mountainous and rural far periphery, where villages are relatively backward and underdevelopedand distinctly less modern in their sociocultural attributes. As noted earlier, the Upper-Yangzi boasts two metropolises, Chengdu and Chongqing, and it will be noted that each is surrounded by an inner core zone. Zones of the core-periphery system appear as concentric circles around the metropolises. At the level of the outer core (zone 3), the two inner cores are joined to form a horseshoe-shaped regional core. The finger of the periphery (zone 6) jutting from the northern rim southwestward toward the geographic center is roughly equidistant from the two metropolises, at the rim of their respective maximal hinterlands. The most peripheral areas (zone 7) are remote from either metropolis at the rim of the macroregional economy. One way to think of the core-periphery structure, then, is in terms of effective distance from the metropolis, metropolitan influence being greatest in the inner core and weakest in the far periphery.

**Table 2. Northwest China macroregions:
Mean sex ratio and mean household size of cities
and towns, by level in the urban hierarchy, 1990.**

Hierarchical Level	No. of cities/towns	Sex ratio (means)	Household size (means)
Metropolises	6	110.9	3.72
Regional Cities	19	110.8	3.79
Greater Cities	67	119.8	3.91
Local Cities	187	128.4	3.99
Central Towns	228	140.1	4.21
Market Towns	389	169.6	4.61
Total Urban	896	116.5	3.83

Turning back to Figure 1, it is apparent that gender differentials in educational attainment are strongly shaped by position in relation to the urban hierarchy. In rural counties at the far periphery of the macroregion (the lower-right cell), that is, in counties most remote from urban influence, whether from the metropolis or from lower-order cities, the sex ratio of the well educated is sharply skewed: for every 100 women with a senior middle-school education there are 279 men. As one moves diagonally across the chart toward the upper left, the female disadvan-

Core- periphery structure of the Upper Yangzi macroregional system, 1990

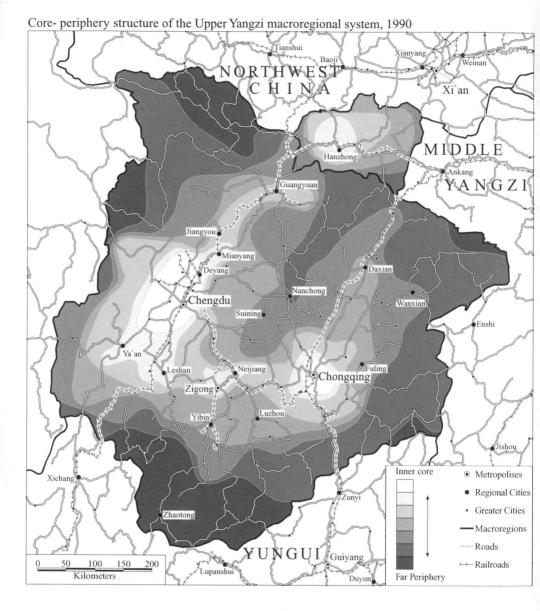

**Map. 2. Core-periphery structure of the Upper Yangzi macroregional
  system, 1990.**

Figure 1. Sex ratio* of the well-educated (senior middle school and higher), Upper Yangzi macroregion, 1990

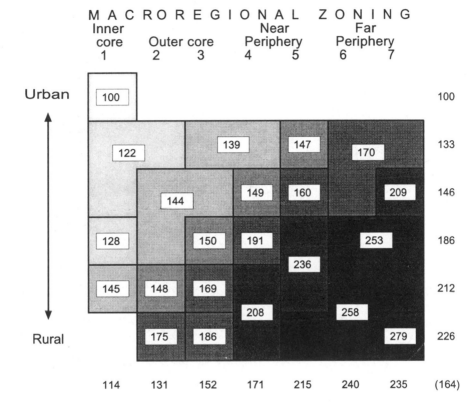

* Males per 100 females, age 6 amd older.

G. WILLIAM SKINNER

Figure 2. Sex ratio* of technical/professional personnel, Upper Yangzi macroregion, 1990

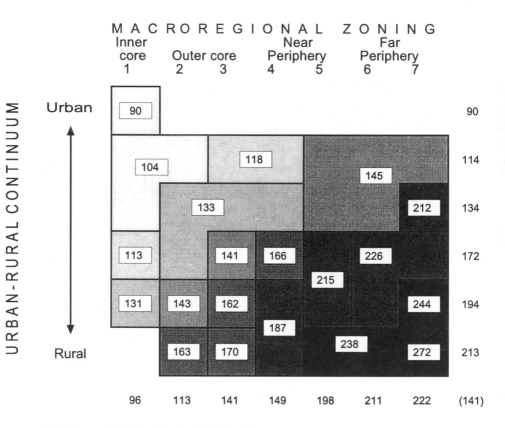

* Males per 100 families in the labor force.

tage grows steadily smaller, with parity achieved only in the upper-left cell, in the two metropolitan cities. The units containing regional cities, (urban centers at the level just below metropolises), are positioned in the second row of the chart, where it can be seen that the female disadvantage increases with distance from the metropolises, the sex ratio of those with senior middle-school education increasing from 122 in the inner core to 170 in the far periphery.

Figure 2 displays in the same matrix the sex ratio of technical and professional personnel (whether in government agencies, state-owned industry, collective enterprises, or the private sector). The general order of magnitude and the patterning of sex ratios within this high-status occupational category closely parallel those for high educational attainment. Sex ratios for other occupations not shown here confirm that gender discrimination within the labor force is at a minimum in metropolitan cities, increasing steadily down the urban hierarchy and out from urban centers into their rural peripheries.

I have not yet analyzed the data on family structure available in the 1990 census returns, so I limit myself here to some very general remarks on family change. Urban youth today have a much greater say in their choice of spouse than had been the case in the 1890s, and the age at marriage is considerably later for both sexes (Whyte 1993). (I am able to show from 1990 census data that, on average, age at marriage is later in cities than in the countryside and that mean age at marriage declines as one descends the urban hierarchy.) The sharp class differentials in family structure that obtained in the 1890s (as between the literati and tradesmen) have largely disappeared. The closest approximation to the traditional joint family system in metropolitan cities today is found among officials and high-level Party cadres (Unger 1993). However, the proportion of stem families is probably no smaller today than a century ago. For most of the big-city population, housing is so restricted that even if desired, it is usually unfeasible for more than one married son to share an apartment with his parents. A not uncommon co-residential sequence amounts to what might be called a hiving-off stem family system. A daughter-in-law is brought in for the eldest son, with the couple occupying a loft or a second bedroom if there is one. When the second son is married, the older brother's conjugal unit hives off to establish a separate household. Ideally the younger or youngest son and his wife remain in the stem family arrangement, caring for the senior couple as they age. Recent social surveys suggest that separate residence of a conjugal family need not imply independence (Davis 1993). A married son may regularly drop off his children at his parents' apartment for care during the working day, and his wife might deliver cooked dishes. Cash and gifts may flow either way according to income and need. A century ago, urban sojourners typically returned to their native places on retirement, while the elderly in urban literati families relied on their married sons. Today, the urban elderly are for the most part pensioned and hence less reliant on married sons for support in old age. Nonetheless, retirement homes are rare, and the great majority of the dependent elderly live with a married child (Ikels 1993). Yet, urban households on average are much smaller today than in the 1890s. The mean size of households in metropolises throughout China ranged (in 1990) from 3.3 in Shanghai and Tianjin to 3.9 in Taiyuan and Nanchang. In all regional systems, mean household size increases as one descends the urban hierarchy; in general, lower-order cities and towns are characterized by housing markets that are less tight, offspring sets that are somewhat larger, and family structures that are more complex. The data shown in Table 2 for Northwest China are typical.

Having described a few of the main social characteristics of China's urban hierarchy, I can now compare how Hong Kong fits into this system of cities. In matters of family, gender, and education, Hong Kong is a bit distinctive, but in most respects it falls within the range exhibited by mainland metropolises. In Hong Kong, it is among the high-echelon business elite (rather than high-level cadres) that we find the closest approximation of the traditional joint family system, and, since a significantly smaller proportion of the elderly are pensioned than in mainland cities, we also observe a somewhat higher incidence of intact stem families. Nonetheless, in terms of averages, household size in Hong Kong (3.4) falls near the low end of the range for Chinese metropolises and contrasts with Guangzhou (mean household size 3.9) and other cities in Lingnan, where urban as well as rural households are on average larger and more complex than in any other Chinese macroregion. With respect to educational attainment, too, it is instructive to compare Hong Kong with its twin metropolis Guangzhou[6] Of the population age 15 and older, 17.9 percent have received some higher (post-secondary) education in Hong Kong, as against 13.1 percent in Guangzhou; at the same time, illiteracy rates are also higher in Hong Kong: 12.9 as against 6.9 percent. This is precisely the contrast one might expect between the two systems: greater investment in higher education and sharper class differentials in capitalist Hong Kong vs. a higher floor and lower ceiling in "socialist" Guangzhou. A more surprising finding, given the Maoist emphasis on gender equality in education, is that Hong Kong's educational system is less sexist than Guangzhou's: females constitute 79 percent of all illiterates in Guangzhou but "only" 72 percent in Hong Kong; more significantly, among those with any higher education the ratio of males to females is 2.02 in Guangzhou as against only 1.28 in Hong Kong.

Let me turn, finally, to the demography of urban populations. In the case of Chinese cities, the century in question encompassed the entire demographic transition from very high mortality and moderately high marital fertility in the 1890s to low mortality and below-replacement fertility in the 1990s. The demographic transition in China has been far more dramatic for the urban than for the rural population.

We may begin with mortality. As in all pre-modern agrarian societies, it was high, but the point to be stressed here is that it was generally higher in cities than in rural areas; specifically, that mortality was highest in inner-core metropolises, declining down the urban hierarchy and through the zones of the core-periphery structure to the far periphery. I offer three reasons for expecting mortality to be highest in large cities in the inner cores of regional systems and lowest in their rural far peripheries. The first is a direct function of occupant density. In densely populated cities, interpersonal contact was frequent and living conditions were crowded. Extensive contact guaranteed a higher level of exposure to airborne pathogens, while crowding facilitated the spread of water-and filth-borne pathogens. The second reason follows from the fact that regional systems took shape within drainage basins and, apart from Yungui, had lowland, riverine cores. The risk of infection from polluted water increased as one moved from uplands to the plain. The danger of water-borne disease was especially great in spring, when rivers tended to flood and drive surface water into wells. As noted earlier, with the exception of Kunming, the major Chinese metropolises were sited in the riverine lowlands of drainage basins. This factor interacts with occupance density in that sewage disposal was a particular problem in cities. The third reason follows from the fact that migration flows were generally from less to more urban settlements and from peripheral locales toward the core. More often than not, the migrants attracted to inner-core cities came carrying a fresh supply of new pathogens and had little resistance to those already present.

I have not documented in any detail the following hypothesis concerning the mortality transition, but I believe some version of this story will fit the Chinese case. The biomedical revolution provided the knowledge to eradicate or control most of the diseases that kept mortality high in premodern times. The practical techniques of preventive medicine (such as inoculation, pasteurization, sewage disposal, insect control, and measures to minimize food contamination and purify the water supply) together with the development of a modern system for health-care delivery made possible a dramatic lowering of mortality. But virtually every one of these medical innovations was introduced in metropolises, spreading only gradually to lower-order cities and surrounding rural areas. The development of a network of hospitals and clinics and of medical schools largely recapitulated the urban hierarchy, as did the distribution of modern doctors and modern pharmacies. Effective health-care delivery to villages was slow in coming, especially to those remote from cities and poorly served by the transport net. In short, we may posit with some confidence that benefits of the biomedical revolution diffused within a regional system down the urban hierarchy and, at each level, out from the urban center into the rural hinterland. The first localities to see a drop in mortality were inner-core cities, where mortality had been the highest; the last localities to benefit were remote villages in the far periphery, the healthiest parts of the realm in the 1890s. One can imagine a magic moment in the diffusion process, perhaps in the 1950s, when, with mortality in the urbanized inner core lowered to levels traditionally enjoyed in a far periphery as yet untouched by biomedicine, mortality levels would be uniform through the regional system. However, as the potential of biomedicine came to be more fully realized in the urbanized inner core at a time when it had barely penetrated the rural far periphery, the balance quickly shifted in favor of the former. At that juncture, although mortality in the far periphery might be no higher than in premodern times, in relative terms the patterning within the internal structure of the regional system had been reversed. The very localities that once enjoyed the highest life expectancies were now burdened with the lowest. And it was precisely in inner-core metropolises that the mortality transition was most dramatic, with life expectancy at birth increasing from around 30 years in the 1890s to over 70 in 1990.

The fertility transition story is both less conjectural and more simply told. Available evidence suggests that at the end of the nineteenth century and, indeed, on through the Republican period, marital fertility was somewhat lower in cities than in the countryside. Be that as it may, it is clear that modern fertility control in marriage first appeared in China among the better educated strata in the major metropolises (Lavely and Freedman 1990). Fertility decline was already under way in the higher reaches of the urban hierarchy prior to the start, in 1970, of the *wan-xi-shao* program, which promoted delayed marriage, wider spacing between children, and fewer births overall. When the one-child policy was introduced in 1979, most families in inner-core metropolises were motivated to limit the number of offspring, and in any case enforcement of the policy was much stricter and more effective in tightly organized municipalities than in towns and a fortiori in rural villages. Figure 3 displays general fertility rates for the Upper Yangzi in the matrix already introduced. The particular fertility measure used is the number of births per 1,000 women age 15–44, and as you can see it varies sharply across the matrix, being lowest in Chengdu and Chongqing, the region's metropolises (in the upper-left cell), and increasing steadily down the urban hierarchy and through the zones from the inner core to the far periphery. A more detailed analysis of parity progression ratios shows that in the metropolises of Chengdu and Chongqing combined, the proportion of women with one child who go on to have a second fell below 10 percent in 1982 and has been below 5 percent since 1987. This level of fertility is lower than that recorded for cities anywhere in the world outside China.

Similar to the previous comparisons, Hong Kong's demographic trends are in line with those of other metropolitan regions in China. It is especially interesting in this regard that fertility levels in contemporary Hong Kong are no higher than

Figure 3. General fertility rates,* Upper Yangzi macroregion, 1989-90.

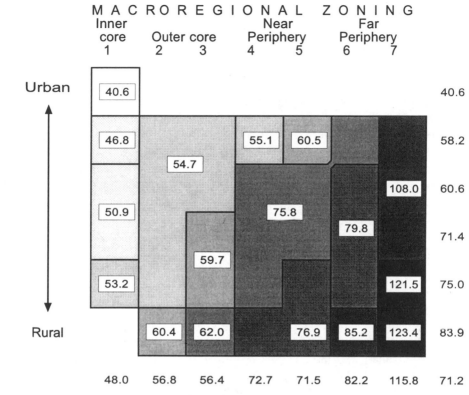

* Males per 100 families in the labor force.

in mainland cities where the one-child family policy has been strictly enforced. Indeed, the general fertility rate in Hong Kong is a bit lower than in Guangzhou: 43 vs. 48.[7]

To summarize: It is precisely the cities in China that have seen the most dramatic changes during the past century—in the family system, in the occupational structure, in education, in the demographic regime, and in gender relations, which crosscuts all the others. In all these respects, the magnitude of the transformation during the past century has been greatest in the metropolitan cities at the apex of regional hierarchies, declining down through the urban hierarchy and with distance from the metropolis. These dimensions—level in the urban hierarchy and position in the macroregional core-periphery structure—are critical for analyzing differentiation among cities, in the 1990s as in the 1890s. And I have argued here that the very extent of social transformation experienced by particular cities is a function of the same spatial logic. The most significant continuity during the past century is to be seen in the continued salience of China's regional systems of cities. The cities themselves are virtually unrecognizable across the century, and their populations, too, have been fundamentally transformed. It is the spatially grounded hierarchical structure of urban systems that has endured.

Let me close with a coda on Hong Kong's changing role in Lingnan's urban system. During the first four decades of the twentieth century, Hong Kong experienced rapid population growth through in-migration from Lingnan and almost equally dramatic development of its entrepôt economy. On the eve of the Sino-Japanese War, Hong Kong's pretensions to metropolitan status had largely been realized, and it was more closely integrated into Lingnan's economy than ever before. Events of the next 15 years, however, fostered the industrialization of Hong Kong's economy and led to its eventual isolation from the mainland (M. Chan 1995; Endacott 1973; Liu 1997). Hong Kong's entrepôt trade was badly hurt by the Japanese occupation (1941–45), the subsequent civil war in China (1946-49), and the ban on trade with China imposed by the colonial government (at American instigation) after the outbreak of the Korean War in 1953. Hong Kong's industrialization benefited twice from the influx of Chinese businessmen fleeing Shanghai and Guangzhou, bringing their capital and technology with them: first in the late 1930s, when these mainland cities were conquered by the Japanese, and second a decade later when they were occupied by the People's Liberation Army. Its labor pool was also greatly augmented by the flood of refugees from the Delta during the period of 1948–56. By the late 1950s, Hong Kong's transformation from entrepôt port to industrial center was complete. Hong Kong manufactures, increasingly high-technology products after 1970, were exported not to China but to Southeast Asia and the West. Hong Kong's links with the mainland were greatly attenuated throughout the Maoist era of self-reliance, when Guangzhou was indisputably the sole metropolis of Lingnan's stagnant macroregional economy.

However, the onset of Reform in 1978 precipitated a dramatic restructuring, and Hong Kong's reintegration with the Lingnan economy has proceeded at astonishing speed. Hong Kong industrialists began moving their production north to the Delta in 1980, and today 80 percent of Hong Kong's manufacturing is done on the mainland, most of it in the core areas of Lingnan. Hong Kong also quickly regained its stature as entrepôt. As of 1988, the entrepôt trade surpassed that of locally made products in both volume and value, and by 1994 it accounted for over 80 percent of total exports (Liu 1997). Today, Hong Kong and Guangzhou are twin metropolises of Lingnan, their respective strengths largely complementary. If anything, because of its technological edge and international orientation, not to mention its superiority in shipping, banking, and insurance, Hong Kong is likely to prove the dominant metropolis. In contrast with a century ago, Hong Kong now provides regional-city-level urban functions for a hinterland that incorporates the very areas from which its population largely originated. And in even sharper contrast with a century ago, Hong Kong is today *the* cultural center of all Lingnan.

NOTES

1.   Estimates of China's population during the second half of the nineteenth century are based on an official series of provincial statistics for 1850. Recent scholarship has shown that the official 1850 figures for many provinces systematically overstate the actual population (Skinner 1987). The total cited here for China Proper represents a province-by-province downward revision of the 394 million estimated for 1893 in my earlier study of regional urbanization (Skinner 1977a).

2.   The figure for the 1890s given here differs from that in Skinner 1977a because of the inclusion of Manchuria. The count of central places in both years undoubtedly misses out on a number of towns in the 2,000–4,000 range.

3.   The estimated urban population of 230 million is smaller than that given by other analysts on the basis of 1990 census data. My figure is based on the actual count of urban residents in each city and town (some 12,000 central places in all of China), whereas other China-wide estimates are based on the population of territorial units (municipalities and townships) that often include extensive rural areas. One of the more careful and conservative of the estimates based on data for administrative units (K. W. Chan 1994: 153) suggests an urban population of 313 million. Of the extensive "floating" population in the urbanized cores of China's macroregional economies, only a small proportion represent a net increase in the aggregate urban population (K. W. Chan 1994: 46), and of these many were counted by the census. Extending the estimate to include "floaters" missed by the census would probably add 5–8 million to the total urban population of China proper as of 1990, yielding

an urbanization index of 20.2.

4. In fact, this cross-time comparison is biased by an expansion in the territorial extent of the Lower Yangzi macroregion during the intervening century. Since the incorporated areas on the northern and southern peripheries are relatively underurbanized, the percentage of urbanization in 1990 is lower than it would be if calculated for the smaller territory of the 1890s macroregion.

5. For a brief explication of the methodology, albeit applied to 1982 rather than 1990 data, see Skinner (1994).

6. The Hong Kong data in this paragraph, taken from *Hong Kong 1991 Population Census Main Report*, are for the entire colony, including the small rural population of the New Territories. To enhance comparability, the data presented for Guangzhou, taken from my computerized datafile for 1990, were applied to the municipality, which includes periurban villages, rather than to the central city per se.

7. The general fertility rate is the number of births in a given year divided by the number of women of childbearing age. This is usually taken to mean women 15–44, but the rate for Hong Kong as given in the 1991 census report was calculated for women 15–49. The figure given for Guangzhou is a recalculation with the same denominator.

REFERENCES

Beers, Burton F. 1978. *China in Old Photographs, 1860–1910*. New York: Scribner.

Boerschmann, Ernst. 1982. *Old China in Historic Photographs*. New York: Dover.

Chan Kam Wing. 1994. *Cities with Invisible Walls: Reinterpreting Urbanization in Post-1949 China*. Hong Kong: Oxford University Press.

Chan, Ming K. 1995. "All in the Family: The Hong Kong–Guangdong Link in Historical Perspective." in *The Hong Kong-Guangdong Link: Partnership in Flux*, edited by Reginald Yin-Wang Kwok and Alvin Y. So, pp. 31–63. Armonk, N.Y.: M. E. Sharpe.

Davis, Deborah. 1993. "Urban Households: Supplicants to a Socialist State," in *Chinese Families in the Post-Mao Era*, edited by Deborah Davis and Stevan Harrell, pp. 50–76. Berkeley: University of California Press.

Elvin, Mark. 1974. "The Administration of Shanghai, 1905–1914," in *The Chinese City between Two Worlds*, edited by Mark Elvin and G. William Skinner, pp. 239–262. Stanford, Cali.: Stanford University Press.

Endacott, G. B. 1973. *A History of Hong Kong* Rev. ed. London: Oxford University Press.

Hong Kong Census Planning Section. 1993. *Hong Kong 1991 Population Census: Main Report*. Hong Kong: Census and Statistics Department.

Ikels, Charlotte. 1993. "Settling Accounts: The Intergenerational Contract in an

Age of Reform," in *Chinese Families in the Post-Mao Era*, edited by Deborah Davis and Stevan Harrell, pp.307–333. Berkeley: University of California Press.

Lavely, William, and Ronald Freedman. 1990. "The Origins of the Chinese Fertility Decline," *Demography* 27: 357–367.

Lee, Robert H. G. 1970. *The Manchurian Frontier in Ch'ing History*. Cambridge, Mass.: Harvard University Press.

Liu Shuyong. 1997. "Hong Kong's Economic Development," *China Today* 46, no. 6: 30–33.

Rowe, William T. 1984. *Hankow: Commerce and Society in a Chinese City, 1796–1889*. Stanford, Cali.: Stanford University Press.

Schipper, Kristofer M. 1977. "Neighborhood Cult Associations in Traditional Tainan," in *The City in Late Imperial China*, edited by G. William Skinner, pp. 651–676. Stanford, Cali.: Stanford University Press.

Skinner, G. William. 1977a. "Regional Urbanization in Nineteenth-Century China," in *The City in Late Imperial China*, edited by G. W. Skinner, pp. 211–249. Stanford Cali.: Stanford University Press.

———.1977b. "Cities and the Hierarchy of Local Systems," in *The City in Late Imperial China*, edited by G. W. Skinner, pp. 275-364. Stanford, Cali.: Stanford University Press.

———.1977c. "Urban Social Structure in Ch'ing China," in *The City in Late Imperial China*, edited by G. W. Skinner, pp. 275-364. Stanford, Cali.: Stanford University Press.

———.1987. "Sichuan's Population in the Nineteenth Century: Lessons from Disaggregated Data." *Late Imperial China* 8: 1–79.

———.1994 "Differential Development in Lingnan," in *The Economic Transformation of South China*, edited by Thomas P. Lyons and Victor Nee, pp. 17–54. Ithaca, N.Y.: Cornell East Asia Program.

Thomson, John. [1873/4] 1982. *China and Its People in Early Photographs*. New York: Dover.

Unger, Jonathan. 1993. "Urban Families in the Eighties: An Analysis of Chinese Surveys," in *Chinese Families in the Post-Mao Era*, edited by Deborah Davis and Stevan Harrell, pp. 25–49. Berkeley, Cali.: University of California Press.

Whyte, Martin King. 1993. "Wedding Behavior and Family Strategies in Chengdu," in *Chinese Families in Post-Mao China*, edited by Deborah Davis and Stevan Harrell, pp. 189–216. Berkeley, Cali.: University of California Press.

4 / Between China and the World

Hong Kong's Economy before and after 1997

BARRY NAUGHTON

The People's Republic of China resumed sovereignty over Hong Kong on July 1, 1997, ending 150 years of colonial rule. The transition has multiple historical, cultural, and political implications that will resonate and unfold for a long time. However, for many, the single most striking and surprising aspect of the change is the contrast between the economies of China and of Hong Kong. Although China is taking over Hong Kong, in comparing the two economies, the advantage appears to be always with Hong Kong. Hong Kong's prosperous and successful capitalist market economy was recently ranked number one in the world on a major index of economic freedom (Heritage Foundation). Hong Kong continues to have a strong legal system, which, combined with active anti-corruption efforts, has kept corruption relatively low. And until the recent downturn in Asian economies, Hong Kong enjoyed rapid, sustained economic growth that gave it the highest per capita income—after adjustment for real purchasing power differences—of any economy in Asia. By contrast, China's economy, while rapidly growing, is still poor and inefficient. It is hobbled by residual elements of the mostly discarded socialist system, including a pervasive pattern of government involvement in the economy on all levels, which has inevitably led to serious corruption problems. To be sure, the leaders of China have pledged that Hong Kong's system will remain unchanged for 50 years. But such reassurances only make it more strikingly apparent that the losing system seems to be taking over the winning system. Skeptics ask whether the losers can be trusted to keep their hands off the accumulated gains of the winners. Optimists follow a different line of reasoning: Since the new rulers are dependent on their new subjects for the secrets of success, they can be trusted not to kill the goose that laid the golden egg. In this respect, the emphasis is inevitably on the benefits that Hong Kong can bring to China, and on the closely related question of whether China can enjoy those benefits without destroying the system that created them.

This sharp contrast between the economies of the People's Republic of China and Hong Kong is certainly real, and the interactions between these two distinct economic systems will shape the economic destiny of southern China for the foreseeable future. However, it is also possible to overemphasize and oversimplify the contrast between the two economies, and, as a result, to misunderstand the challenges, threats, and opportunities that Hong Kong faces in the coming years. The economies of Hong Kong and the People's Republic of China have been deeply intertwined for many years. Indeed, it is impossible to understand the recent development of either economy without reference to the other. The synergies generated between the two economies have been greatly beneficial to both, but perhaps especially so to Hong Kong, certainly on a per capita basis. The increasingly dense network of interactions between these two jurisdictions means that while the two maintain many separate characteristics, they have long since ceased to be two separate economies and in many respects form a single complexly interdependent unity. Inevitably, this means that the spectacular economic success of Hong Kong depends at least partially on its relations with China. A crucial issue for Hong Kong is thus whether it will be able to maintain its privileged position vis-à-vis China in the future. Future challenges will depend primarily on the changing balance of interests and incentives within this complicated relationship, rather than simply on the extent to which Chinese government policies impinge on the freewheeling Hong Kong economy.[1]

In order to provide a glimpse into this complex economic relationship, this chapter looks at the Hong Kong–China economic relationship from a variety of different perspectives. First, I will discuss Hong Kong's role as the entrepôt and gateway to China, and examine the changing balance between trade and manufacturing in the Hong Kong economy. This section presents what might be thought of as the ordinary economics of the Hong Kong–China relationship. It examines the growth of trade and investment, the dramatic restructuring of the Hong Kong economy, and the enormous interdependence that already exists between Hong Kong and China. The second section probes one of the deeper strata in the relationship between Hong Kong and China, stressing the major flows of investment that link the two. While it is well known that Hong Kong is the largest "foreign" investor in China, it is less commonly stressed that China is also the largest "foreign" investor in Hong Kong. There is a substantial two-way flow between the two. An important feature of these two-way flows is the ability of Hong Kong actors to engage in what I call "property rights arbitrage." For a long time, Hong Kong agents have been in a peculiarly advantageous position to profit from the distortions and partial openings of China's economic reform. One result has been large inflows of capital from China to Hong Kong.

The third section takes off from the observations of the previous section. The existence of property rights arbitrage means that Hong Kong has been in the position to earn substantial locational rents from its relationship with China. That is, by virtue of its unique position, businesses and individuals in Hong Kong are able to earn above-normal returns on their skills and efforts, as well as on some of their assets. The overall level of locational rents is increased by some of the peculiar incentives that Beijing possesses vis-à-vis Hong Kong: since Hong Kong's retrocession is widely regarded as a bellwether of Beijing's ability to manage a complex, internationally dependent market economy, Beijing has an enormous incentive to stabilize and guarantee the prosperity of Hong Kong. Inevitably, the process of stabilization costs money, and some of that money flows into the pockets of Hong Kong people.

In the final section, I speculate on the implications of the preceding analysis for Hong Kong's role in the world economy. Hong Kong's future depends not simply on whether China can keep its hands off Hong Kong's prosperity but more importantly on the specific features of the relationship between China and Hong Kong. Hong Kong, I argue, is torn between a steadily deepening involvement with China and the need to increase its efficiency as a world city. To a certain extent, these trajectories conflict. The only way they can be reconciled is through further reform and social progress in China.

THE HONG KONG PARADOX

Yun-wing Sung has written extensively about what he calls the "Hong Kong paradox." The paradox consists of the following: Before China began economic reforms, a significant proportion of China's external trade—and especially of China's exports—was channeled through Hong Kong. One would have expected that liberalization in China would lead to a proliferation of opportunities and channels for export and import, and rapid growth of trade in all parts of China. Therefore, one would expect that although trade between Hong Kong and China would grow rapidly, Hong Kong's *relative* position in China's trade would decrease, simply because of the relatively faster rise of alternate trade opportunities. Instead, the opposite happened: between 1978 and 1993, the proportion of China's trade sent to or through Hong Kong increased steadily and dramatically from 11 percent to 48 percent. The share of Chinese exports going through Hong Kong increased from 21 percent to 52 percent (see figure 1). For Sung, this paradoxical result reflects, above all, the outstanding efficiency of the Hong Kong economy and the presence of economies of scale and scope in an urban center. In Sung's analysis, Hong Kong has attracted the bulk of China's trade to itself simply because it so efficient in carrying out the role of middleman (Yun-wing Sung 1991a, 1991b, 1997).

Sung's pathbreaking analysis provides the elements necessary to understand

Figure 1: Hong Kong's Share of China Trade

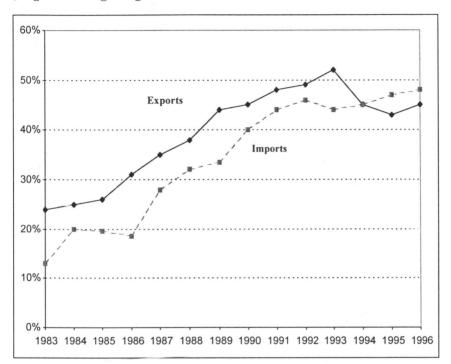

the Hong Kong–China relationship. We can build further on his analysis to point out that Hong Kong's growing role in China trade is due not only to Hong Kong's efficiency as a trader but also to the simple fact that much of "China trade" is in fact a geographic displacement of past "Hong Kong trade." That is, Hong Kong's success as the key China trader is, in fact, founded upon Hong Kong's past success as a manufacturer and upon the transfer of Hong Kong manufacturing capacity to China, especially to Guangdong province. This presents us with a complete historical cycle: Hong Kong first established its prosperity in the nineteenth century by serving as an entrepôt for the China trade and had little or no manufacturing capability. As this section will show, Hong Kong's evolution has essentially been from entrepôt to entrepôt in three generations.

Hong Kong did not develop significant manufacturing capabilities until after 1949. Indeed, Hong Kong indirectly owes its initial manufacturing base to the Chinese Communist Party, because the initial seeds of Hong Kong manufacturing were planted by emigrant industrialists from Shanghai immediately following the 1949 revolution (Wong Siu-lun 1988). Shanghai industrialists brought their familiarity with modern labor-intensive manufacturing, especially in the textile industry. These skills meshed nicely with Hong Kong's existing commercial networks, which were accustomed to transmitting the demands and caprices of world markets to local producers. New industries grew up alongside the transplanted Shanghai textile industry: plastic flowers and rattan furniture led gradually to electronics and precision machinery (Turner 1996). By the early 1980s, it was common to think of Hong Kong as predominantly a producer and exporter of labor-intensive manufactures, and the manufacturing labor force totaled almost a million workers.

During the mid-1980s, economic reforms in China opened up the China coastal region to foreign investment and trade just at the time when rising wages and costs and currency realignments were creating pressures to restructure for exporters in the successful East Asian newly industrializing countries (NICs), including Taiwan, Korea, and Singapore, as well as Hong Kong. Hong Kong businesses were extremely well placed to take advantage of this opportunity, and they responded with a flood of business into the People's Republic of China (PRC), especially into neighboring Guangdong province. Hong Kong investment poured into Guangdong, creating thousands of new foreign-invested enterprises, many of them exporters. Moreover, Hong Kong businesses pioneered new trade arrangements of "outward processing," by which they supplied raw materials and components to Chinese domestic enterprises (often township and village enterprises) for processing and re-export. Thus, there was a massive transfer of manufacturing capacity to the PRC, and especially to Guangdong province.

In 1985, Guangdong produced only 11 percent of China's exports (including most of the 1 percent of exports produced by foreign-invested firms). By 1994, Guangdong produced a staggering 44 percent of China's total exports. Foreign-invested enterprises (FIEs) had grown to produce nearly 30 percent of China's exports, and Guangdong produced more than half of all of those exports. Perhaps even more impressive, Guangdong's domestic enterprises (state-owned firms, collectives, and, increasingly, private firms) had increased their share of Chinese domestic exports (i.e., those not produced by FIEs) to 39 percent (China General Administration of Customs). Thus, behind the growing role of Hong Kong in China's foreign trade is Guangdong's growing role in China's export production. A massive transfer and buildup of capacity has occurred in Guangdong. Since Hong Kong is the natural export outlet for Guangdong manufacturing capacity, it is not surprising that Hong Kong's importance in trade has increased along with Guangdong's growth in manufacturing. More fundamentally, Guangdong's development is itself the result of the restructuring and geographic expansion of Hong Kong's existing manufacturing networks (Naughton 1996).

In turn, that restructuring has fundamentally transformed the nature of the Hong Kong economy. Most obviously, the importance of manufacturing carried out within

Hong Kong has declined dramatically. The manufacturing labor force has fallen by over 60 percent, from nearly a 1,000,000 to only 386,000 at the end of 1995, which represents a drop of from 45 percent to 16 percent of the workforce. Hong Kong itself is increasingly specialized in business services, providing finance, marketing, transport, and communications services to an industrial economy that sprawls throughout Guangdong, and increasingly throughout the entire China mainland.

During the years 1995-1997—the runup to Chinese resumption of sovereignty over Hong Kong—the growth of this industrial complex slowed substantially. Some slowdown was inevitable, simply because the restructuring process had been so thorough. There are simply not that many labor-intensive producers left in Hong Kong—most such activity has already been relocated to neighboring Guangdong province. But other factors are at work as well. Rapid growth has pushed up wages and other costs inside China, and especially in Guangdong, reducing export competitiveness. Nevertheless, additional foreign investment, drawn by the lure of the vast China market, continues to pour in, and the inflow of capital has tended to keep the Chinese currency appreciating in real terms, further squeezing exporters (Naughton 1996). In Guangdong, economic success has led to increasing congestion and rising costs. Guangdong's share of Chinese exports declined after 1994, reflecting reductions in Guangdong's share both of domestic firm exports (from 39 percent to 33 percent in 1996) and of FIE exports (from 57 percent to 49.9 percent) in two years.

Thus, the economies of Hong Kong and (at least) Guangdong are already highly integrated. Integrating these two disparate economic systems is not the challenge facing Hong Kong post-1997. Rather, the challenge is to improve the productivity and competitiveness of an existing export economy. The export economy is centered on Hong Kong but sprawls across the border into Guangdong. The export complex has lost the benefits of extremely low labor costs that provided the basis for the first period of very rapid growth. It now needs to find a basis for enhanced competitiveness by improving efficiency and technological capacity.

PROPERTY RIGHTS ARBITRAGE

At the same time that the restructuring of Hong Kong manufacturing has taken place, the opening of China has created another type of opportunity for Hong Kong. This is the opportunity to engage in what I call "property rights arbitrage." In this business, Hong Kong residents profit from the existence in Hong Kong of a secure and transparent system of property rights, in close proximity to the vague and uncertain property rights regime in China. Hong Kong has benefited from the wholesale transplantation of the British property rights regime and the full panoply of supporting legal and commercial institutions, which evolved in Britain over hundreds of years. An effective and generally fair judiciary, with clear enforcement powers, was supplemented in 1974 by the creation of the powerful Independent Commission Against Corruption (Chan 1997). As a result, commercial transactions in Hong Kong take place in a legal regime that is as clear and transparent as any developed market economy. By contrast, despite the progress that has been made in China during nearly 20 years of economic reform, property rights there remain vague, difficult or impossible to enforce, and always ultimately uncertain. Distribution of ownership and control rights is rarely precise, and interested parties only occasionally have recourse to third-party adjudication in disputes about control rights. Even when courts can be brought in to make civil judgments (as in contract disputes), they are often unable to enforce their judgments (Clarke 1996), which results in a persistent demand within China for secure property rights. Hong Kong, by virtue of its proximity to China, its cultural similarities, and its excellent property rights regime is in a position to satisfy this demand.

PRC residents come to Hong Kong in a steady stream, looking for opportunities to transform assets over which they have uncertain claim into secure and liquid assets. In return, these PRC residents are prepared to provide "inside information," which they possess in abundance, to those who can assist them. The basic act of arbitrage is the exchange of inside information for the opportunity to transform existing control rights into secure ownership under Hong Kong's legal system. Inside information should be understood here as knowledge about economic opportunities—both socially productive and socially unproductive—which those residents would exploit openly if they had access to secure property rights over the return thereby generated. PRC residents may hesitate to exploit these opportunities in the absence of secure claims over the resulting return. However, they will be happy to share those opportunities with "outsiders" who can offer them a secure claim to a portion of the resulting returns. In the current Chinese context, those outsiders are often from Hong Kong.

There is a broad spectrum of activities that fit into this general description. At one extreme, Hong Kong serves as a safe haven for assets plundered from the public. Exploiting political position and family ties, individuals in the PRC move essentially stolen capital into Hong Kong, where nobody asks questions. At the other end of the spectrum, public and privately owned businesses in China move assets to Hong Kong in order to increase their operational autonomy, learn about new property rights procedures, and access information about the world market. In the latter case, formal ownership doesn't change, but the way that ownership is exercised does. In this situation, even publicly owned corporations can benefit from the Hong Kong property rights regime, since it provides a set of procedures and examples for specifying control rights and thereby improving managerial autonomy and incentives.

It is important to maintain the right balance between cynicism and enthusiasm in examining the process of property rights arbitrage. This process includes both laundering (money) and learning (new commercial institutions), as well as many other activities in between. For example, even state-owned firms in China maneuver to gain greater autonomy and more secure managerial control over their own assets. When they establish Hong Kong subsidiaries, those subsidiaries can invest back in China with the status of "foreign investors." Ventures entered into in China by these bogus foreigners (*jia yangguizi*) qualify for tax breaks and expanded autonomy. This round-tripping of investment is sometimes referred to with a snicker, as if the economic transactions being reported were somehow phony or inflated. In fact, such transactions are an important part of the success of China's economic reforms. Public enterprises maneuver for greater autonomy, and in the process establish new institutional forms—and new forms of accountability—that contribute to the transition to a new property rights regime within China.

Indeed, the establishment of a stronger and more clearly specified property rights regime is a necessary part of the transition to an open market economy. Every economy making the transition from socialism faces difficult decisions about the extent to which state-appointed managers may be allowed to transform their effective political control over nominally public assets into private ownership. In the long run, the transition to a market economy clearly and inevitably implies the conversion of most formerly public assets into private property. While it would be nice to think that this process could be entirely fair, it is unlikely that it ever will be. Some managers will be able to convert a portion of the value of assets they control into their own private property. Moreover, even in a perfect world, it would probably not be desirable to reduce to zero the incidence of such conversion of public assets to private ownership. To do so would simply do too much to inhibit the development of productive potential by those in a position to identify and exploit it. Thus, in China, as in other transitional economies, there will always be politically powerful and influential individuals who are able to convert their privileged positions into economically valuable assets. What is distinctive about China is that Hong Kong is so clearly the superior venue in which to carry out this transformation.[2]

We can gain important insight into the process of property rights arbitrage by examining Chinese firms in Hong Kong. By early 1997, there were about 3,700 Chinese enterprises in China, active in all sectors and pursuing a variety of objectives and commercial strategies (Huchet 1997; also Wong 1993). The mainland firms in Hong Kong that have attracted the most attention lately are the so-called red chips. The term refers to 62 firms with a predominant PRC ownership stake, which are now based in Hong Kong and are listed on the Hong Kong stock exchange. During 1996, the red chips appreciated by an average of 70 percent, significantly outperforming the booming Hong Kong market. By the spring of 1997, the red chips accounted for more than 7 percent of Hong Kong's stock market capitalization and were again outperforming the market in the runup to July 1. Of course, listing on the Hong Kong exchange is a way for these firms to attract financing, and indeed, over $1.4 billion was raised in 1996–97. But this capital is attracted with the expectation of access to mainland China properties. Indeed, according to one calculation, the total valuation of the red chips, at $32 billion, reflects an "excess" valuation of $11 billion relative to the market's average price-earnings ratio. This reflects both the implicit valuation placed by the market on the red chips' politically influential connections and the expectation that mainland parents will transfer significant assets to their subsidiaries. "Large goodwill premiums may be justified if an influential Chinese parent is likely to inject under-priced assets in exchange for over-priced shares in its listed subsidiary, as happened with CITIC Pacific." ("Red chips" 1997; Ridding 1997). Alternately stated, red chips are favored by the Hong Kong stock market because they are viewed as a way for the average investor to participate in the ongoing process of property rights arbitrage.

CITIC Pacific is by far the largest of the red chips, with a stock market capitalization equivalent to over US$10 billion in May 1997. Its holdings are extensive (see figure 2), and CITIC Pacific has gradually expanded its investments to give it a large stake in the regulated monopolies of the Hong Kong economy. In early 1997, CITIC Pacific had substantial stakes in both of Hong Kong's airlines (Cathay Pacific and Dragonair), Hongkong Telecom, and Hong Kong Light and Power.[3] These deals—all joint ventures with existing Hong Kong companies—provide interesting benefits to both sides. CITIC Pacific can claim, with some justification, to be investing in infrastructure in Hong Kong and the mainland, as Chinese policy deems preferable. CITIC Pacific's partners hope to gain an influential partner in Beijing, so they have a clear pipeline to exert influence. At the same time, CITIC Pacific often appeared to get "sweetheart" deals in its purchase of stakes for precisely this reason.[4]

A second aspect of Hong Kong business can be loosely grouped under the rubric of property rights arbitrage. Hong Kong has developed an enormous business providing information about China to the world business community. Just as China's property rights regime is opaque, so information about commercial opportunities in China is sketchy and difficult to interpret. Hong Kong firms and individuals serve as middlemen, introducing foreign companies to opportunities and partners in China. Some of this is pure consulting work, translating terms and legal concepts into Western languages. But much of it is far more extensive deal making. Hong Kong firms serve as investment bankers, matching up foreign businesses and Chinese clients. Some of this can be quite lucrative.

Figure 2. Citic Pacific: expanding empire

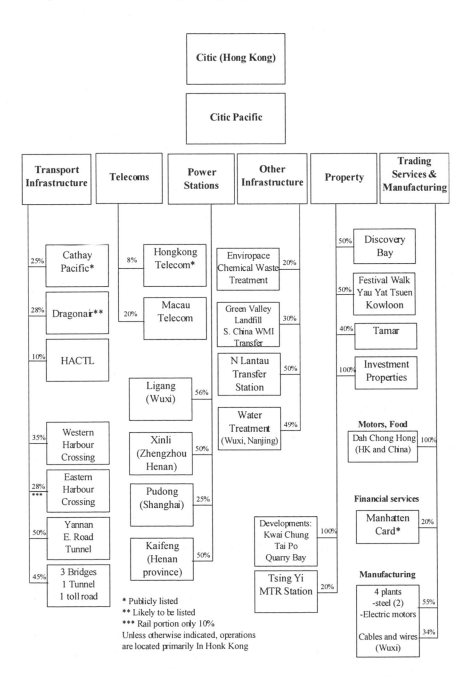

The operations of the U.S. transnational corporation Avon Cosmetics is an example of this type of activity. Avon tried without success for several years to get into China. Ultimately, the company went through a Hong Kong banker, David Li of the Bank of East Asia, who was able to structure a deal with a small Guangzhou cosmetics factory and obtain the necessary approvals. In return, Li and a Hong Kong associate received 5 percent of the value of the resulting joint venture, which is now a substantial business (White 1991; Laidler 1994). Clearly, Li provided real information and assistance of substantial value to Avon. More crucially, he was also able to provide something useful to the relevant decisionmakers in China. After all, they could simply have accepted Avon's earlier overtures, but something was lacking, presumably the opportunity to attract all the necessary decisionmakers to a package that offered something for each of them. Li was able to succeed not only because he could determine who all the relevant decisionmakers were, but also because he could structure a deal that had something for all of them. Undoubtedly, he was assisted in this process by the abundant, secure opportunities in Hong Kong, to which he could make explicit or implicit promises of access.

Most of the property rights arbitrage in which Hong Kong has engaged has probably resulted in increased productive activity and improved living conditions for the people of Guangdong, Beijing, and Hong Kong. The gains made from opening up China and combining available low-cost labor with world markets and capital were simply so enormous that even if individuals skimmed off part of the benefit, there was plenty left for the public good. Hong Kong has played a significant role in this process. It is not quite enough to say that Hong Kong benefited from the rule of law and secure property rights; it did so benefit, but it benefited even more from the fortuitous combination of protected property rights in Hong Kong and insecure property rights inside a China in transition.

A final type of transaction that might perhaps be placed under the general rubric of property rights arbitrage is smuggling. Granted that smuggling is different in kind from the activities previously discussed, it does bear some important similarities. Goods are brought into Hong Kong legally, efficiently, and cheaply and required only one quick and relatively inexpensive step to be smuggled into China. Smuggling is lucrative precisely because legal imports to China are limited by high tariffs and a tangle of difficult-to-navigate administrative restrictions. Again, Hong Kong earns locational rents from its position as the superior jumping-off station for smuggling into China. Huge contraband traffic flows are known to exist in cigarettes (Smith 1996), fruit (Iritani 1997), and consumer electronics (Huang 1993). In all these instances, Hong Kong agents play a pivotal role and earn substantial revenues.

It is appropriate to end this section by reviewing the overall magnitude of the processes discussed above. Some idea of the relevant magnitudes can be achieved from examining China's balance of payments (Table 1). In 1995, China's current account was approximately in balance. A trade surplus of $18 billion was enough to pay for freight charges of almost $9 billion and profit remittances of $10 billion. Hong Kong, as a service provider, was a major earner of freight charges and a major recipient of profit remittances. Capital poured into China, almost $39 billion. But despite the balanced current account, China's foreign exchange reserves increased only $22.5 billion. Errors and omissions added up to a staggering $17.8 billion net outflow (errors and omissions have been approximately $10 billion or more since 1993). Errors and omissions were equal to about 12 percent of China's total exports and equivalent to the total export surplus. Errors and omissions basically reflect three factors: (1) smuggling into China, (2) flight of capital out of China, and (3) services purchased outside of China that do not get recorded by the formal statistical system. A plausible guess might be that the above list reflects the relative ranking of factors as well. For our purposes, what is important is that in each of these flows, Hong Kong agents play a crucial and lucrative role.[5]

Hong Kong's entanglement with the Chinese economy permits us to trace other

Table 1. China's Balance of Payments 1995
(Billion US Dollars)

Current Account	**1.62**
Trade	18.05
Freight	-8.67
Tourism	5.04
Investment	-11.77
of which: Profit	-9.95
Transfers	1.44
Capital Account	**38.67**
Errors and Omissions	**-17.81**
Change in Reserves	**-22.48**

Source: State Statistical Bureau 1996: 620-621

interactions as well. One important way in which capital is moved across borders covertly is through over-invoicing of imports and under-invoicing of exports. There is no simple way to detect under-invoicing but there are some interesting numbers that allow us to estimate the joint impact of under-invoicing and the real economic advantages that Hong Kong possesses. In 1995, Hong Kong imported US$67.2 billion of commodities from China and re-exported $82.3 billion of Chinese commodities (Census and Statistics Department 1996: 80). This is not impossible. Hong Kong shippers and marketers add value to commodities brought in from China. However, keeping in mind that about 8 percent of Chinese imports are retained in Hong Kong, these numbers, taken at face value, would imply that Hong Kong re-exports added, on average, 33 percent to the value of commodities from China. This is a lot of value to add, and the relationship does not hold for any other country's re-exports through Hong Kong.

Consider a related set of numbers. In the same year, exporters inside China imported US$58.4 billion worth of duty-free components and raw materials for export production. Most of these exporters were foreign-invested firms; most of the foreign investment comes from Hong Kong. These producers then exported commodities made with duty-free imports to the value of $73.7 billion (not all of this through Hong Kong). That is, the value of their exports was 26 percent greater than the value of their imports (General Administration of Customs 1995). These data imply that for goods "manufactured in China" and re-exported through Hong Kong, a greater share of the value is retained in Hong Kong than is retained in China.[6] While we cannot say anything definitive about who ought to be earning the net revenues from exporting, we can say that the agents who control the transactions choose to have the majority of those net revenues accrue in Hong Kong, even though the bulk of the manufacturing activity, at least, is performed inside China.[7] Moreover, we can begin to understand another piece of the "Hong Kong paradox." Hong Kong has increased its share of China's trade despite reform in part because traders prefer to divert transactions to Hong Kong in order to take advantage of Hong Kong's more accommodating property rights regime.

THE EMERGING PARTNERSHIP BETWEEN
HONG KONG AND BEIJING

The previous section discussed the impact of property rights arbitrage, an activity that reflects the interests of individuals and individual businesses or organizations. In addition, though, economic exchanges between China and Hong Kong are influenced by the interests of the Beijing government through officials acting in an official capacity.

Politically, the return of Hong Kong is an event of great importance. If it is bungled, it will reflect extremely poorly on the Beijing leaders who are responsible. No individual Beijing leader is likely to survive politically if he appears to have mishandled Hong Kong's prosperity. Moreover, because the PRC is a huge investor in Hong Kong through thousands of legitimate and illegitimate, public and private channels, and because Hong Kong is so important to China's export economy, there are substantial reasons to try to guarantee the economic functioning of Hong Kong.

As a result of these intersecting political, economic, and personal factors, the PRC is far more likely to try to prop up the Hong Kong economy in case of adversity than it is to try to extract resources from it. In that respect, the post-1997 reality will be a continuation of the pre-1997 reality. The Beijing government will step in to insulate the Hong Kong economy from some of the fluctuations occasionally induced by its free-market economy. Indeed, Beijing has already earmarked a potential "rescue fund" to shore up the Hong Kong stock exchange. This follows earlier Chinese intervention in October 1987 and June 1989 to protect the Hong Kong market in the face of external shocks, of U.S. and Chinese origin, respectively (Lucas 1996). In the sphere of currency intervention, the Asian business crisis revealed China's resolve to hold to its agreement to support the Hong Kong dollar, even while promising that Hong Kong funds will not be used to rescue the PRC in case of fluctuations there (Sheng 1997). According to one insider account, during the first half of 1997—the runup to the July 1 retrocession—Beijing spent the equivalent in Hong Kong dollars of US$12 billion in order to support the property and stock markets in Hong Kong (Luo Bing 1997).

For the Chinese government, such investments have a dual motivation. The first is simply to stabilize a potentially unstable market, in a situation in which instability would have adverse consequences for Chinese policy. The second motivation is to secure what the Chinese government sees as "strategic" influence over the Hong Kong economy. Chinese leaders unquestionably see the Hong Kong economy as dominated by U.S. and British corporations, including long-standing Hong Kong corporations that are descendants of British hongs. In this respect, the Chinese government engineered a stunning conversion of control over Hong Kong's strategic industries in little more than a year. Beginning with the purchase in April 1996 of a stake in Cathay Pacific Airlines, Hong Kong's flag carrier, and ending with the purchase in June 1997 of 5.5 percent of Hongkong Telecom by China Telecom, close affiliates of the Beijing government gained a minority interest in all the main utilities and communications firms in Hong Kong.

The expansion of Beijing interests in Hong Kong inevitably implies a flow of resources into Hong Kong. Initially, this may not be evident, because Beijing has been able to acquire many of these assets at bargain prices, because China is and will continue to be an enormous opportunity for businesses in Hong Kong. Thus, the owners of each of Hong Kong's strategic industries were willing to pass on a minority stake at bargain prices, perceiving this transaction as a way to open the door to further business on the Chinese mainland. Currently, a wave of restructuring is taking place in Hong Kong, as businesses there try to position themselves to benefit from future opportunities in the new policy environment. Many Hong Kong corporations, most notably Li Kashing's Cheung Kong Holdings, are going through restructuring processes designed to position them closer to channels of influence leading to Beijing and thus able to take advantage of new opportunities decided increasingly by the government in Beijing. This is generally not a defensive restructuring, but rather an aggressive effort to position companies to take advantage of new opportunities. Private interests seek to accommodate Chinese government interests and to profit thereby. Profit may be particularly easy to attain because the Beijing government also seeks to woo Hong Kong capitalists to support the new regime. In this respect, Beijing seeks to replicate the traditional British power structure and ensure a policy in which business interests are the primary support of the post-1997 regime (Beja 1997).

THE FUTURE?

What, then, of Hong Kong's future? I hope the preceding pages have convinced the reader that Hong Kong's economy is already engaged in a complex, multifaceted collaboration with businesses and government in the PRC. As a result, we cannot reasonably reduce the question of Hong Kong's economic future to the question of whether China will be able to leave Hong Kong's economic system alone to flourish. An alternative perspective would be to see Hong Kong as poised between two contrasting economic futures: Hong Kong–International and Hong Kong–China (Business and Professionals Federation of Hong Kong, 1993). Hong Kong has been remarkably successful as an international city, building first an export base and subsequently an international service corporation of exemplary efficiency. Particularly since the mid-1980s, the success of Hong Kong–International has been reinforced by the lucrative and successful business of Hong Kong–China, as Hong Kong has reaped the locational rents provided by its unique access to the emerging Chinese market and production base.

As of 1997, the two alternative visions of Hong Kong–International and Hong Kong–China are beginning to show signs of conflict. One source of conflict is purely economic. As described above, rising costs are eroding the competitiveness of the Hong Kong–Guangdong export complex, even as further market openings within China attract more foreign (and Hong Kong) investment to China. As a result, the appeal of business in China is increasingly drawing Hong Kong businesses, and especially the biggest Hong Kong businesses, into tight collaboration with the PRC. The danger of an excessive orientation toward China exists, not because of governmental controls but because of the very lucrative opportunities that continue to be found there.

Moreover, if economic reforms in China stall, Hong Kong agents will continue to engage in property rights arbitrage, but ultimately this will hurt them. Resources will continue to flow into Hong Kong so long as the PRC cannot provide secure property rights. However, in order to protect mainland businesses, Hong Kong companies would be drawn more and more deeply into corrupt arrangements in China, and further and further away from the alternative future envisaged in "Hong Kong–International." Moreover, in this type of scenario, as Huchet (1997) points out, even as Hong Kong retains its overall prosperity, Hong Kong companies will have less of a comparative advantage over Chinese companies in Hong Kong. Chinese enterprises in Hong Kong are better prepared, Huchet argues, to process Chinese economic interests in Hong Kong. The lure of real opportunity combined with special privileges may draw Hong Kong into an intensified collaboration with China that might cause Hong Kong to become less oriented toward providing efficient commercial and intermediary services to the East Asian region as a whole. Hong Kong is still small: its labor force and land area are tiny, and it probably cannot be all things to all people. If its political and economic leaders pursue the vision of a Hong Kong that predominantly serves the Chinese economy, this will almost certainly mean a relative diminution in Hong Kong's international role. This does not necessarily mean a less prosperous, or an unhappy, Hong Kong. But it might mean one that plays a less distinctive role in the world economy than Hong Kong does today.

One path through which this might occur is an interventionist attempt to build Hong Kong's technological capability in order to infuse the Hong Kong–centered manufacturing network with an additional competitive advantage. Moreover, pressures to do so are inevitable, given the rising costs being experienced in the Hong Kong–Guangdong production complex and the apparent decline in the rapid growth of labor-intensive manufactured exports. Recently, two major studies, commissioned by important Hong Kong agencies, have recommended related policies (Berger and Lester 1997; Enright 1997). Such proposals for an activist government policy to foster technological upgrading are said to regarded favorably by the new chief executive, C. H. Tung ("Riding the Next Industrial Wave," 1997). Government support for such an industrial policy, combined with concessionary access to opportunities on the mainland, could prove an irresistible lure for Hong Kong businesses.

On balance, this scenario would be somewhat negative for Hong Kong's development, and indirectly for that of China. China would be better served by a more comprehensive opening up, rather than a type of "hothouse development" with Hong Kong playing a catalytic, but controlled, role. Hong Kong's past movement from entrepôt to manufacturing power to entrepôt shows that the past does not determine the future. With the benefit of good human skills and physical infra-structure, Hong Kong, like any successful economy, should be able to remake itself over and over again, adapting to the changing mix of opportunities and chal-lenges. Moreover, Hong Kong residents have dispersed around the globe, consti-tuting an international network of potentially huge value to Hong Kong's future development.

In an alternative scenario, further reforms in China would make Hong Kong's position less special. Hong Kong would enjoy fewer locational rents, and there would be a smaller influx of flight capital and strategic investments. Hong Kong's property market, still expensive despite easing off during the Asian business cri-sis, might continue to lose more of its value because it would not be necessary to concentrate so many activities in Hong Kong's tiny land space. But in compensa-tion, Hong Kong's prosperity would ultimately be less precarious than in the first scenario. Hong Kong companies and individuals would be able to bring their skills into play throughout China and the world. Rather than managing the Hong Kong–Guangdong export complex, Hong Kong people would serve as catalysts for a broad-based process of economic growth throughout southern China. In a dynamic growth process of this kind, the conflict between Hong Kong–China and Hong Kong–International would be less fundamental, and Hong Kong would be able to mediate a productive development synthesizing the needs of both.

NOTES

1. For example, the tendency to see the Chinese and Hong Kong economies as fundamentally separate recently led the Speaker of the U.S. House of Representatives, Newt Gingrich, to propose using China's most favored nation (MFN) trading status as a reward for good Chinese behavior toward Hong Kong. Gingrich proposed a six-month conditional MFN status for China, while its behavior toward Hong Kong was closely monitored. The problem with using MFN status as a reward or punishment for China's conduct toward Hong Kong is that it fails to recognize that the economies are so intertwined that cancellation of the MFN designation for China would be even more devastating for Hong Kong. Gingrich's proposed sanction provoked the polite, but essentially caustic, reminder from Chris Patton that "for the people of Hong Kong there is no comfort in the proposition that if China reduces their freedoms, the United States will take away their jobs." Paul Blustein and John E. Yang, "Hong Kong Leaders Reject GOP Plan," *Washington Post*, May 9, 1997, p. 1.

2. In any case, the weak property rights and unfair distribution of control over nominally public assets that create this profitable arbitrage are, after all, characteristics of the PRC legal regime, not that of Hong Kong. There is no point in blaming Hong Kong for it.

3. The stake in Hongkong Telecom was sold to another red chip, China Everbright in May 1997. China Everbright might plausibly be considered to have even closer ties to the current Beijing leadership than CITIC Pacific. Since Cable & Wireless, the parent of Hongkong Telecom, subsequently sold an additional 5.5 percent stake to China Telecom, a corporation wholly owned by the Chinese Ministry of Post and Telecommunications, it is reasonable to interpret this subsequent reshuffling of assets as bringing Hongkong Telecom more directly into the sphere of Chinese government interest.

4. Ironically, the head of CITIC Pacific, Larry Yung, is often labeled a "princeling" who traded on the influence of his family, since his father Rong Yiren, besides being the founder of CITIC, the Beijing parent of CITIC Pacific, was also a vice president of China. However, this criticism is misguided. Rong Yiren was first and foremost a Shanghai capitalist who chose to stay in Shanghai while most of the rest of his family relocated to Hong Kong (see Wong Siu-lun 1988). For this service he was—after the tribulations of the Cultural Revolution—rewarded with money and influence. But this did not thereby bring his family into the inner circle of Communist Party leaders.

5. See Gunter (1996) for a heroic attempt to untangle some of the factors relating to capital flight from the PRC.

6. The fit between these two sets of numbers is not perfect. The Chinese numbers refer to transactions that are known in Hong Kong as "outward processing." Outward processing accounted for an estimated 82 percent of Hong Kong's re-exports of Chinese origin in 1995. Thus, while no precise comparison between the numbers is possible (or attempted here), they refer to broad categories of goods that generally overlap.

7. There is no point in going further to disentangle this data, which reflect a combination of factors. First, because Hong Kong specializes in higher-skilled stages of the value-added chain, it earns much higher returns on its productive inputs and claims a surprisingly large share of total value-added. By contrast, China contributes predominantly unskilled labor, with little earning power. In either case, though, agents based in both China and Hong Kong choose to transfer revenues from China to Hong Kong by understating the value of the commodities shipped from China to Hong Kong (i.e., by "under-invoicing") to take advantage of a favorable taxation and property rights regime. Again, Hong Kong benefits due *both* to its superior efficiency and its status as a property haven. The figure for value-added within China is also lower because some duty-free imports are diverted to the domestic market and are never used in export production at all. This does not directly affect Hong Kong interests, except to the extent that Hong Kong businesses specialize in such activities. In fact, there is substantial evidence of such activity by specialized Hong Kong businesses, which are called channel providers.

REFERENCES

Beja, Jean Philippe. 1997. "Hong Kong Two Months before the Handover: One Territory, Two Systems?" *China News Analysis 1583,* April 15.

Berger, Suzanne, and Richard K. Lester, eds. 1997. *Made by Hong Kong.* Hong Kong: Oxford University Press.

Business & Professionals Federation of Hong Kong. 1993. *Hong Kong 21: A Ten-Year Vision and Agenda for Hong Kong's Economy.* Hong Kong: Business & Professionals Federation of Hong Kong.

Census and Statistics Department, Government of Hong Kong. 1996. *Annual Review of Hong Kong External Trade 1995.* Hong Kong: Census and Statistics Department.

Chan Kin-man. 1997. "Combating Corruption and the ICAC," in *The Other Hong Kong Report 1997,* edited by Joseph Y.S. Cheng, pp. 101–121. Hong Kong: Chinese University of Hong Kong Press.

Clark, Donald C. 1996. "Power and Politics in the Chinese Court System: The Enforcement of Civil Judgments," *Columbia Journal of Asian Law* 10, no. 1: 1-92.

Enright, Michael J. 1997. Hong Kong Advantage. Hong Kong: Oxford University Press.

General Administration of Customs. 1995. *China Customs Statistics.*

Gunter, Frank R. 1996. "Capital Flight from the People's Republic of China," *China Economic Review* 7, no. 1 (Spring): 77–96.

Heritage Foundation. Report on economic freedom, as reported by Hong Kong Trade and Development Council website at http://www.tdc.org.hk/hktstat/ 97index.htm.

Huang Weiding. 1992. *Zhongguo de Yinxing Jingji* (China's Hidden Economy). Beijing: Zhongguo Shangye.

Huchet, Jean-Francois. 1997. "Les entreprises chinoises à Hong Kong: Des partenaires ambigus dans l'avenir du Territoire." *Perspectives Chinoises* 41 (May/June): 54–66.

Iritani, Evelyn. 1997. "U.S. Orange Trade with China Sour and Sweet," *Los Angeles Times,* August 12, pp. A1, A6.

Laidler, Nathalie. 1994. "Mary Kay Cosmetics: Asian Market Entry." *Harvard Business School Case Study, 9-594-023.*

Lucas, Louise. 1996. "Beijing plans fund to shore up Hong Kong market," *Financial Times,* October 30, p. 6.

Luo Bing. 1997. "Hong Kong: Beijing supports the market with billions," *Zhengming* 236 (June), translated by Jacques Seurre in *Perspectives Chinoises* 41, (May/June): 52–53.

Naughton, Barry. 1996. "China's Emergence and Future as a Trading Nation," *Brookings Papers on Economic Activity* 2: 273–344.

Pritchard, Simon. 1997. "Way forward is with feet firmly on the floor," *South China Morning Post*, 1 July, p. B18. ·

"Red chips" 1997. "The Lex Column," *Financial Times*, March 27, p. 16.

Ridding, John. 1997. "Red Chips and Dark Horses," *Financial Times*, February 24, p. 15.

"Riding the Next Industrial Wave," 1997. *The Industrialist* (February): 11–17.

Sheng, Andrew. 1997. "Hong Kong Will Remain a Free Market after 1997," *Transition* 8, no. 2 (April): 1–3.

Smith, Craig. 1996. "Smugglers Stoke B.A.T's Cigarette Sales in China: Company Condemns Illicit Trade, but Churns Out Smokes to Supply It," *The Wall Street Journal*, December 18, p. A16.

Sung Yun-wing. 1991a. "Hong Kong's Economic Value to China," in *The Other Hong Kong Report 1991*, edited by Sung Yun-wing and Lee Ming-kwan, pp. 477–504. Hong Kong: Chinese University of Hong Kong Press.

———. 1991b. *The China–Hong Kong Connection: The Key to China's Open Door*. Cambridge: Cambridge University Press.

———. 1997. "Hong Kong and the Economic Integration of the China Circle," in *The China Circle: Economics and Technology in the PRC, Taiwan, and Hong Kong,* edited by Barry Naughton, pp. 41–80. Washington, D.C.: The Brookings Institute.

Turner, Matthew. 1996. "Hong Kong Design and the Roots of Sino-American Trade Disputes," *Annals of the American Academy* 547 (September): 37–53.

White, George. 1991. "Hong Kong Bankers Help Open Doors to China," *Los Angeles Times,* July 1.

Wong, John. 1992. "PRC Business in Hong Kong: A Prelude to Economic Take-Over?" Institute of East Asian Philosophies Internal Study Paper No. 4 (March), National University of Singapore.

Wong Siu-lun. 1988. *Emigrant Entrepreneurs: Shanghai Industrialists in Hong Kong.* Hong Kong: Oxford University Press.

5 / Hong Kong

Cultural Kaleidoscope on a World Landscape

HELEN F. SIU

THE MEANING OF 'SOVEREIGNTY' AT THE MARGINS: THEN AND NOW

On June 1997, the world watched Hong Kong go through the ritual of reuniting with China, and the dynamic energies that had to do with sovereignty, the physical embodiments being the flag and the national anthem. At midnight of June 30, the blue flag of Hong Kong with the British crown was lowered and the red flag with the five stars raised. No individual preferences could have reversed the solemn occasion, which was shaped by larger structures of history and power.

Although these physical symbols cannot be arbitrarily changed, empires have related to subject populations with notions of the political quite differently from those of modern nation-states. The meaning of sovereignty at the political center also differed from that in the margins. Numerous historical landmarks related to these notions have churned the cultural kaleidoscope we now call Hong Kong. We are all-too-familiar with how the political history of these events is told today. I would, however, explore the social and cultural meanings of people's lives on the ground, which may not always fit political categorizing.

Chinese official documents consistently use a neutral phrase, "China resumes sovereign control over Hong Kong," to describe the political handover. However, the popular term "reunification" (*huigui*) is loaded with emotions. The question is, while sovereignty is resumed, should historical experiences be reclaimed? The notion "one country, two systems" is a unique one. "One country" refers to sovereignty. "Two systems" on the other hand involves complex histories and contradictory sentiments.[1] If the region's populations are urged to trace their ancestral roots (*renzu guizong*) and exert their nationalistic commitments toward a political center, shouldn't they begin by respecting and appreciating their own historical experiences? Maybe only on that basis can the "two systems" side of the political formula be realized.

One often associates sovereignty with images of stately capitals and national pride, with clear-cut notions of "we" and "they." In 1842, however, the emotions of local populations on the South China coast might have been ambivalent. Who was in the region then? Although at the margins of empires, Hong Kong was not a barren rock when the British came. There were historic sites in the general area around Hong Kong. Tuen Mun, Fat Tong Mun, and Kap Sui Mun were along major trade routes during the Tang and Song dynasties. Traders came from Europe, the Middle East, and Southeast Asia on their way to China. Local settlements developed unique cultures and occupations. They produced commodities ranging from salt and lime to pearls and incense. Imperial officials kept their disdainful distance, except for occasional excursions to punish real or imagined rebels. History tells us that battles were fought that determined dynastic fortunes. Those between the supporters of the child emperor Bing of the Southern Song dynasty and the pursuing Mongols were the most prominent. They left a repertoire of myths and memories.

During the Ming and Qing, commerce in the area grew with agricultural development. River marshes in the delta were sought after by single-surnamed territorial groups who claimed origins from the Central Plains. Market towns mushroomed. Land and trading rights were contested. Local elites used the imperial metaphor to support their claims and to create alliances. These land-based settlements developed a cultural complex strongly identified with the literati and authority. Similar processes took place in the New Territories.[2]

While landed elites eagerly sought Confucian cultural symbols, unorthodox trading networks thrived along the South China coast and in Guangzhou, Macao, and the Pearl River delta. One would have found Chinese junks flying Dutch and Portuguese flags for convenience and protection. Foreign traders came to conduct business with China and used the region's waters for replenishing their fleets. Local populations did the provisioning.[3] There were conflicts, but local and foreign traders were also partners in many ways. The extent of their involvement and their multiethnic affiliations alarmed officials, who often termed them "*yiyu jiangun*," and lamented that "this situation in the south had always meant trouble."[4]

Encounters with foreigners in the general area were not limited to the material. Missionaries who aimed to sink roots in local society encouraged indigenization.[5] One may summarize that from the sixteenth century onward, despite official displeasure, there was much cultural borrowing and tolerance. Identities were fluid. Emergent Han lineages, mobile and multiethnic traders, religious practitioners, pirates, and officials competed and mingled in this open and diversified ecology.

On the eve of the Opium War, the livelihoods and cultural affiliations of people on the South China coast were tied to imperial and foreign interests in complicated ways. Take Xiangshan county as an example. Its proximity to Macao and the commercial networks of Guangzhou prompted officials to comment with dismay that its residents "had been tainted with foreign ways" (*jianran yisu*). But many innovative comprador/officials in Guangzhou and Shanghai came from this county—the prominent ones were Yung Wing, Zheng Guanying, Xu Run. Modern historians have noted their progressive political beliefs and entrepreneurial energies.

When Hong Kong was ceded to Britain, local traders in the area were, at best, intrigued bystanders quite beyond the reach of formal state apparatus. No doubt conflicts arose from competition and prejudices among the settlers, and between them and foreign interests. But one wonders if the populations at the southernmost frontier of the empire shared the wounded pride of those at the political center.[6] According to official Chinese historical accounts, the Sanyuanli incident in Guangzhou in 1841 was an anti-imperialist patriotic act by local masses, just as the occupation of Guangzhou by British and French forces in 1857 and 1860 was regarded as national humiliation. However, a closer look at the culture of local resistance reveals divergent meanings: acts against foreign encroachment did not necessarily mean loyalty to the imperial center. No doubt the residents of Sanyuanli fought the British troops. The reason could have been simple: when someone pressed against one's door and looted one's property, resistance could only be expected. Community feuds could have triggered similar actions. Moreover, in 1899, major lineages in the New Territories fought the British for fear that the "barbarians" would take their land and side with their competitors. The significance of the dispute revolved around "lineage land" rather than the emperor's land. Would the aggressors be regarded as representatives of Britain as a country, or as "bandits" who happened to be foreign acting in their own interests? These emotions were probably too complicated to explain as local patriotism. Moreover, for the governments involved, their sense of humiliation or triumph had less to do with the territory's fate than their own. In fact, both officials at the negotiating table, Qishan and Charles Elliot, were disgraced for having chosen Hong Kong as a point of departure.

WHAT WERE THE EMOTIONS ON THE EVE OF 1997

In 1997, the stakes were much higher, because the fortunes and sentiments of millions were now rooted in the territory. A colonial perspective downplayed the role of either China or the local populations before the Opium War and it claimed credit for the miraculous transformation of the territory.[7] On the other side, like any sovereign state, China was eager to reestablish authority. At a time when its own legitimacy on the mainland was being redefined, it was most concerned about the integrity of its territory. The government wanted reassurance that subject populations "at the margins" could identify with the center as its own people. As Ernest Gellner (1985) said, when culture and power are combined to define a homogenizing, exclusive political unit, one finds nationalism. These contests were not limited to formal pronouncements on each side of the political divide. They have been diffused into everyday life—even in the naming of streets, in public ceremonies, and in proposals for civic or patriotic education in the schools.[8]

For this momentous plunge into the future, subject populations also looked back to evaluate the territory they have traversed and selectively retrieved memories. True to the Hong Kong spirit, the scholarly community and the popular media have already presented competing histories. Books on Hong Kong's past have appeared with increasing frequency.[9] Emotions among the general populace have been mixed. Some staged exhibitions and made plans for various commemorations. Others watched with unease the crowds on the mainland celebrating the impending return of Hong Kong. As the clock at Tiananmen Square ticked away the minutes, designers for the Hong Kong room in the Great Hall of the People debated whether Ming and English furniture should be juxtaposed. A "reunification plaza" as a historical landmark in the Central District in Hong Kong was no longer a farfetched proposal.

The idea of a plaza leaves one with a sense of déjà vu. Harbin, after prolonged Russian occupation, was reclaimed by a warlord in the 1920s. Some Chinese merchants erected a temple in the city center, which was lined with Russian churches, schools, and a cemetery. The Jile Si (Temple of Paradise) was a monument with which the residents could work themselves into the orbit of China. They were eager to present, in their view, a Chineseness appropriate to the rising nationalism.[10] The efforts of these Chinese residents of a "Russian" city paralleled an occasion in 1847, when merchants in Hong Kong enlarged a Man Mo Temple in the Taipingshan area where Chinese residents congregated. Associated with the Tung Wah Hospital in 1869, the complex became a powerful "public arena" for Chinese elites to negotiate with the colonial government on the affairs of an emergent Chinese community. Between the construction of the Man Mo temple in 1847 and the plans for the reunification plaza in 1997, there is a history of Hong Kong I would like to tell. It is a narrative in which events concerning China's territorial concerns have continued to redraw a local cultural landscape. It defies the imposition of any clear-cut lines of commitment in nationalistic terms.

COLONIAL EXPERIENCES REVISITED

Narratives about Hong Kong have been increasingly politicized in the period immediately before and after the handover. Complicated social and cultural experiences are framed in dichotomous terms. The crucial political event is presented as the end to a partitioning of China imposed by foreign imperialism, which marked the subjection of Chinese populations to colonial discriminations. Despite the maturing of a post-war generation of Chinese who may identify more with Hong Kong than China, 1997 has been seen as the moment that washes away national humiliation as the territory returns to its motherland.[11] The first part of the nationalistic story expresses the wounded pride of the political center—be it the Qing dynasty, the Nationalists, or the regime in Beijing today. It also assumes that conflicts that arose from the day-to-day encounters of the colonizers and colonized rigidified along racial and national lines. "The British" appear as a category of relentless profit seekers who have conspired against "the deserving but wounded Chinese." The tenuous relationships between governments and their own people are left unexplored. The creative energies used by local populations to weave components of their worldly activities into a unique ethos are also ignored by such rhetoric.

Historical evidence of course tells of a more nuanced process. From the start, Chinese business elites played significant mediating roles. Like the traders in the previous centuries, their operations were worldly. They could also afford to buy orthodoxy. As with many sojourning merchants, they were eager to cultivate an identity with their native place, real or imagined. Attached to a territorial base that displayed the language of lineage, land, charity, and academic honors, they and the imperial order held common ground. One may say that wealthy merchants were co-opted into the imperial system before they could be effective challengers. On the other hand, they could subvert that system with their worldly resources, Aiming in all sincerity to find themselves respectable places within the empire. The cover photograph of Dr. Elizabeth Sinn's book *Power and Charity* (1989) illustrates this dynamic process. It was taken in the 1850s and shows the Tung Wah Board of Directors, in Qing official attire, presiding over the planning of a hospital, an institution quite foreign to the Chinese at the time and later legitimized by the Hospital Ordinance under British law. The question is, how "colonial" were their Hong Kong experiences, at once marginal and committed to the imperial enterprise?

Moreover, both foreigners and Chinese worked to build institutions that had lasting impact. No doubt many colonial administrators were discriminatory. The government moved slowly on enfranchising the Chinese on the formal political front. British merchants were major beneficiaries. That was the nature of empires: frontiers were exploited rather than incorporated. However, with unrelenting effort, the Chinese sought opportunities. Tens of thousands chose to arrive within the first two decades—pirates, fishermen, craftsmen, and wealthy families escaping from the Taipings. They shrewdly used British commercial law in Hong Kong and their trading networks in China to extend business worldwide. In the 1860s, the first Chinese newspaper *Zhongwai xinbao* was established to provide shipping and commodity information, headed by Huang Sheng and Wu Tingfang. Following this the *jinshan zhuan* (239 in number) and *nanbei hang* (84 in number) were founded. They were guilds representing the largest group of import-exporters. By the 1870s, the Chinese, supporting a population of over 150,000, moved into real estate.[12] According to a correspondence of then Governor Sir John Pope-Hennessy in 1880, Chinese residents paid over 90 percent of government taxes. Moreover, a government gazette in 1882 noted that of the 20 largest property owners and ratepayers (in 1881), 17 were Chinese.[13]

The important point here is that through a combination of efforts from all sides, intentional or otherwise, the Hong Kong environment provided unique opportunities for people to extend themselves. Creative energies unbound to link two merchant cultures. Amidst boom and bust, Chinese merchants sank roots in the territory side by side with foreign interests.[14] This was due partly to their ability to speak the colonizers' language. Many of their children went through local schools to become bilingual, bicultural professionals.[15] The real advantage was their links to the Chinese mainland, as shown by the strength of the import-exporters. Yuan Fat Hang and Kintyelung were prime examples of these enterprises, which maintained roots in China, Hong Kong, Thailand, Southeast Asia, and North America. In 1847, The Man Mo Temple signified the merchants' entry into the political arena. The Tung Wah Hospital, the guilds that were corporate board members, the Po-Leung Kok, the Chinese schools, and the District Watch Committee, were woven into a complex of culture, power, and charity for the Chinese community in Hong Kong.[16]

The merchants' contribution to their native place on the mainland, real or imagined, was also significant. For example, Chen Xuanyi, the founder of Kintyelung, invested in substantial ancestral estates in his native village of Qianxi, Chaozhou (Chiuchow), only ten years after they established themselves in Hong Kong.[17] Yuan Fat Hang, under the leadership of Gao Man-wah, started in Hong Kong around 1853. His businesses included shipping, banking, import and export, warehouses, and numerous properties. Gao was elected to the first board of the Tung Wah Hospital. His grandson, a nationalist at the turn of the century, invested in modernizing Shantou's (Swatow's) city infrastructure—electricity, tap water, mail, and modern banking services. Would it be appropriate to brand these commercial energies as merely colluding with colonial interests? These merchants worked with foreigners, but not always for them.

STRADDLING THE WORLD AND THE NATION

The merchants' success could not have been secured without the services provided by a generation of Hong Kong–educated professionals. They were accountants, lawyers, educators, public health workers, surveyors and builders, specialists on shipping, and banking. By the time Wu Tingfang, Huang Sheng, Sir Kai Ho Kai, and Wei Yu were appointed as members of the legislature from the 1880s on, Chinese commercial and professional circles had representative voices in the formal political processes.[18]

Like the merchants, they had impact in China and the West. Wu Tingfang (1842–1922), a native of Xinhui county in Guangdong who spent his early years in Singapore, was educated in St. Paul's and Central College in Hong Kong through missionary connections. He went on to study law in England and graduated in 1877. After returning to Hong Kong, he was appointed a legislator in 1880. Two years later, he joined Li Hongzhang in China and in 1896 was ambassador to the United States, Spain, and Peru. Not only did he negotiate major treaties, he also restructured civil, commercial, and criminal law codes in the late Qing. In the early Republican years, he stood by Sun Yat-sen against the warlords.

Sir Kai Ho Kai (1850–1914) was a graduate of Central College in Hong Kong who went to England in 1872 to study law and medicine. He returned to Hong Kong to practice law and promoted Western medicine. In 1887, he financed the building of the Alice Memorial Hospital and played a key role in the establishment of Hong Kong's first medical college. A constitutional reformer, he was active in publishing new political works, such as *True Interpretations of Political Reform (Xinzheng zhenquan)*. He later turned to support the Republican revolution, influenced by his student, Dr. Sun Yat-sen.[19]

Even Sun Yat-sen himself, in his speech to students at the University of Hong Kong in 1923, pointed out how he could envision positive links between his Hong Kong experiences and China's future. The speech may sound anachronistic under the present circumstances but is worth contemplating:

> "On returning to Hong Kong this time, it feels like coming home. I was educated here.... People have asked me, where did you get your revolutionary ideas? To be honest about it: they came from Hong Kong.... Although China had a revolution twelve years ago, there was hardly any improvement, and people's suffering deepened.... Now Hong Kong's six hundred thousand residents live in relative comfort. This is due to good government. I earnestly hope that all of you who pursue studies in Hong Kong consider the West and Hong Kong as your models in order that when you return to the motherland, you can help build a good government..."[20]

These professionals, among others, had contributed to the institutional bases of Hong Kong society and to China's modernity and nation building.[21] All of them were Chinese nationalists. They gave China what they had gained from the unique environment of Hong Kong. Moreover, they were comfortable with their multicultural qualities and did not harbor a colonial chip on their shoulders. At times, they fought against colonial abuses with a sense of social justice that came, ironically, from their Western education. Peers from China and the West respected them. Would it be fair to ignore the positive aspects of their Hong Kong background, label them merely colonial products, and belittle their multifaceted contributions to China?

It should not surprise us to find their contemporaries from the mainland dwelling on these politicized sentiments.[22] Famous intellectuals—Wen Yiduo, Lu Xun, and Ba Jin, among others—visited the colony in the 1920s and 1930s. Many took refuge due to persecution and war on the mainland. One detects tension in their perceptions—a sinocentric subjectivity, reinforced by acute nationalism in the wake of the May Fourth Movement. Hong Kong was censured for not being China— not the real China then embroiled in turmoil, but rather the ideal China held firmly in the minds of the visitors. They saw Hong Kong as bearing the blood and tears of the Chinese for over a hundred years. Although they were impressed with her cosmopolitan civility and orderliness, she was despised as a "bastard," and pitied as "orphaned." As Lu Wei-luan, a scholar of Hong Kong literature observes, "Whenever there were major upheavals in the Mainland, Hong Kong displayed unusual capacities to accommodate visitors. The sojourners brought her advantages, but their hearts belonged elsewhere. They hated this place of temporary residence more than they loved it. This intertwined quality of interdependence and distance is Hong Kong's melancholy." In their eyes, Hong Kong was objectified as a place that reminded China (and them) of hurt and humiliation. However, this view tells us more about the speakers themselves than the subject of their description.

I can sympathize with the sentiments of Lu Xun and others. The 1930s, was a trying time for nationalists and revolutionaries alike. Torn apart by foreign aggression as much as by warlords, China was on her knees. Some also encountered personal harassment from petty officials, both in Hong Kong and on the mainland.[23] But today, must we dwell on mentalities that have transcended their historical circumstances?[24] If we do, we may as well equate the predicaments of Hong Kong with those of a traditional Chinese woman: patriarchy judges her for her many uses, but seldom appreciates her for what she is. She is condemned if her background and sentiments do not match the agenda of the beholder who claims her.[25]

POST-WAR BABY BOOMERS AND THEIR HONG KONG IDENTITY

If a nationalistic mind-set prevents us from appreciating the Hong Kong cultural universe of the past, have we allowed it to shape our assessment of the present and future? Some may dismiss the issue. They argue that people today see through political rhetoric and ignore its straitjacketing. However, others point to the ways in which everyday language frames the way we see the world around us. Their uncritical use can put a limit to "what is thinkable." In view of the recent debates on the Hong Kong identity and the surge of nationalistic emotions, we should examine our lenses and assumptions all the more urgently.

I would argue that a pluralistic cultural universe has continued through the efforts of post-war generations in the territory—local-born immigrants and emigrants who have created a unique ethos from their diaspora. This universe is connected to the world as much as it is attached to the real or imaginary China. Their efforts in the last 40 years tell a different story from traditionalist, colonial, or nationalist narratives. The identities and emotions are as complex and energized as those of the generations before them. If experiences do not fit into highly charged political categories, we should take a moment to appreciate them on their own terms.

Public opinion across the ideological spectrum would agree that from the 1960s on, a distinct Hong Kong ethos emerged. It came with a generation of post-war baby boomers whose education and professional achievements had been tied to the territory at a time when China was turned inward, with Hong Kong projected to the world almost by default. This coincided with the Hong Kong Government's decision to invest heavily in the territory's future after long-neglected social issues exploded in the riots of the late 1960s. Hong Kong's eventual role as an Asian financial hub triggered a surge of upward mobility from the late 1970s on. Life in Hong Kong became brashly luxurious, and its impact diffused through popular media and conspicuous consumption worldwide. The values, emotions, and identities of these cosmopolitan Hong Kong residents were relatively shielded from those of the mainland Chinese. Although few would deny their Chinese ancestry or cultural bearing, many have made it clear that cultural identification does not automatically lead to unquestioned political commitment. In my ethnographic encounters in China, I also detect a change in the popular term for Hong Kong residents, which has been shifting since the mid-1980s, from "Gang Ao tongbao" (Hong Kong and Macao compatriots) to "Xianggang ren" (Hongkonger).[26] These mutual perceptions of difference zoomed into sharp focus on the eve of 1997.

Whether these differences can be bridged depends a great deal on how we view the Hong Kong experience.[27] I am quite surprised by some of the extreme positions taken in recent debates.[28] Most of us probably would not share these positions, but they are emerging in public forums. First, Hong Kong's cosmopolitan city-life and associated Western civic values are posed against a reified "Chineseness." The commercial ethos, which has always been seen in positive union with Confucian values to fuel a business ethic in Hong Kong, is treated with a touch of disdain—as lacking cultural depth or a collective sense of mission. Second, Hong Kong's political arena, based on liberal assumptions of institutional procedure, social justice, and respect for the individual before the law, is seen as a colonial product working against Chinese nationalistic agendas. The third extreme position is more implicit. If one tries to transcend the colonial and nationalistic frameworks to appreciate Hong Kong on her own terms, one is often accused of harboring Hong Kong chauvinism against a Chinese identity.

Again, historical evidence refuses to be discussed in these terms. On the cultural ethic front, both Yü Ying-shih and William Tay have argued strongly that despite the severing of ties with mainland China, post-1949 Hong Kong provided a space for intellectual contemplation unmatched in China or Taiwan. From the late 1940s to the 1970s, the political persecutions under the Kuomintang in Taiwan and the equally intense campaigns on the mainland denied even loyal opposition. Hong Kong was the precious little island, linked to networks of the Chinese diaspora, which kept intellectual discourse alive. Qian Mu (Qien Mu), Quan Hansheng (Ch'uan Han-sheng), Luo Xianglin (Lo Hsiang-lin), Jian Youwen (Chien Yu-wen), Tang Junyi (Tang Chun-yi), Mou Zongsan (Mou Chung-san), and Xu Fuguan (Hsu Fu-kuen) were intellectual giants associated with the new Confucianism—a philosophical force that has swept China with a vengeance today.[29] These scholars enjoyed an environment relatively free of ideological impositions, as Xu Fuguan was said to have commented that "the government and he were non-existent for each other."[30] Moreover, one wonders if their "escape from predicament"—the creative fusion of scholarly integrity and mission with modern agendas—has been shaped by their experiences in a society in which personal vulnerability is minimized by the respect for law, professionalism, a liberal frame of mind, cosmopolitan civility, and worldly horizons.[31] Those years in Hong Kong were not marked by material affluence, but the intellectual richness contrasts favorably with the tragic, last 20 years of Chen Yinke's life across the border.[32]

One may say that philosophical musings were limited to a privileged few, while the rest of the society remained mired in vulgar materialism. However, recent support for Hong Kong's Olympic gold medalist, Lee Lai-shan, tells a different story. The "Hong Kong spirit" is equated with Lee's achievements and enthusiastically promoted in the media. There was extensive commentary on the fact that the 1996 ceremonies were the last occasion at which the Hong Kong flag would be raised. Political rhetoric framed the issue as a contest between Hong Kong chauvinism and Chinese patriotism. But if we go beyond the political, the emotions of these ordinary citizens crystallize an appreciation for an unrelenting work ethic and respect for professional and personal integrity, which have been major ingredients to Hong Kong successes. I recently came across a photographic album of life in Hong Kong in the 1960s and 1970s by Yau Leung (Qiu Liang). I was as deeply moved by the poverty of a vast majority of the population as I was by the human warmth, sense of community, self-respect, and the innocence on children's faces.

These emotions are still very much woven into our lives. They occasionally resurface amidst the brash consumerism of the 1980s and 1990s, and allow us to appreciate the hardships generations of Hong Kong residents went through to achieve their positions today. It also makes an important point: in the foreseeable future, Hong Kong will remain a land of immigrants and emigrants. If Hong Kong cannot maintain its existing social order and legal institutions, the new immigrants may not have any reasonable and healthy way to settle into mainstream Hong Kong life. Ironically, the "get rich quick by whatever means" mentality, as opposed to the Lee Lai-shan spirit, seems to be closely tied to Hong Kong's reintegration with a post-Mao China reeling from decades of deprivation.

Last but not least is the issue of the Hong Kong identity. In contrast to the nationalist narrative, the Hong Kong experience has been neither entirely colonial/Western or narrowly territorial. In education, Choi Po-king and Bernard Luk have pointed to the significant Chinese component in the schools. In ritual practices, elements of tradition continue to be recycled in an urban setting. In popular culture, scholars emphasize its multi-cultural, all-encompassing qualities. Growing up in such an environment, where the population continues to be made up of immigrants and emigrants, where family processes are truncated and personal choices reconfigured in the world metropolis or in cyberspace, the territory's residents have acquired overlapping identities of Hongkonger, Cantonese, Chinese, and global citizen. In sum, the Hong Kong identity is attached to a territory without clear boundaries. It constitutes fluid layers of social meaning, economic interests, and political preferences and has grown global without losing its Chinese bearing.[33] The world, as much as China, engages this identity in order to communicate. In the 1970s, Hong Kong students who demanded social reforms were swept up in radical thinking worldwide. Many were inspired to look to China for the socialist utopia. In the 1990s, the world's interest in China as market became a lifeline for a post-industrial Hong Kong. What Hong Kong has offered in this unique position has fueled China's reentry into the world community.

As Elizabeth Sinn comments, "Hong Kong culture grew in a unique environment full of historical contradictions. Hong Kong is a window to the world for China, as well as a one for the world to look into China. In Hong Kong, the Chinese, the foreign, the new, the old, the orthodox, and the unorthodox are mixed in a melting pot, with various contradictions as catalyst, out of which arises a pluralistic, fluid, exuberant cultural uniqueness. If we used a one-dimensional, flat, nonprocessual framework to understand it, it may be too narrow, too unfair."

I have tried to show that from the Ming dynasty to the end of the twentieth century, local populations have been quite beyond the reach of formal state apparatus and have foiled any serious imposition of rigid categories. Interacting with these state efforts, the merchants, the turn-of-the century professionals, the revolutionaries, the refugees, the post-war baby boomers, and the new immigrants have exerted tremendous ingenuity to accommodate, to maneuver, and to absorb. They have created the phenomenon we now call Hong Kong. I sincerely hope that there is no closure to the historical narrative. If one asks what Hong Kong can contribute to China, I suggest that Hong Kong should insist on the social institutions it has built and bring the world to the territory on that basis in order to engage China positively in the nexus. That has been Hong Kong's historical role, and its residents should have the self-confidence to maintain that role in the future.

In a way, Hong Kong is fortunate to be at the margins of empires. Although physically cramped, its residents, migrants and local born, have collectively created an unusual cultural and political space, where they can choose and act on agendas most meaningful to them. The history of Lingnan (south China) tells us a similar story. From the Ming dynasty on, a unique regional culture evolved with local elites who willingly grappled with the cultural symbols of central authority in order to seek legitimate places in the imperial order. By the eighteenth and nineteenth centuries, one saw a "Chinese" culture that was intensely diverse yet, once embraced, offered a unifying sense of identification. The relationship between region and center is a dialectic one: if the center is confident enough to accommodate the region by giving it the necessary space and allowing multiple systems to exist on their own terms, the authority of the political center can in fact be appreciated.

Every turn of political events has triggered a remarkable churning of cultural energies. My story will be only one among many. Wherever we choose to place our faith, I hope that this story can be testimony to the open society of Hong Kong, where public forums are vibrant and different voices respected. May be we should not build anything at all in the future reunification plaza—let it be that open, tolerant "public space" representing what is truly a Hong Kong experience.

NOTES

This chapter is based on a talk given in the Hong Kong Lectures, the University of Hong Kong, December 7, 1996.

1. For a similar argument, see Bai Shi (1997).

2. See the works of Maurice Freedman and later scholars on the lineage complex in south China and the New Territories of Hong Kong. For recent revisions of the lineage complex, see David Faure and Helen Siu (1995).

3. In the Ming, the language for trading in the general area was Portuguese. It was later replaced by a Cantonese version of pidgin English. At times of conflict, the Chinese government had threatened to order local populations not to provision foreign ships. See Chen (1894: 10–12).

4. On Guangdong coastal trade with Southeast Asia during the Ming, see Li

(1985); in the same volume, see also the essay by Zhang (1985). In the early Qing, Zhangzhou traders often manned Dutch boats operating in and out of Guangzhou. For more on this, see Zhang (1985: 317), who quoted Qu Dajun [1700]. Zhang also notes that the collaboration between *jian* and *yi* in the Ming was as intense as on the eve of the Opium War, and that scholar/officials at the time saw it as a serious problem which was difficult to resolve (Zhang 1985: 319).

5.   Benedict Anderson, in a talk on Philippine nationalism, concurred with this idea about the indigenizing missionary agendas. Also see Bays (1996) and Leung (1993).

6.   See Chapter 26 in *Hong Kong 1996* (Howlett 1996) for some hint of this. By the time the New Territories were leased in 1898, lineages there did resist. Their fears were specific: land rights and the potential loss of revenue from their "mixed surname" tenants. Their reactions were different from those of the merchant community in the city and of literati elites on the mainland. The local "Chinese" were by no means united in their "nationalistic sentiments." See also Tsai (1993); he makes a useful distinction between anti-foreign, patriotic, and nationalistic sentiments. These sentiments were also crossed with other factors such as class and gender.

7.   Scholars try to counter the image of the "barren rock" in colonial narratives. See Chan (1993).

8.   A colonial history can also be diffused into everyday life. Take the naming of streets, for example. On Hong Kong Island, most streets are Chinese translations of British names, associated with particular colonial officials. Those in Kowloon are mixed. New Territories street names are mostly English translations of Chinese names. See Leung To's study (1992) of street names in Hong Kong. See also the cynical explorations in Lo Dayou's popular music in the films of Tsui Huk and Cheung Kin-ting. The recent debates on "national" and "civic" education put these narratives in sharp focus. See Choi (1996a, 1996b) and, in the same volume, Lin (1996) and Lau (1996); see also Yuen (1996) on the different facets of nationalistic emotions. See also Ren (1997) on museum exhibits in the narration of Hong Kong history.

9.   Many are from colleagues from Hong Kong—Drs. Fok Kai-cheong, Ming Chan, Elizabeth Sinn, Choi Po-king, and Rey Chow, among others.

10. This is the topic of a dissertation by Jay Carter, a student in the History Department at Yale University.

11. Again, see the essays by Choi (1996a, 1996b), Lin (1996), and Lau (1996). See also an essay by King (1997).

12. On the history of this period involving merchants, foreign traders, and laborers, see Elizabeth Sinn (1989). See also Tsai (1993) and Chan (1991).

13. See Yu (1994) p. 330. See also similar observations in Lin (1993).

14. Many scholars have argued that Hong Kong has a double-tracked colonialism, under which Chinese interests were not always subordinated. For instance, see Fok (1992).

15. Efforts to set up Chinese schools were not lacking. In fact, Wah Yan, with the help of the Jesuit fathers, represents one such effort to balance the achievements of the Queen's College. For government support for Chinese schools in the early decades, see Ng (1984). For a more detailed history of the different school systems, see A. Sweeting (1990).

16. Another overlapping arena for the flexing of political muscles was the District Watch Committee. Beneath the appearance of its formal mundane duties was the politicking that earned it the name of "The Chinese Executive Council." See Ng (1984).

17. Their business network linked Chaozhou, Hong Kong, and various Chinese communities in Southeast Asia through the rice trade, remittances, and shipping, among other ventures. Chen started as a fisherman who became a boatman for a sea merchant, Gao Yuansheng of Chaozhou (Choi 1995).

18. See the records of the meetings of the Pok Leung Kok, where Sir Kai Ho Kai interacted confidently with the Registrar General as a professional equal. The records are included in a manuscript prepared by David Faure (1996). On Sir Kai Ho Kai, see also G. Choa (1981), and Linda Pomerantz-Zhang (1992)

19. See G. Choa (1981).

20. The speech, "Guofu yu Xianggang Daxue yanjiang jilue," was originally published in *Huazi ribao,* 1923, February 21. It was been reprinted in Lu (1983: 243–245).

21. For examples, see Wu Ting-guang (1922a, 1922b). See Fok Kai-cheong (1992) for numerous examples of prominent Hong Kong Chinese who contributed to China's nation building. Others have emphasized the efforts of the Hong Kong laboring classes that stood with Chinese workers on the mainland. See M. Chan (1994) and Tsai (1993).

22. The labels, such as "comprador" (*maiban*), "colonial lackeys" (*nucai*), or even "coolies", and "laboring masses," are terms with specific historical context and are loaded with political meanings. Using them uncritically as analytical language is problematic. See Faure (1994) for a review of Tsai's book. See also Choi Po-king and Ho Lok-sang (1993) for a critique of the modern version of this mentality. The essays in the volume, according to Choi (1993: xxiv) are wary of the ethnic and cultural purists who harbor a restrictive nationalism and related anti-foreignness.

23. See Lu Xun, "Lue tan Xianggang" and "Zai tan Xianggang," about his trip to Hong Kong and the harassment from customs officials, reprinted in Lu Wei-luan (1983).

24. See, for instance, Hong (1997) and Xu (1997).

25. Margaret Ng made this point in a public talk given at Yale University in October 1996.

26. Pamela Crossley has made similar observations.

27. On the cultural front, see Sinn (1995). For the sociological and political-economic front, see Ming Chan and Postiglione (1996); also see Choi Po-king and

Ho (1993).

28. See the essays in the *Ming Pao Monthly* volumes. Some authors dwell on dichotomous categories, while others look for mediating frameworks.

29. These were Chinese scholars who took refuge in Hong Kong after 1949 and who trained a generation of Confucian scholars under the auspices of the Xinya Yanjiusuo. Some were later associated with the New Asia College of the Chinese University of Hong Kong, and others with Academia Sinica in Taiwan.

30. Personal conversations with William Tay. See also Yü Ying-shih (1993), who argues that one has to maintain a world perspective in order to appreciate the tremendous intellectual space Hong Kong has historically provided.

31. The formal political processes may not be democratic in practice, but the Hong Kong government is more or less held accountable to a democratic tradition in Britain.

32. Chen Yinke was an intellectual giant in China—historian, literary critic, philosopher, and linguist. He was regarded as a "national treasure" and given special treatment during the difficult years. He spent his last years in Zhongshan University in Guangzhou and died in the early 1970s. See Lu Jiandong (1995).

33. On the issues of how meanings about space and place are established, and how identities are increasingly de-territorialized, see a theoretical piece by Gupta and Ferguson (1992). Using that framework, I published an essay on "Cultural Identity and the Politics of Difference" (Siu 1993).

REFERENCES

Bai Shi. 1997. "Xunzhao Xianggang wenhua de genyuan," in *Ming Pao Monthly* (January): 23–26.

Bays, Daniel, ed. 1996. *Christianity in China.* Stanford: Stanford University Press.

Chan Hoi Man. 1995. "Popular Culture and Political Society: Prolegomena on Cultural Studies in Hong Kong." in *Culture and Society in Hong Kong,* edited by Elizabeth Sinn, pp. 23–50. Hong Kong: The Center for Asian Studies, The University of Hong Kong.

Chan Kai-cheung. 1993. "History," in *The Other Hong Kong Report,* edited by Choi Po-king and Ho Lok-sang, pp. 455–484. Hong Kong: The Chinese University Press.

Chan Ming, ed. 1994. *Precarious Balance, Hong Kong between China and Britain, 1842–1992.* Armonk, N.Y.: M. E. Sharpe.

Chan Ming and Gerard Postiglione, eds. 1996. *The Hong Kong Reader: Passage to Chinese Sovereignty.* Armonk, N.Y.: M. E. Sharpe,

Chan Wai-kwan. 1991. *The Making of Hong Kong Society: Three Studies of Class Formations in Early Hong Kong.* Oxford: Clarendon Press.

Chen Huixun. 1894. *Xianggang zaji* pp. 10–12.

Choi Po-king. 1996a. "Minzu jiaoyu de miusi" (The misunderstandings of nationalist education) *Ming Pao,* August 9, 1996.

———. 1996b. "Zhengzhi de jiaoyu, jiaoyu de zhengzhi" (Political lessons and the politics of education), *Ming Pao Monthly* (September): 28–31.

Choi Po-king and Ho Lok-sang, eds. 1993. *The Other Hong Kong Report.* Hong Kong: The Chinese University Press.

Choi Chi-cheung. 1995. "Dongnanya huaren jiazu qiye de jiegou: Qiantailong yu Yuanfa hang de bijiao yanjiu" (The structure of Southeast Asian Chinese family firms: A comparative study of the Qiantailong and Yuanfa hang), in *Dongnanya huaren yu Zhongguo jingji yu shehui* (Southeast Asian Chinese and Chinese economy and society), edited by Lim Hou-seng, pp. 91–108. Singapore: Singapore Society of Asian Studies.

Chow, Rey. 1993. *Writing Diaspora: Tactics of Intervention in Contemporary Cultural Studies.* Bloomington: Indiana University Press.

Faure, David. 1996. "History of Hong Kong." Unpublished manuscript prepared for the Open Learning Institute, Hong Kong.

———. 1994. "Review" of *Hong Kong in Chinese History* by Tsai Jung-fang, *Journal of Asian Studies* (May) v.53, pp. 543–44.

Faure, David, and Helen Siu. 1995. Introduction to *Down to Earth: The Territorial Bond in South China,* edited by David Faure and Helen Siu, pp. 1–19. Stanford, Cali.: Stanford University Press.

Fok Kai-cheong. 1992. *Xianggang yu jindai Zhongguo.* Hong Kong: Commercial Press.

G. Choa. 1981. *The Life and Times of Sir Kai Ho Kai: A Prominent Figure in Nineteenth Century Hong Kong.* Hong Kong: The Chinese University Press.

Gellner, Ernest. 1985. *Nations and Nationalism.* Ithaca, N.Y.: Cornell University Press.

Gupta, Akhil, and James Ferguson. 1992. "Beyond 'Culture': Space, Identity, and the Politics of Difference," *Cultural Anthropology* 7, no. 1: 6–23.

Hong, Qingtian. 1997. "Zhongguo ying zenyang dui Yingguo baochou" (How should China take revenge on Britain?), *The Hong Kong Economic Journal,* January 30, 1997, p. 19.

Howlett, Bob, ed. 1996. *Hong Kong 1996.* Hong Kong: Government Printing Department.

King, Ambrose. 1997. "Xianggang yü ershiyi shiji Zhongguo wenhua," *Ming Pao Monthly* (January): 18–22.

Lau Siu-kai and Kuan Hsin-chi. 1988. *The Ethos of the Hong Kong Chinese.* Hong Kong: The Chinese University Press.

Lau Siu-kai, 1996. "Yiguo liangzhi xia de guomin jiaoyu," *Ming Pao Monthly* (September): 19–20.

———. 1997. "'Xianggang ren' huo 'Zhongguo ren': Xianggang huaren de shenfen rentong 1985-1995," in Liu Qingfeng and Guan Xiaochun, eds. *Hong Kong in Transition: The Continued Search for Identity and Order* (in Chinese). Hong Kong: The Chinese University Press.

Leung Ka-lun. 1993. *Christian Education of Guangdong Province (1807–1953).* Hong Kong: The Alliance Bible Seminary.

Leung To. 1992. *Origins of Hong Kong Street Names.* Hong Kong: Urban Council.

Li Longqian. 1985. "Ming dai Guangdong duiwai maoyi ji qi dui shehui jingji de yingxiang," in *Ming Qing Guangdong shehui jingji xingtai yanjiu,* edited by Guangdong lishi xuehui, pp 279–312. Guangzhou: Guangdong renmin chubanshe.

Lin Cong, 1996. "Yi xin, li xin, shangxin: Gangren shenfen zai sikao," in *Ming Pao Monthly* (September): 9–11.

Lin Yulan. 1983. *Xianggang shihua.* 3rd edition. Hong Kong: Shanghai yinshuju.

Lu Jiandong. 1995. *Chen Yinke de zuihou ershi nian.* Beijing: Sanlian chubanshe.

Lu Wei-luan, ed. 1983. *Xianggang de youyu.* Hong Kong: Huafeng shuju.

Luk Hung-kee. 1996. "Zhimindi jiaoyu yu suowei zhengzhi lenggan" (Colonial education and the so-called political apathy) *Ming Pao Monthly,* August 9.

Ng Lun Ngai-ha. 1984. *Interactions of East and West: Development of Public Education in Early Hong Kong.* Hong Kong: The Chinese University Press.

Pomerantz-Zhang, Linda. 1992. *Wu Ting-fang (1842–1922): Reform and Modernization in Modern Chinese History.* Hong Kong: Hong Kong University Press.

Ren Hai. 1997. "Kan de bianzheng: zhanlanchu zhong de Xianggang," in *Hong Kong in Transition: the Continued Search for Identity and Order* (in Chinese), Qingfeng and Guan Xiaochun, eds. Hong Kong: The Chinese University Press, 1998.

Sinn, Elizabeth. 1989. *Power and Charity: The Early History of the Tung Wah Hospital, Hong Kong.* Hong Kong: Oxford University Press.

———. ed. 1995. *Culture and Society in Hong Kong.* Hong Kong: The Center for Asian Studies, The University of Hong Kong.

Siu, Helen. 1993. "Cultural Identity and the Politics of Difference," *Daedalus* 122, no. 2 (Spring): 19–43.

———. 1996. "Remade in Hong Kong: Weaving into the Chinese Cultural Tapestry," in *Unity and Diversity: Local Cultures and Identities,* edited by Tao Tao Liu and David Faure. pp.177–197. Hong Kong: Hong Kong University Press.

Siu Kwok-kin. 1990. *Xianggan qiandai shehui.* Hong Kong: Zhonghua shuju.

Sweating, A. 1990. *Education in Hong Kong: Pre-1841–1941, fact and opinion: materials for a history of education in Hong Kong.* Hong Kong: Hong Kong University Press.

Tsai Jung-fang. 1993. *Hong Kong in Chinese History: Community and Social Unrest in the British Colony, 1842–1913.* New York: Columbia University Press.

Wong Wang-chi, Li Siu-leung, and Chan Ching-kiu. 1997. *Hong Kong Unimagined: History, Culture and the Future,* Taipei: Rye Field.

Wu Ting-guang. 1922a. *Wu Ting-fang.* Shanghai: Wenhai chubanshe.

———. 1922b. *Wu xiansheng (dieyong) gongshu.* Shanghai: Wenhai chubanshe.

Xu Yongxuan. 1997. "Helai chiru" (Where is the humiliation?), *The Hong Kong Economic Journal,* February 12, 1997.

Yu Shengwu and Liu Cunkuan, Eds. 1994. *Shijiu shiji de Xianggang* (Nineteenth-century Hong Kong). Hong Kong: Qilin shuye youxian gongsi.

Yü Ying-shih. 1993. "Xianggang yu Zhongguo xueshu yanjiu," in Liu Qingfeng and Guang Xiaochun, eds. *Hong Kong in Transition: the Continued Search for Identity and order.* Hong Kong: The Chinese University Press.

Yuen, Shen-bong 1996. "Minzu zhuyi de lizhi yu qinggan," *Ming Pao Monthly* (August): 25–28.

Zhang, Wenyin. 1985. "Ming Qing Zhongxi maoyi yu Zhongguo jindai maiban de qiyuan," in *Ming Qing Guangdong shehui jingji xingtai yanjiu,* edited by Guangdong lishi xuehui, pp. 313–348. Guangzhou: Guangdong renmin chubanshe.

6 / Chineseness

The Dilemmas of Place and Practice

WANG GUNGWU

Some years ago, I was invited to write an introduction to a reference volume on China and was given the subject "The Chineseness of China." My first response was to say that since everything in China was Chinese, it was a non-question for the Chinese people, and what was there to write about? But I was challenged to rethink that topic. So I set out to explore whether or not there was such a thing as Chineseness. Two factors led me to write the essay (Hook 1982). Firstly, as a historian, I was sure that the land called China, with a continuous history, must surely have produced something that could be pointed to as Chineseness. Secondly, as a Chinese who was born and grew up outside of China, I assumed that all Chinese outside China would have something in common with those inside China, and that would be Chineseness. In fact, I found it easier to find the Chineseness rooted in history than in the shared qualities among people known as Chinese around the world.

IDENTIFYING CHINESE

The Chineseness in people is much harder to pin down. It calls for judgments about identity and meaning. It is my subject today, and it is still a difficult problem for me. So you will understand if you find me struggling with it. About the only thing that encourages me to try again is that it is an outsider's question and, being part of the Chinese diaspora myself, the outsider in me remains intrigued by it. Parts of this volume of essays are concerned with the origins of the Chinese diaspora. Other parts seek to describe what that diaspora looks like now. What is being studied are questions such as, how have the different communities of the diaspora changed in response to the demands of their adopted countries? What kinds of ethnic identities are being constructed to deal with other people's sense of nationhood? Does Chinese nationalism still mean anything for ethnic minorities outside China?

These are far-ranging questions, and I do not propose to deal with all of them. I have argued that outside the borders of China, Chinese ethnicity derives from cultural identity and is subjectively determined (Cushman and Wang 1988: 10–15). Apart from official population statistics set out according to local legal definitions and requirements in their adopted countries, the only reliable tests of a person's identity is that a person's self-identity as a Chinese, and other people agreeing that the person is Chinese, even to the point of insisting on it whether the person likes it or not. The former centers on aspects of psychology and the latter largely on physical attributes. This would certainly be true of those of Chinese descent in Southeast Asia and North America. These concerns, however, are different from those that would be of interest to Chinese within China. For them, Chineseness is of little interest unless it is changing or is forced to defend itself against change. And underlying the changes that have been the most meaningful for them this past century are the forces of modernization.

I shall approach this difficult subject by looking at the differences produced by place and practice. By place, I refer to the locality and environment in which people live. Each place obviously has its own set of practices. I shall focus on changes in practice over time and the ways in which each ethnic community coped with those changes. In the context of place and practice, does being Chinese always mean the same thing, or does it change from time to time and place to place? Do we begin with variations and adaptations of the Great Chinese Tradition that has always been associated with the power and intellectual centers of North China in the past? Do we assume that modern urban Chinese today have moved away from all that? Could we still say that numerous small traditions of rural China, with their distinctive sets of local practices, may each be more directly and quintessentially Chinese? Or is Chineseness something more abstract, a collection of cultural traits that can be isolated and used to measure each person's willingness to acknowledge them whether they lived inside Chinese territory or not?

These questions bring out the relationship between the concrete experience of being Chinese and the abstract qualities of Chineseness. They imply that being Chinese is not absolute. One could be more or less Chinese at any one point in time. One could remain stationary, true and unwavering in maintaining what one believes to be vitally rooted in tradition. That suggests an act of will, without which one could become less Chinese. This also means that if found to be inadequately Chinese, one could correct that by acquiring cultural attributes that would intensify the qualities that make one Chinese. This implies a "scientific" approach that tries to determine, however inexactly, the attributes that make someone Chinese and to measure the degrees of change that could either diminish or enhance one's Chineseness.

You may be pleased to know that I have retreated from that line of inquiry. There is no way I can quantify those attributes, and I do not want to mislead others about how accurately one can weigh something like Chineseness. I shall stay with a simple historical approach, noting changes over time in different places. But I confess that the above questions of relative quality have been unavoidable. All I ask is that you note that my efforts at answering some of them have been impressionistic and many not attain a high degree of accuracy. I shall also be experimenting with direct comparisons between the Chinese overseas and samples of those who live in Chinese territories, and have chosen four large urban clusters for discussion in this chapter: Singapore and the Bay Area around San Francisco, on the one hand, and Shanghai and Hong Kong, on the other. My starting point is that Chineseness in the former underwent changes quite different from those in the latter during the past half century.

WHO ARE "OVERSEAS CHINESE"?

This leads me to make a correction to recent writings that define the "overseas Chinese" as all Chinese outside the People's Republic of China (PRC), including those of Taiwan and Hong Kong.[1] This would immediately separate Hong Kong from Shanghai and place Hong Kong together with Singapore and San Francisco. This makes no sense where Chineseness is concerned. Also, many of the writings that take this approach show carelessness and ignorance. Others may have had an economic, or an ideological, agenda for separating "capitalist" Chinese from "communist" Chinese. The most striking example of this usage was the espousal by *The Economist* in 1992 of this distinction as a hard economic fact (Shambaugh 1995). According to that counting, the populations of Taiwan and Hong Kong–Macau were added to the estimated 25 million people of Chinese descent around the world which led to the author's total of over 50 million "overseas Chinese."

There are several problems with this definition and with the figures for Chinese. Firstly, although isolating all other Chinese from the PRC may serve the interests of Taiwan as the Republic of China, the Taipei government totally rejects the inclusion of the people of Taiwan as "overseas Chinese." Their own use of the term *"huaqiao"* (that is, overseas Chinese) has a long history going back to the beginning of this century, the decade before the Republic was founded in 1912. It referred to Chinese citizens who were temporarily living outside Chinese territories and under foreign governments, or who were so regarded by a series of Chinese governments (Wang 1981: 124–126). Adding to the confusion, the Taipei authorities have always treated Hong Kong Chinese as their *huaqiao*, for these same historical reasons, since Hong Kong was ruled by the British. However, the Hong Kong people do not consider themselves overseas Chinese, although many had once been overseas Chinese or still have family ties overseas. Some of them have, however, accepted the Taiwan usage because *huaqiao* status confers certain benefits in Taiwan, especially for entry into Taiwan's more prestigious universities. In contrast, where the PRC is concerned, the greater advantage for Hong Kong and Macau people comes from being called *tongbao* (compatriots). Indeed, in the PRC, the Taiwanese are also consistently called *tongbao*. In no way could Taiwanese be considered overseas Chinese, which would imply that they lived in foreign territory.

Secondly, even the lower figure of 25 million Chinese who live outside the PRC, Taiwan, and Hong Kong–Macau assumes an accurate definition about who is and who is not Chinese that begs the question. For Southeast Asia alone, the 1992 figure is 23 million. Of this, only the census figures for Malaysia and Singapore define ethnic Chinese more or less consistently, but none of the other estimates can be considered reliable. What is remarkable is that Chineseness is equated with descent and blood, and ignores all questions of identity and the significance of cultural and social attributes. It fails to note the high percentage of mixed marriages in Thailand, the Philippines, Vietnam, and Myanmar that produced progeny who considered themselves local and only incidentally Chinese. Nor does it take into account the effectiveness of the national education that was introduced after the independence of each of the new nation-states. Thus, if this misleading figure is linked with political loyalties and the potential for subversion, as it was during the period of the Cold War, it could be most alarming to China's neighbors. Strategic and diplomatic considerations aside, this way of counting heads is dangerously close to a kind of racism that resembles anti-Semitism. I refer to the prejudice that, in modern times, turned into a systematic discrimination and political persecution that began by identifying every Jew in pseudo-scientific ways, in the name of social biology, breeding, even eugenics.

As far as the Chinese themselves are concerned, only those who live outside Chinese territories, especially those who have settled in foreign countries and become their citizens, might be included in the idea of a Chinese diaspora. More accurately, in order to avoid calling them *huaqiao,* or sojourners, these citizens of Chinese descent are referred to as "Chinese overseas" or are described as hyphenated Chinese—Malaysian Chinese, Sino-Thai, and Chinese-Americans, for example. But clearly, for them, the term *huaqiao* (conventionally translated as "overseas Chinese") is a misnomer, for it implies that such "overseas Chinese" are really citizens of China temporarily residing outside China. In the PRC, Taiwan, and Hong Kong today, these Chinese tend now to be called *"haiwai huaren,"* or *"huaren"* for short. This has been rendered as "ethnic Chinese" in more recent scholarly writings—and is strongly preferred by L. Suryadinata (1995 and 1997)— but it must be said that the term *"haiwai huaren"* still causes confusion because it is the literal translation of "overseas Chinese." Allow me to simplify the matter thus: the diaspora or Chinese overseas do not include the people of Taiwan and Hong Kong–Macau, nor those, whatever their descent, who deny that they are Chinese and have nothing to do with the rituals, practices, and institutions associated with the Chinese.

PLACES AND PRACTICES

I mentioned earlier that I shall compare the diaspora with some communities in China and concentrate on four cities. Two of them, Shanghai and Hong Kong, are clearly Chinese; their Chineseness is entwined with problems of modernization. The other two, Singapore and San Francisco, have large Chinese communities for whom Chineseness means cultural identity, and this subject has divided each community as to how Chinese they are and ought to be. Before I proceed with these large cities, it is important to remember that the dilemmas of place and practice can be just as complex where Chinese communities are small as where they are large. I shall use three examples to illustrate that point.

In Tahiti in French Polynesia, the Chinese number about 10,000, almost 10 percent of the population (Moench 1963). More than 100 years ago, they had come as laborers and small businessmen from the villages and townships of the Pearl River delta just north of Hong Kong. They became well-off, and in some cases immensely wealthy, during the Second World War when the United States took over from the Vichy French and gave the Chinese some exclusive agencies and contracts. Since the end of the war when the French returned, the leading families have been true to their Chinese past and remained successful by positioning themselves in the middle, politically with the French and economically with the American companies that helped them get started. Among the young, however, there is intermarriage and conversion to Christianity, even sympathy for Tahitian independence, but also emigration to Europe and North America. Inevitably, this has caused a loosening of their ties with the community. This tight and small community consists mainly of Hakkas, who are particularly proud of the way they have carried their Chineseness with them wherever they have gone. There is concern that the younger generation should maintain their Chineseness. The generational struggle over being Chinese is no less intense, partly because the elders have tried hard to make up for their isolation in one corner of the South Pacific.

At the other end of the world, in mobile and cosmopolitan Britain, the Chinese are but one of many minorities and they do not have economic dominance over the native population as they do in Tahiti. Also, the Chinese have not clustered there as much as they have in some other parts of Europe (Parker 1998a, 1988b). The links with Hong Kong, from which most of them have come, are strong and maintaining their cultural identity is much easier. The bulk of the Chinese are first-generation immigrants. Among them are many whose educational backgrounds ensured upward social mobility for their children. Chinese language skills, including the ability to write Chinese, have been kept up and global ties with other Chinese communities have been encouraged. The serious test will come when another generation grows up. Stable politics and a sound economy in Britain will guarantee a high degree of tolerance toward the Chinese, which should increase the opportunities to assimilate.

The story is somewhat different in Japan, another native but non-colonial setting on a group of islands where the Chinese community is small and dispersed. It is also a stable and economically prosperous country, albeit in Asia. The major difference is that the Chinese in Japan moved into a country whose people once acknowledged a great cultural debt to China. But modern Japan has always been more restrictive about immigration than Britain, and much more reluctant to assimilate their immigrant workforce. In contrast to their harsh policies toward Korean residents, however, the Japanese have shown great ambiguity in their treatment of the Chinese. The unique mixture of respect and contempt that the Chinese experience there aggravates the dilemmas of place and practice: a place that is proximate and even culturally familiar, and a practice that is hierarchical, discriminatory, and highly controlled. The diaspora experience there is not only totally different from that in the other two territories, but also markedly different from that in Southeast Asia (Shiba 1995; Tad 1980). All of them remind us that, even for the smallest communities, being Chinese is not simple.

FOUR CITIES

Now for the four cities. The people of the four cities can be distinguished as the Hongkongers and Shanghainese who live on the edge of the China coast, and as Singaporeans and the Bay Area Chinese-Americans who live far away. As people living in different environments, with different political and cultural systems, they are obviously not the same. What kind of Chineseness then can be identified in all of them? The difference in place determines a great deal of what people do and think, how they live, and what loyalties they owe. But the fact that all four are great cities, and the regional centers of urban, commercial and cultural activity, bring out much that is common to all global cities. In an increasingly large number of areas, notably in business, technology, and academia, similar goals prevail and it hardly matters whether or not one is Chinese. Wealth, work, education, and certain levels of cultural pursuits bring the cities and their successful people together, making Chineseness far from essential for their respective successes.

Nevertheless, two factors remain important in challenging this prototype of Chinese who are urban, and middle class, and who may also be described as capitalistic, or people servicing a capitalist economic system. The first is that in a spectrum ranging from those who are obviously Chinese to those who are only barely recognizable as Chinese, the Shanghai Chinese, who are the pioneers of modern Chineseness, would be closest to what may be seen as historically Chinese. Along such a spectrum, Hong Kong Chinese today, despite having been ruled by the British for so long, would not be all that distant from those of Shanghai. Those who have settled in Singapore and the Bay Area are further along the spectrum because they have many more complex non-Chinese variables in their lives with which to contend.

The second factor is that political identities and practices still count for a great deal and will be more evident as an increasingly nationalistic China makes more specific demands on Shanghai and Hong Kong Chinese. Such demands may also influence the thought and behavior patterns of Chinese outside China, but there are good reasons why the Chinese in Singapore and San Francisco would be able to resist them. Of particular importance is the more general question, how will regional and global responses to a resurgent China impact ethnic Chinese residents in Southeast Asia and North America?

SHANGHAI

Although they are relevant, I shall not try to answer all these questions. For the rest of this essay, I shall concentrate simply on how the two factors of place and practice apply to the four varieties of Chinese. I begin with Shanghai because, by any criterion, its people are Chinese and have always been seen as Chinese (Wei 1987; Marie-Claire Bergere 1981). Chineseness for them simply means leading the way toward becoming modern Chinese. Shanghai became the model of a modern Chinese city for all Chinese inside and outside China. Its people were also considered the very models of modern Chinese. If there are dilemmas there, they stem from the question of how far modernization should go for its people. As an integral part of China, there were constraints on how much faster they could go without leaving their compatriots behind. Shanghai began by welcoming a wide range of Chinese from all over China, especially those from the wealthiest and best-educated peoples of the Yangzi delta. The city thus attracted a galaxy of creative and innovative talent who were drawn by its openness and a miscellany of practices that allowed far more leeway to challenge convention with innovation.

The Chinese who want to identify themselves as Shanghainese may be described as those who mastered the earliest challenges of the West's impact on China and indubitably became the first examples of modern Chinese. Their city was the first truly international city in Asia. Their success in learning and adapting from the West without losing their Chinese identity was greatly admired throughout China. But there was more, much more, that was contradictory and perplexing to the Chinese in the interior. Shanghai was home to both nationalism and revolution; it also produced some of the keenest minds, who proceeded to instruct the rest of China about the most advanced ideas in science and the arts from all parts of the world. Paradoxically, it was also the first city in China to symbolize the negative images of what had been borrowed from the West. It stood for extravagance and waste, glitter and shallowness, cosmopolitan rootlessness and disloyalty, betrayal of Chinese values, even treachery toward China itself. In short, identity of a modern Chinese in all its manifestations can be said to have evolved in Shanghai.

After the Communist victory in 1949, cosmopolitan Shanghai came to an end, although it remained the most modern city in the PRC for the next 40 years. Four decades of resinification followed for the people of Shanghai. They were not asked to return to being Chinese in the Great Tradition, but to make their contribution to that curious mix of peasant simplicity and socialist experimentation that Mao Zedong imposed on all of China. In Shanghai, there was a conscious effort to eliminate all the dross of foreign capitalist practice and residual feudal values, while retaining the skills necessary for a basic industrialization modeled on another foreign example, that of the Soviet Union. When this experiment was declared a failure in the late 1970s, an older Shanghai tried to be reborn. Interestingly, this recrudescence did not seek to restore traditional Chinese culture but to rejuvenate something of the amalgam created by Shanghai earlier this century. That had been the peak of modern Chineseness, which was seen as the hallmark of the Shanghainese. And they are well on their way to succeeding in the opinion of most people who have been to Shanghai recently.

HONG KONG

In comparison, Hong Kong was marked by its beginnings as the colonial backwater of a single power, the British. Its small Chinese villages remained remarkably parochial and stubbornly impervious to modern influences. Thus, Chineseness in early Hong Kong was not associated with modernization. It remained traditional and provincial up to the 1940s. Whatever modernity the place could produce was either Anglo-Chinese or largely an imitation of the new Chinese practices that were emerging in Shanghai (Wong 1988).

Hong Kong's translation to a global meeting place of goods and services, peoples and cultures came about only after the 1950s. Since then, radical changes have given the place a multidimensional appearance. Certainly, what is Chinese there today is no longer easy to describe or understand because several processes took place at the same time. Although many modern Chinese from Shanghai brought their dynamism and creativity to Hong Kong, the place was also flooded by people who came out of traditional villages of the Pearl River delta in search of work in the newly developed industries. People voted with their feet against the Maoist revolution in the PRC. For the first time, there was a consensus in Hong Kong that modernization was to be found in the open, international, market-economy. It was another beginning of, a second chance for, an alternative Chineseness anchored in modern entrepreneurship and new standards of material and technological success (Leung and Wong 1994).

Given this new inspiration, the heart of this modernity came less from place than from practice. By practice, I refer to the Anglo-Chinese system of authority and management, marked in particular by efficient administration and the rule of law (Leung, Cushman and Wang 1980; Scott and Burns 1988). This modern system enabled rapid changes to occur without disorder and instability, and the Hong Kong people came to admire and depend on it. Although the system had begun with a foreign overarching authority, most Hong Kong people today accept it as a vital part of their modern heritage, a valuable accretion to what Hongkongers may eventually bring to another kind of Chineseness.

After the 1950s, British colonial policies were modified in response to the closure of Shanghai and the new opportunities thus provided. The new practices offered a unique experience of openness to restless and dynamic people who could readily come and go. But events in China after 1949 continued to bring uncertainty to Hong Kong. A series of campaigns and disturbances followed, which came to a climax during the Cultural Revolution. Although most of the subsequent surprises were more benign, they did not cease, not even after the tragedy at Tiananmen Square in 1989. The increasing tension in Sino-British relations is simply one of the symptoms of the underlying uncertainty.

For example, when the "one country, two systems" formula was elaborated in the Basic Law, it became a severe test of loyalty; its success depended on whether or not the Hong Kong people were sufficiently patriotic to accept it. The decolonization process has followed British practice closely, but the workability of having a colonially trained administration in a Chinese jurisdiction is unknown and the effects are quite uncertain. It is expected that gradual sinification in mode and style will occur. The results may not be easily recognizable as Chinese, but the accepted practices of a city that has become part of China must be seen as Chinese in time, no matter how they evolve.

When a place and its practices are subject to external pressures for change as Hong Kong has been, its people face the dilemmas involved in having to choose what kind of modern Chinese they wish to become (Lau and Kuan 1988). This may mean asking whether to stay or leave, whether to change with the times or stand firm, whether to be passive and receptive, or whether to actively seek to identify with China or not. Several of the other papers in this volume deal with this issue, so it is not necessary to cover the ground again. What does need saying, however, is that the dilemmas stem from many causes. The standards and qualities in the modern values to which people aspire must be placed in the context of trying to be both modern and Chinese on the periphery of China. The Hong Kong Chinese can claim to have developed their own version of a new Chineseness during the past four decades. The question is, will they be rewarded for that contribution? Or will they have to pay a price for having gone their own way?

SINGAPORE

Let me now turn to Singapore, another city with a Chinese majority that has gone its own way but, unlike Hong Kong, has been fortunate enough to become an independent state. The city began in 1819 as a free port where varieties of Chinese, already in the neighboring territories, quickly gathered. Within decades, they were joined by large numbers of Chinese who came directly from China. Many later came via Hong Kong, since the British connection helped make that city the most convenient outlet for emigrant Chinese (Wang 1992: 22–28). Chinese and other businessmen then used Singapore as a transit stop from which Chinese laborers were distributed to the Malay States and the Netherlands East Indies.

The Singapore Chinese formed a commercial community that was the freest and most active in Southeast Asia (Sandhu and Wheatley 1989). Interactions with the neighboring areas of Java, Sumatra, Borneo, the Malay Peninsula, and Thailand laid the foundations for the role the island was to play thereafter—the provider of trading services. The first Chinese leaders of the Straits Settlements came from the small Baba (local-born) communities that had left China generations earlier. Most of them had lost the use of the Chinese language, but, together with those of the Malay Peninsula, they retained close links with traditional Chinese organizations. Despite their ties to the British administration, they showed a willingness to support Chinese causes when there was occasion to do so. We might mention examples of loyal supporters of Sun Yat-sen who readily sacrificed their lives for China, and others later on who did likewise in the service of the Communist Revolution. Indeed, this phenomenon continued beyond the Second World War (Lee 1996) and was even truer of those first-generation Chinese who knew little or no English, as well as the thousands of others who were educated in local Chinese schools up to the 1950s. The latter were adept at using modern methods of organization and communication to bring much needed help to China. During the first 150 years of Singapore history, most of these Chinese considered themselves Chinese, and the question of Chineseness posed no problems for them (Chew and Lee 1991).

This was true not only in territories of the British empire. What distinguished local British practice in the Straits Settlements were the legal and administrative measures, the relative media freedom, and the mix of public and private education systems that produced many of the modern skills that China wanted. The links with another British colony, Hong Kong, brought the two cities close together and enabled a degree of coordination that facilitated common action. They thus shared Anglo-Chinese features in the way their peoples responded to modernization. Also the advanced business methods they imbibed from the capitalist world gave them distinct advantages when they returned more recently to be active on the China coasts.

During periods of grave uncertainty, traditional values provided some solace and sanity. The motley clutch of ideas that promoted modernization but was derived from multiple sources was more difficult to handle. In fact, in colonies open to many forces, new people came and went who had little expectation of permanence. They were migratory and pragmatic (Hassan 1976). For such Chinese, the institutional features of the Great Tradition had largely been left behind, and their personal cultural baggage was light and adaptable. This is the source of their strength, the willingness to adjust to any place and any practice if necessary.

After the Second World War, we see this strong adaptability among the growing number of Chinese who settled in Singapore. They had preserved what they could of Chinese culture without much difficulty. But in the 1960s, they were forced to surrender parts of that heritage in order to take up the unexpected opportunity to become the political majority of a small Southeast Asian city-state (Lee 1996; Chua 1995). As Singaporeans, those of Chinese descent now face a different destiny. Their loyalties are to their new nation, whose survival has depended on looking outward. Apart from the immediate region, they have looked for their economic development in the international market economy. No less than the commercial and industrial cities of Shanghai and Hong Kong, they have turned to global business networks in which the Chinese connections have become important (Pan 1990: 225–274). Thus, when modernity is secure, it is in this direction that the new Chineseness has turned.

SAN FRANCISCO

In comparison with the other three cities, San Francisco's Chinese population is not dominant but forms a significant minority. Although it is on another continent, it has also attracted clusters of different kinds of Chinese, especially during the second half of this century. The Chinese of San Francisco began by meeting the harshest tests of Chineseness. They had to endure hostile conditions for three generations before the United States' revision of its Chinese immigration policies brought new life to the Bay Area (Nee and Nee 1972). Thus, a century after the Chinese first arrived in California, Chineseness became legitimized for a strong and distinct minority in an immigrant country of European cultural origins. The story is one of many paradoxes.

On the one hand, there was the near disappearance of Chinese community life. Despite the strenuous efforts of small numbers of the local-born and educated to find acceptance as Americans through assimilation and to fight for the rights of other Chinese, the exclusion policies persisted (Chung 1988). They affected social attitudes toward Chinese at all levels, which led to the truncation or division of many families. This brought isolation for many, especially for the old who rejected Western ways yet did not wish to return to China. Nevertheless, tenacious links with relatives in China and Hong Kong managed to heighten certain kinds of Chinese loyalty (*Chinese America* 1994: Him and Chan). On the other hand, new arrivals after the 1950s enriched the new communities, reminiscent of the way the cities of Shanghai and Hong Kong became great amalgams of all kinds of Chinese. In addition to newcomers from cities of mainland China such as Shanghai, or from elite families of Taiwan, the population was also augmented by the relatives of earlier immigrants from Hong Kong and the Pearl River delta.

Will this new mix bring a unique brand of Chineseness peculiar to Chinese-Americans? The new community has continued to grow, and more and more of its members are participating fully in the modern political and social practices of the country (Tu 1994; Wang and Wang 1998). If this process continues, it could eventually offer new elements of modernity from which the Chinese elsewhere in Shanghai, Hong Kong, or even Singapore might be willing to learn. But it may also be that the Chineseness of China will always be considered the only authentic kind, and those outside must choose to return or forever confront their dilemmas of place and practice.

TOWARDS MODERN CHINESENESS

I have not tried to cover all four cities and their groups of Chinese equally. Each group in each city faces its own unique set of practices. In the cultural spectrum of Chineseness, the Shanghai Chinese would be at one end and the Singapore and San Francisco Chinese at the other, with the Hong Kong Chinese somewhere in between. The cultural gaps between Shanghai and Hong Kong, and those between them and the Singapore–San Francisco variety, are uneven and difficult to measure. But all Chinese faced modern transformations in this century, and the idea of Chineseness was exposed to the modern forces of international capitalism.

There is a presumption that modern capitalism requires common conditions and that increasing dependence on this powerful phenomenon by Chinese of whatever origins means that they will share certain goals and methods. If this is true, the Chinese in all four cities would seek upward mobility and would be increasingly alike in the way they conduct their businesses and in the professional careers they seek for themselves in a borderless world. But I hesitate to draw that conclusion. From the history of the Chinese in these cities, it seems unlikely over time that they will be modern Chinese in similar ways, or that their loyalties to their local place and practice will be diminished by their economic concerns (Tu 1994:

145–146; *Chinese America* 1996: 11–16, Wang and Him).

Events inside and outside of China will develop beyond the control of any of these groups, and much within their own respective localities will undergo change. Many will ask, what matter if they were more Chinese or less? Or whether they were rich or poor in tradition? Or, in some cases, even if they were Chinese at all? But if, after all that, others still treat them as Chinese and they continue to be proud to consider themselves Chinese, then they can well stand up and say that a resilient modern Chineseness has been reinforced. Each group could claim that theirs is the start of new tradition.

The four cities are now key nodes in the extensive business and professional networks established during the past two decades. But Hong Kong, whose people are not yet as fully Chinese as their compatriots in Shanghai, and also clearly not "overseas" as are those in Singapore and San Francisco, provides a valuable test of the politics of identity. Differences in practice will pull the cities in different directions. For example, Shanghai retains socialist goals for the market economy it is trying to build, and a new kind of modern Chinese may come of that experiment. At the other extreme, the Bay Area, is lodged deeply in the strongest capitalist economy in the world. Its Chinese population has by now fully absorbed the values there and can be expected to sustain its own brand of modified Chineseness in that environment (Wang and Wang 1998). In contrast, the city-state of Singapore has integrated public and private enterprise most successfully, and its mixed form of capitalism has taught Singaporeans to look at the value of being Chinese in more utilitarian ways.

Hong Kong's experience of capitalism is clearly of a different order. The fact that it stood as a sort of front line for the capitalistic world was nothing if not a strong political act, an affirmation of economic ideology. Diluting their concern for their Chineseness was the price the Hong Kong people had to pay. But they have demonstrated the strengths and virtues of capitalism. Now they need to show that with this new culture of place and practice, which is contingent on dynamic global factors unknown in the past, they can still pass the test of loyalty to a modernizing China.

Hong Kong's dilemmas at the handover remind us that Hong Kong people will have to face issues of being Chinese that are quite different from those confronting people in Singapore or San Francisco. Despite the capitalistic intercourse that might bring Chinese peoples together, location and the distance in political practice alone preclude the sharing of a common Chinese identity. Instead, being Chinese in Hong Kong hereafter may be compared with what Shanghai people had to face in the past (Wang and Wong 1997). Shanghai's role as an international city that led the way in creating a modern Chinese identity may be the nearest example for Hong Kong to emulate. Most Hong Kong people will choose to stay and turn toward that former Shanghai model. Some who left earlier have already returned, and many more may do the same. If they do, and join in the task of modernizing China as Shanghai will continue to do, they will have decisively discarded the superficial "overseas Chinese" image that foreigners have tried hard to project on Hongkongers in recent years.

Finally, for a variety of reasons that we cannot predict, there will be Hongkongers who will choose not to follow the Chineseness of new Shanghai but to leave China altogether (Skeldon 1994). If and when they do, they will be choosing to become ethnic Chinese in foreign countries, setting out to eventually lose themselves among non-Chinese or looking for a vision of universal Chineseness among the millions spread around the world (Tu 1994). If they truly want to pursue that quest, it is not obvious that such Hongkongers would find their way to Singapore, even though the city-state has a Chinese majority and is geographically closer to Hong Kong and China. Singapore's place in the Malay Archipelago is ultimately alien to people accustomed to a vast Chinese hinterland. Hong Kong people would tend to feel confined in space and limited in opportunity without a continental backdrop. Although it has far fewer Chinese, San Francisco, together with other similar cities in North America and Australia, may be more attractive to Hongkongers, not only because these cities promise more of the freedoms they have learned to enjoy but also because the Chinese there are more recent immigrants. As such, they display a familiar kind of modern Chineseness that makes them people with whom Hongkongers could more easily relate and, ultimately, the kind of Chinese overseas they themselves would like to become.

NOTE

1.   There are many journalistic essays that take this view, notably *The Economist* (November 21, 1992). It is less comprehensible when serious studies follow this usage (Reading 1990: 23–24; East Asia Analytical Unit 1995; and Lever-Tracy, Ip, and Tracy 1996). For an earlier effort to correct this, see Shambaugh (1995).

REFERENCES

Benton, Gregor, and Frank N. Pieke, eds. 1998. *The Chinese in Europe*. New York: St. Martin's Press.

Bergere, Marie-Claire. 1981. " 'The Other China': Shanghai from 1919 to 1949," in *Shanghai: Revolution and Development in an Asian Metropolis*, edited by Christopher Howe, pp. 1–34. Cambridge: Cambridge University Press.

Chew, Ernest C.T., and Edwin Lee, eds. 1991. *A History of Singapore*. Singapore: Oxford University Press.

Chinese America 1988, 1994, and 1996. *Chinese America: History and Perspectives.* Essays by Sue Fawn Chung (1988), Him Mark Lai (1994, 1996), Sucheng Chan (1994), and Wang Gungwu (1994, 1996). San Francisco: Chinese Historical Society of America.

Chua, Beng-Huat. 1995. *Communitarian Ideology and Democracy in Singapore.* London: Routledge.

Cushman, Jennifer, and Wang Gungwu, eds. 1988. *Changing Identities of the Southeast Asian Chinese since World War II.* Hong Kong: Hong Kong University Press.

East Asia Analytical Unit. 1995. *Overseas Chinese Business Networks in Asia.* Canberra: Department of Foreign Affairs and Trade.

Hassan, Riaz, ed. 1976. *Singapore: Society in Transition.* Kuala Lumpur: Oxford University Press.

Howe, Christopher, ed. 1981. *Shanghai: Revolution and Development in an Asian Metropolis.* Cambridge: Cambridge University Press.

Lau Siu-kai and Kuan Hsin-chi. 1988. *The Ethos of the Hong Kong Chinese.* Hong Kong: The Chinese University Press.

Lee Ting Hui. 1996. *The Open United Front: The Communist Struggle in Singapore, 1954–1966.* Singapore: South Seas Society.

Leung Chi-keung, J. W. Cushman, and Wang Gungwu, eds. 1980. *Hong Kong: Dilemmas of Growth.* Canberra and Hong Kong: Australian National University and Centre of Asian Studies.

Leung, Benjamin K.P., and Teresa Y.C. Wong, eds. 1994. *25 Years of Social and Economic Development in Hong Kong.* Hong Kong: University of Hong Kong Centre of Asian Studies.

Lever-Tracy, Constance, David Ip, and Noel Tracy. 1996. *The Chinese Diaspora and Mainland China: An Emerging Economic Synergy.* New York: St. Martin's Press.

Lim, Linda Y.C., and L.A. Peter Gosling, eds. 1983. *The Chinese in Southeast Asia,* 2 volumes. Vol. 1: *Ethnicity and Economic Activity.* Vol. 2: *Identity, Culture, and Politics.* Singapore: Maruzen Asia.

Moench, Richard Ulmer. 1963. *"Economic Relations of the Chinese in the Society Islands"* Unpublished Ph.D. dissertation, Harvard University.

Nee, Victor G., and Brett de Bary Nee. 1972. *Longtime California': A Documentary Study of an American Chinatown.* New York: Pantheon Books.

Pan, Lynn. 1990. *Sons of the Yellow Emperor: A History of the Chinese Diaspora.* Boston: Little, Brown.

Parker, David. 1998a. "Emerging British Chinese Identities: Issues and Problems," in *The Last Century of Chinese Overseas,* edited by Elizabeth Sinn, pp. 91–114. Hong Kong: Hong Kong University Press.

———. 1998b "Chinese People in Britain: Histories, Futures and Identities." in *The Chinese in Europe,* edited by Gregor Benton and Frank N. Pieke, pp. 67–95. New York: St. Martin's Press.

Redding, S. Gordon. 1990. *The Spirit of Chinese Capitalism*. Berlin: Walter de Gruyter.

Sandhu, Kernial Singh, and Paul Wheatley, eds. 1989. *Management of Success: The Moulding of Modern Singapore*. Singapore: Institute of Southeast Asian Studies.

Scott, Ian, and John P. Burns. 1988. *The Hong Kong Civil Service and Its Future*. Hong Kong: Oxford University Press.

Shiba, Yoshinobu. 1995. *Kakyo* (The Overseas Chinese). Tokyo: Iwanami Shoten.

Sinn, Elizabeth, ed. 1998. *The Last Century of Chinese Overseas*. Hong Kong: Hong Kong University Press.

Skeldon, Ronald, ed. 1994. *Reluctant Exiles? Migration from Hong Kong and the New Overseas Chinese*. Armonk, N.Y.: M. E. Sharpe.

Suryadinata, Leo, ed. 1995. *Southeast Asian Chinese and China. 2 volumes*. Vol. 1: *The Politico-Economic Dimension*. Vol. 2: *The Social-Cultural Dimension*. Singapore: Times Academic Press.

———. ed. 1997. *Ethnic Chinese as Southeast Asians*. Singapore: Institute of Southeast Asian Studies.

Tai Kuo Hui. 1980. *Kakyo: 'rakuyo kikon' kara 'rakuchi seikon' e no kumon to mujun*. (Overseas Chinese: the agonies and contradictions, from sojourning to settlement). Tokyo: Yamamoto Shoten.

Tu Wei-ming, ed. 1994. *The Living Tree: The Changing Meaning of Being Chinese Today*. Stanford, Cali.: Stanford University Press.

Wang Gungwu. 1981. *Community and Nation: Essays on Southeast Asia and The Chinese*. Singapore and Sydney: Heinemann Educational Books and George Allen & Unwin Australia.

———. 1982. "Introduction: The Chineseness of China," in *The Cambridge Encyclopedia of China*, edited by Brian Hook, pp. 31–34. Cambridge: Cambridge University Press.

———. 1988. "The Study of Chinese Identities in Southeast Asia," in *Changing Identities of the Southeast Asian Chinese since World War II*, edited by Jennifer Cushman and Wang Gungwu, pp. 1–21. Hong Kong: Hong Kong University Press. Also reprinted in Wang Gungwu, 1991. *China and the Chinese Overseas*, pp. 198–221. Singapore: Times Academic Press.

———. 1992. *Community and Nation: China, Southeast Asia and Australia*. New Edition. St. Leonard's, N.S.W.: Allen & Unwin.

———. 1994. "Among Non-Chinese," in *The Living Tree: The Changing Meaning of Being Chinese Today*, edited by Tu Wei-ming, pp. 127–146. Stanford, Cali.: Stanford University Press.

———. 1995. "Greater China and the Chinese Overseas," in *Greater China: The Next Superpower?*, edited by David Shambaugh, pp. 274–296. Oxford: Oxford University Press.

Wang Gungwu and Wong Siu-lun, eds. 1997. *Hong Kong in the Asia-Pacific*

Region: Rising to the New Challenges. Hong Kong: Centre of Asian Studies, University of Hong Kong.

Wang Ling-chi and Wang Gungwu, eds. 1998. *The Chinese Diaspora: Selected Essays.* Two volumes. Singapore: Times Academic Press.

Wei, Betty Peh-t'i. 1987. *Shanghai: Crucible of Modern China.* Hong Kong: Oxford University Press.

Wong Siu-lun. 1988. *Emigrant Entrepreneurs: Shanghai Industrialists in Hong Kong.* Hong Kong: Oxford University Press.

7 / Deciding to Stay, Deciding to Move
Deciding Not to Decide

WONG SIU-LUN

Hong Kong had a date with destiny.[1] On July 1, 1997, the territory ceased to be a British colony. It became part of China again. The changeover was a historical event, which signified the end of Western imperialism and colonization in Asia. At the same time, it represented an unprecedented case of a capitalist economy being subsumed under a socialist polity. Hong Kong has been promised a large measure of autonomy within the framework of "one country, two systems." Innovative as it is, that framework remains untried. Because of the inherent uncertainty and suspense, the world continues to watch the territory with keen interest and concern. In the period leading up to the handover, those of us from Hong Kong became accustomed to the standard questions posed by outsiders. The usual opening query was "What will happen after 1997?" Then the inevitable follow-up: "Are you leaving Hong Kong?"

To leave or not to leave? As Hong Kong residents, we agonized over that question for a long time. It was a favorite topic for local opinion polls. In one of the last ones, conducted on April 30, 1997, exactly 62 days before the changeover, about 19.1 percent of the respondents said they would leave Hong Kong if given a free choice. Of the remainder. 77.6 percent said they would stay, and 3.3 percent answered that they did not know (*Asia Television News*, April 30, 1997).

These findings are in line with those reported in previous studies. For instance, in the 1991 emigration survey in which I took part, about 13 percent of our respondents expressed a wish to leave, 77.2 percent said they would stay, and 9.8 percent were undecided (Lam, Fan, and Skeldon 1995: 116). The only significant difference between the two sets of findings is that the proportion of people who decided not to decide has shrunk in the intervening years. As the fateful date drew near, more and more people apparently felt that they had to make up their minds.

Some of these decisions were already translated into action before the July 1 handover. After the Sino-British agreement over the future of Hong Kong was signed in 1984, there was a gathering wave of emigration. The number of emigrants rose from about 22,400 in 1980 to 30,000 in 1987. Then came the Tiananmen incident in China in 1989, which dealt a great blow to popular confidence in Hong Kong. Gripped by depression and panic, many people in the territory flocked to various consulates to apply for emigration. The number of people who were leaving doubled the following year. It reached a peak of 66,000 in 1992 and hovered at this level till 1994. Since then, the outflow has subsided. For 1996, the number of emigrants came down to 40,300. But it is still too early to say whether this represents just a temporary ebb in the flow, or whether it signifies that the peak of the exodus is over (on these emigration figures, see Wong 1994a; *South China Morning Post*, September 12, 1996, p. 1; *Ming Pao Daily News*, May 2, 1997, p. A16). Whatever the case may be, we can certainly say that Hong Kong has averaged an annual loss of approximately 1 percent of its population through emigration during this decade.

The sense of loss is induced not simply by the scale of the outflow. It is compounded by the quality of the emigrants, who are predominantly yuppies—young, educated, middle-class professionals who are bilingual and possess other skills. Their popular destinations are the "migrant states" (Wang 1993) of Canada, the United States, and Australia, which are actively recruiting talented immigrants throughout the world. There has been some alarm in Hong Kong over the apparently harmful effects of this depletion of local elites. But as I have argued elsewhere (Wong 1992), I believe such an alarm, pertaining in particular to the problems of brain drain, social anomie, and legitimacy crisis, is largely exaggerated and misplaced. More importantly, the alarmist view betrays narrow vision. It is too engrossed with the internal impacts of the current wave of emigration and thus loses sight of the wider significance of the phenomenon.

In a forum I attended in April 1997 in Manila on the transition in Hong Kong, a participant invoked the familiar specter of the worst case scenario—what if catastrophe strikes, Hong Kong collapses, and its people run amok? Has the Philippine government prepared any contingency plan, he asked, to repatriate the large number of Filipinos working in the territory? The official in charge of labor and employment in the Philippines gave an eloquent answer that cut to the heart of the matter. He said, "Hong Kong is an idea. Hong Kong is a dream. Hong Kong is a reality. It will not disappear after the handover. If worse comes to worst, it will resurrect itself elsewhere." Then he added, "There will always be employment opportunities for Filipino domestic workers."

What the Philippine official tried to capture is an entrepreneurial spirit that the Hong Kong emigrants carry with them, a spirit that is highly mobile and resilient. Many of these emigrants are turning themselves into entrepreneurs and small businessmen after their relocation. They are spinning transnational business networks that bind their host countries with Hong Kong and China. Thus the present wave of emigration is actually enhancing the global reach of the Hong Kong economy by spawning a host of cosmopolitan capitalists abroad. In the process, it creates a strong force that contributes to the invigoration of what Hamilton (1996) calls "overseas Chinese capitalism," a form of capitalism that is not domestic in nature, that defies national and geographical boundaries. But what constitutes this strong force? The key sources of dynamism, I shall argue, spring from the interaction between ambivalent identities and family strategies, the use of personal networks as a form of capital, and the changing meaning of home as upheld by the Hong Kong migrants.

IDENTITIES AND FAMILIES

In Hong Kong, the desire to emigrate is linked with an individual's sense of identity. But that identity is not simply a product of personal preferences. It is rooted in family experiences and strategies. The family is the basic unit in shaping decisions on whether to leave or to stay. As the key decision-making unit and the bearer of the entrepreneurial spirit, the Hong Kong Chinese family typically seeks to maximize its autonomy and avoid subjugation to state domination. Such an orientation produces a special style of overseas Chinese capitalism that is not dependent on any particular political order (Hamilton 1996).

AMBIVALENT IDENTITIES

In our 1991 emigration survey, we discovered that our respondents, who were all ethnic Chinese, tended to embrace a mixed and ambivalent sense of identity. They were torn between regarding themselves primarily as "Chinese" or "Hongkongese." Their views were split. About 48.4 percent of the sample opted for a basic identity as a Hong Kong person, while some 45.9 percent regarded themselves as Chinese. And their professed identities affected their attitudes toward emigration. As I have observed in an earlier publication,

> "... it was found that those who identified themselves as Hongkongese were actually more likely to consider leaving the territory. Respondents who declared that they would stay were more inclined to regard themselves as Chinese. Such a difference emerged most clearly when respondents were asked about their decisions after 1997. For those who identified themselves as Chinese, 59.9 percent said they would definitely stay. Just 5.1 percent indicated that they would definitely move after 1997. But for those who regarded themselves as Hongkongese, only 45.5 percent said they would definitely stay and about 6.4 percent indicated that they would definitely move. It seems that the Hong Kong identity is a mobile one, not fixed to a locality." (Wong 1994a: 381)

Besides being mixed and mobile, the identities as upheld by the Hong Kong emigrants have several additional characteristics. First, they are tinged with a strong sense of pragmatism. The Hong Kong migrants tend to approach issues of passports and nationalities largely as an instrumental issue. They referred to the acquisition of foreign passports as the purchase of "insurance policies" to guard against political risks. In our 1991 survey, we asked our respondents the question, "As 1997 approaches, some people in Hong Kong are emigrating to foreign countries. Do you think their action is morally right or wrong?" The majority of the sample, about 55.6 percent, would not be drawn into making an answer. They suspended judgment, maintaining that it was neither right nor wrong. For the rest, around 22.5 percent actually approved of the act and only 11.3 percent felt it was wrong (Wong 1994a: 381).

Second, the identities tend to be multiple and pluralistic. Hong Kong migrants are keen collectors of passports and nationalities. In order to maximize options and security, they are seldom content to stick to just one "insurance policy." For instance, the Yip family which I interviewed as part of our emigration project, is quite typical. In the aftermath of the 1989 Tiananmen incident, the Yips rushed to apply for emigrant visas to Australia, New Zealand, Canada, the United States, and Singapore. All these countries accepted them. Then, one by one, the Yips gave up the visas when they were required to move. They held on to the Singapore offer, which did not force them to make up their minds, until several years after 1997.

Third, these identities are often very costly to acquire. Many Hong Kong migrants have to give up their careers or part with their savings in exchange for new sets of passports and identities. In our 1991 survey, we asked respondents who were already working whether they expected their income to increase or decrease if they were to emigrate. Over half of them, 51.9 percent, anticipated a reduction. Only 29.4 percent believed that they would earn more after relocation (Lam, Fan, and Skeldon 1995: 130). In other words, most of them were not economic migrants looking for quick improvements in their livelihood overseas. If they leave, they have to pay quite dearly for their decisions. They either have to accept a lower income, or invest considerable sums in business immigration programs with little hope of profits or even of getting their money back (Smart 1994).

Fourth, the identities are flexible and situational in nature. Migrants from the China coast have perfected the art of managing multiple identities, which is the source of their cosmopolitan charm. Let me just cite as an example the Shanghainese cotton spinners in Hong Kong, whom I interviewed in the late 1970s:

"According to the situation, a Shanghainese can activate regional ties of various scope....
Like insects with a protective coloration, his identity can undergo subtle, and if need

be, rapid changes to suit the context of interaction. In international forums such as textile negotiations, the cotton spinners usually present themselves as industrialists from Hong Kong, a vulnerable free port of the developing region of Asia. *Vis-à-vis* their foreign buyers or the senior British officials of the colony, they are Chinese. Meeting in regional associations, they are people from Ningpo or Shanghai city who enjoy their local cuisine and theatrical entertainment. When they participate in the activities of their trade association, they are modern, Westernized businessmen. (Wong 1988: 111–112)

Then lastly, these identities are effective shields to deflect state domination. Hong Kong migrants tend to use them as bargaining chips when negotiating with political authorities to gain autonomy of action. Modern governments, in their efforts at nation building, are often keen to demand exclusive allegiance from their nationals and to impose rigid classifications of citizenship. But in the case of Hong Kong, the large number of its people holding foreign passports of all sorts have forced the Chinese government to relax its nationality law and adopt a flexible definition of a Chinese national in Hong Kong post-1997. In effect, the Chinese government turned a blind eye to the issue of dual nationality in the territory. It announced that all ethnic Chinese in Hong Kong shall be regarded as Chinese nationals after the handover as long as they do not declare formally to the Hong Kong Special Administrative Region (SAR) government that they are holding foreign passports (*South China Morning Post*, April 5, 1997, p. 1; *Ming Pao Daily News*, April 5, 1997, p. A1). Similarly, foreign governments, such as Australia, have introduced flexible residential requirements to accommodate the high mobility of the new immigrants from Hong Kong and elsewhere.

FAMILY EXPERIENCES

So far, I have been discussing the question of identities mainly at the level of individual attitudes as revealed in survey findings. In our research project, we tried to supplement the survey method with longitudinal in-depth interviews with 30 families selected according to their emigration propensities and socioeconomic backgrounds. Through those interviews, we came to realize that the diverse identities held by our respondents were rooted in their social experiences, particularly those transmitted through their families. We discerned four patterns of these identities and family experiences. We call them respectively the loyalists, the locals, the waverers, and the cosmopolitans.

LOYALISTS

The loyalists welcome reversion, which they see as good for their families. They are not well-to-do. Economic concerns dominate their views. To them, the past means hard times. The closing of the border between Hong Kong and the mainland in the early 1950s divided some of these working-class families. Others later fled rural poverty and entered Hong Kong illegally. They are now grateful that the turn towards privatization in China has improved the position of those family members whom they left behind. They expect China to continue its economic progress after reunification with Hong Kong. Loyalists were born in China and spent their formative years there. Because they emigrated to Hong Kong late in their lifetimes, their ties to Chinese kin are ongoing and dense. They cross the border often to see their Chinese kin, and hope for closer contact after reunification. With few relatives living abroad, the loyalists have no plans to leave. Their attention is drawn to China.

LOCALS

The locals expect China to continue to its economic and political progress, but they have few personal connections to China. Nor do they express an affinity to the British. They are firmly attached to Hong Kong and accept the changeover without fanfare. They were born to working-and lower-middle-class families who were not subject to political movements on the mainland. Most are fairly young. Because they were brought up in Hong Kong, they are politically neutral. They are closely attached to the local cultural lifestyle, which includes wide-ranging personal freedoms and the right to self-expression. Trepidation about reversion is based mainly on their fear of losing this Hong Kong way of life. These locals have most of their important kin in Hong Kong. They no longer have close bonds to China. Few have relatives abroad. Thus, emigrant kin do not form a dense overseas group that these families wish to join. They are not torn in different geographical directions. Their focus is on Hong Kong.

WAVERERS

Waverers are those families that want to emigrate but have been turned down by foreign countries. Over the course of our interviews, many changed their attitudes from critical anxiety to one of "wait and see," and even to acceptance of reversion to China. Waverers are mostly working class. Their lack of resources makes it hard for them to emigrate. Once rejected, they do not have the resources to reapply to other countries. They have not merely given up, however. They modify their attitudes. Cynical and negative about China when we first met them, they are now more optimistic. They expect no immediate change in Hong Kong, and they do not expect their children to suffer. But they distrust the Chinese system and prefer what the British have done in the colony to what they see in China. Although they were born mainly in Hong Kong, many of their kin live abroad and others have applied to emigrate. They recognize few kin across the border on the mainland. Their circle includes those who are thinking of going abroad or who have already gone overseas, which colors their attitude toward the changeover. However, the bitter choice of the waverers is sweetened by Hong Kong's prosperity. They end up reasoning that while they can not leave, at least they will be economically better off in Hong Kong.

COSMOPOLITANS

The cosmopolitans were opposed to reunification with China and preferred life as it was under British rule. They are mostly from political refugee families that fled China. They generally have upper-middle-class backgrounds and were once regarded as class enemies by China. They have deep misgivings about the Chinese political system. Many of their close family members suffered persecution under Chinese communism. The collective memory of losing family properties on the mainland fueled their anxiety about the changeover. But their response was not panic and exit. Instead, they planned their move carefully for years. They organized for emigration well in advance of 1997. Others have not experienced class-based discrimination in China. Yet their experiences as businessmen or professionals in China shook their trust in China's ability to handle the delicately balanced Hong Kong economy. The cosmopolitans were born mainly in Hong Kong. Some were born in China of well-to-do parents and fled after land reform. They lacked ongoing contact with their kin on the mainland because of this politically caused rupture. Most have kin living in the West, as well as close friends and classmates abroad, with whom they keep in contact. They are part of a stratum that spans the seas.

After looking at these thumbnail sketches of the four types of identities, it should be clear that regularities in political views toward the changeover are formed by family experiences. But it is equally evident that socioeconomic status and personal networks also figure prominently. Let us now turn to the significance of networks in influencing decisions to leave or to stay.

NETWORKS AS CAPITAL[2]

In our research, we discover three salient features in the use of personal networks for emigration purposes in Hong Kong. First, there is a quantitative variation in terms of occupational class. On the whole, the higher the class position of the family, the larger the number of social ties that can be mobilized for emigration. Options increase as one moves up the social ladder. Second, there is a qualitative variation, too, in the type of networks used by members of different occupational classes. Working-class emigrants tend to depend heavily on kinship ties, while affluent emigrants are more inclined to activate diverse bonds of friendship. Third, members of the lower middle class, whose livelihood hinges on bureaucratic careers and wages, have the lowest emigration propensity. It seems that the assets they possess are the least mobile and transferable.

These findings suggest that it may be fruitful to regard networks as a form of capital. This idea is akin to the concept of social capital as proposed by scholars such as Pierre Bourdieu (1986) and James Coleman (1988). By putting forth the notion of network capital, we are trying to elaborate on Bourdieu's idea and relate *guanxi* and connections directly to the question of social inequality and class formation. When network capital is put on a par with other forms of capital, such as economic and cultural capital, we may come to a better appreciation of the diversity and fluidity in the class structure of Chinese communities such as Hong Kong. It would also lead us to identify at least three analytically distinct class segments that correspond to the three forms of capital, namely entrepreneurs with networks as assets, capitalists with economic means of production as properties, and professionals with knowledge and skill as resources. These class segments are of course only abstract theoretical constructions or ideal types. In reality, they overlap and seldom exist in a pure form.

INSTITUTIONALIZATION

In comparison with economic and cultural capital, network capital is the least institutionalized form of assets. On the whole, economic capital is institutionalized in the form of property rights, and cultural capital in the form of educational qualifications (Bourdieu 1986: 243). Both forms depend heavily on the reliability of social institutions or system trust. Network capital, on the other hand, is basically a diffused asset. It may sometimes take institutional form as an association of one kind or another, but it is generally lodged in reciprocal relations that may or may not be maintained by the parties concerned. In order to reduce uncertainty and to reinforce mutual obligations, personal trust plays a more prominent role as a cementing force in the accumulation of network capital. Therefore, relatively speaking, network capital is less dependent on system trust though it can never be completely free of this form of trust as resources such as classmate networks are derived from reliable educational institutions. (On the distinction between personal and system trust, see Luhmann [1979] and S. L. Wong [1991]).

Because of the different degrees of institutionalization, the three forms of capital tend to have distinctive patterns of geographical mobility and are drawn to different destinations. The movement of economic capital typically follows the logic of comparative advantage. In the case of Hong Kong, for example, industrialists in the cotton-spinning sector had a tendency to diversify their investments into Southeast Asia, Latin America, and parts of Africa where labor costs were relatively low and textile quotas were available (Wong 1988: 39).

The movement of cultural capital is affected by the recognition of credentials and compatibility with educational systems in host countries. Consequently, as revealed in our study, the most popular destinations for the present wave of educated migrants from Hong Kong are English-speaking countries such as Canada, the United States, and Australia.

Network capital, being less dependent on system trust, has greater scope for diffusion and is better able to transcend boundaries. It tends to spread with the Chinese diaspora through personal connections. It can venture into territories with shaky institutional frameworks for business operations, such as the People's Republic of China and Vietnam, and still manage to flourish (Smart and Smart 1991; Wong 1995).

NETWORK CAPACITY

After contrasting network capital with other forms of capital, it is necessary to examine the heterogeneous nature of networks and its implications more closely. Different types of networks exist, with various capacities for facilitating mobility and economic competition. There are kin and non-kin ties, and there are strong and weak linkages (Granovetter 1982). In our study, we have found that reliance on kin ties and strong linkages is more characteristic of the working class. Members of the affluent class are actually disinclined to make use of such ties and often refuse help from family members and relatives. They tend to draw on diverse, weak ties of friendship instead.

We can say that a restricted and elaborated style of network construction exists among our respondents. Dependence on kin relations and strong ties is the hallmark of the restricted network style, while flexible use of non-kin relationships and weak ties is the key feature of the elaborated network style. An elaborated network style is useful in economic competition because it generates greater access to sources of information and provides more autonomy. It can create networks rich in "structural holes," that is, networks with relationships of low redundancy. Ronald Burt (1992: 21) asserts that such "optimized" networks have two design principles. The first is efficiency, achieved by concentrating on the primary contact and allowing relationships with others in the cluster to weaken until they become indirect relations. The second is effectiveness, attained through differentiating primary from secondary contacts in order to focus resources on preserving the former.

MORAL ECONOMY

The "design" principles as set out by Burt alert us to what may be called the moral economy of network capital. In the attempt to optimize benefits, individuals have to be calculating to manipulate relations in their favor. Granovetter seems to be conscious of the moral ambivalence inherent in network construction when he states wryly, "Lest readers of SWT [Strength of Weak Ties] and this chapter ditch all their close friends and set out to construct large networks of acquaintances, I had better say that strong ties can also have some value" (1982: 113; see also Burt 1992: 262).

This defensive statement reveals the basic reason why those who are skilled at networking, such as entrepreneurs, tend to incur popular hostility and resentment in a society (Yang 1994: 51–64; Chu and Ju 1993: 133–134, 150–3). They appear too cunning and pragmatic. They spurn the sacredness of personal relations, turning ends into means. Thus they are open to charges of undermining social solidarity and eroding group allegiance. These are the dark sides of network capital.

CONVERSION AND REPRODUCTION

Another source of the hostility toward network construction can be traced to the sites of tension with other forms of capital, especially with cultural capital. In Hong Kong society, studies have shown that people tend to seek advancement through two major channels of mobility: the entrepreneurial route of starting one's own business and the credential route of acquiring professional qualifications (T.W.P. Wong 1991: 164–165). Both network capital and cultural capital are apparently valued and sought after. Yet other studies have revealed a strong anticapitalist sentiment and deep distrust of entrepreneurs among the educated and professional elites (S. L.Wong 1994b: 230–232). Evidently friction and rivalry exist between carriers of network and cultural capital.

Such tension draws our attention to the problem of conversion and reproduction of various forms of capital. The conversion of cultural capital into network capital in the process of migration is relatively well documented by now. Research on small factory owners in Hong Kong has found that many of these entrepreneurs were immigrants from China with high educational attainment. But their credentials were not recognized in Hong Kong, thus forcing them to seek advancement through industrial endeavors instead (Sit and Wong 1989: 97–100). In the present wave of emigration from Hong Kong, the educated and professional elites are facing a similar barrier overseas, where their qualifications and experience are not fully recognized. A substantial number of them are thus turning themselves into entrepreneurs by setting up small businesses in destination countries such as Australia (Lever-Tracy et al. 1991).

However, conversion is by no means a one-way process. We have found that our respondents express a nearly universal concern for their children's education. Hong Kong Chinese entrepreneurs, whether potential or actual, share with others the same preoccupation with the cultivation of cultural capital for themselves and among their offspring (Ong 1992). Thus there appears to exist a cyclical, intergenerational process by which network capital is converted into cultural capital and vice versa. But precisely how is network capital reproduced in the family and passed down through the generations? What role does gender in particular play in the accumulation and transmission of this type of capital? We know very little about these issues and more research is clearly needed.

NEITHER EMIGRANTS NOR RETURNEES

Although many Hong Kong people have left the territory in the past few years, a sizable portion of them are coming back. However, the precise magnitude of this reverse flow is not known because the Hong Kong government does not collect systematic migration statistics.

We have an official estimate that about 12 percent of those who emigrated during the 1980s have returned. But an academic study suggests that the return rate for that period is much higher, probably close to 30 percent (Kee and Skeldon 1994). Whatever their exact numbers, they are substantial enough to have confounded the official population projections. In 1996, the Census and Statistics Department in Hong Kong revealed that the local population has grown much more rapidly than expected. It had reached the 6.31 million mark, exceeding the official projection by more than 7 percent. This sizeable discrepancy was attributed mainly to large-scale return migration, which was said to amount to more than 100,000 in the single year of 1995–96 (*Ming Pao Daily News*, September 18, 1996: A2).

Those who are coming back to Hong Kong are often called "returnees." But this is actually a misnomer because nobody knows whether they are coming back to stay (Kwong 1993: 151–152). Furthermore, it is unlikely that they are giving up the citizenship they acquired abroad. For most of them, it seems that the decision of whether to leave or to stay has been deferred indefinitely. They are thus neither "emigrants" nor "returnees" in the strict sense. Rather, they are engaged in a form of "experimental migration" (Wang 1993: 133), made possible by the growing permeability of national borders and advancements in global transportation and communication.

THE "ASTRONAUTS"

The fluidity of their status is better captured by the new and figurative term "astronauts," which carries a double meaning. At one level, it is a Cantonese pun, which means literally "persons with absentee wives," highlighting the fact that many of those who come back are leaving their spouses and children abroad. At another level, it refers to their frequent long-distance flights shuttling back and forth between Hong Kong and their new countries of adoption.

These "astronauts" constitute a novel phenomenon with several significant features. First of all, they tend to possess more versatile skills and valuable assets that set them apart from traditional Chinese migrants who were predominantly coolies and traders. Mostly educated and bilingual, they include quite a number of professionals and entrepreneurs in their midst. Their talents are being actively courted by Hong Kong and various destination countries that compete to attract them to their fold. They can therefore afford to pick and choose, and move to and fro. Together, they form a horde of what I call "roaming yuppies" in the contemporary world (Wong 1994a).

Secondly, they are creating a pattern of migratory movement that is unprecedented in Chinese communities. Instead of individuals, families are now on the move together. In the past, the usual pattern was for able-bodied men to venture overseas to seek a better livelihood. Parents, wives, and children were generally left in their native communities, sustained and cared for by relatives and neighbors. The current practice is to relocate the entire family abroad. In many instances, able-bodied men then return to Hong Kong to work, leaving the women, the young, and sometimes even the old to fend for themselves and adjust as well as they can to their new environment. The gruesome murder of an elderly couple from Hong Kong in their Canadian home in April 1997 provides a poignant example of the unforeseen consequences of this shift in migration pattern. The couple, both in their seventies, were due to return to Hong Kong to celebrate their newly acquired Canadian citizenship when they were apparently beaten to death by burglars. Their eldest son, who emigrated to Vancouver in 1989 and sponsored them to join him in 1992, moved back to Hong Kong with his wife and children in 1995 after securing a job at one of the local universities. Therefore, the elderly couple, living by themselves in their house in Vancouver, was vulnerable to attack (*South China Morning Post*, April 2, 1997).

WHERE IS HOME?

When families rather than individuals are on the move, the notion of home base inevitably undergoes change. Contemporary Hong Kong migrants have to confront the question, where is home? For their predecessors, the Chinese sojourners going overseas in the past, the answer was unambiguous. Home was the native village in China, where one's ancestors were buried. They maintained a distinction between what G. W. Skinner (1971: 275) calls residence and abode. The former was permanent while the latter was temporary. Should they be unfortunate enough to die overseas in their place of abode, it was imperative that their bodies, or at least their bones, be sent home for a proper burial (Sinn 1989: 71).

For the present-day "astronauts" from Hong Kong, however, the matter is far less clear-cut. Their conceptions of home are more divergent. Some still uphold the traditional idea that the most desirable resting place remains the native village.

DECIDING NOT TO DECIDE

Failing that, they should at least be returned to Hong Kong for burial, with the name of their native place engraved on their tombstones as symbolic reminders of home. Then there are those who have uprooted themselves and found their home in their adopted land. A recent obituary published in the *South China Morning Post* is illustrative. It reads: "CHAN, SHUN, born in China, lived in Hong Kong and settled in Vancouver since 1989, passed away peacefully on May 25, 1997. Survived by his loving wife, sons Tom and Caleb, daughters Helen, Esther, and Jacqueline, and 17 grandchildren." The memorial service was held at the University of British Columbia's Chan Shun concert hall, of which he was a benefactor, and he was buried in a cemetery in Vancouver (*South China Morning Post*, May 29, 1997: 8; *The Hong Kong Economic Journal*, May 29, 1997: 14).

Yet, for the majority of the Hong Kong migrants, the idea of home is probably more slippery and less definite. They tend to maintain multiple abodes in various places, being unsure in their own minds of where they would call home. In a study based on in-depth interviews with 18 returned migrants from Canada working in Hong Kong, Wendy Chan (1996: abstract) sums up their feelings of uncertainty and anguish this way:

"The results of my study suggest that the returned migrants were "reluctant exiles" in the first place, and they are now living in a state of migrancy and "homelessness." However, while my subjects have failed to find home in the rationalist sense of the term, they still cannot accept homelessness as celebrated in the postmodernist view, and hence, the search for home continues. For they are "home but not home."

In their search for home as described by Wendy Chan, one place is conspicuous by its absence. They may be agonizing over the choice between Vancouver, Toronto or Hong Kong, but none of them mentions his native village in the Chinese mainland as a possibility to be considered. It is apparent that China is no longer home to them. Such an orientation and sense of estrangement from China has been thrown into relief by Cheung Yuen-ting, the director of the movie *The Soong Sisters*. In the program publicizing the gala premiere of her film, Cheung (1997) writes:

"Born and raised in the British Colony of Hong Kong, I have never set foot on China until 1989, only to discover a country and a people I did not understand.

With the coming of 1997 (the year that Hong Kong will stop being a colony and go back as part of China), I try to re-establish a link with the past, to study the history of China as we step towards the future, and to find out who I really am.

During this search, I discovered three women who lived at the turn of the century, the Soong Sisters, whose situation bore a striking resemblance to our predicament. Sent by their pioneering father to study abroad during their childhood, when most Chinese women still had their feet bound, they came back from the West as total strangers to a country they called their home—a home they hardly recognized, and a home that hardly recognized them ....

As a filmmaker facing the imminent handover, and all the unknowns of the future, I can understand and share the sentiment of these women living a century before me. And by writing about them and China of the time, it seems that I have come to understand more about myself and China now."

CULTURAL AFFINITY AND ECONOMIC RATIONALITY

It is this weakened emotional attachment that has enabled many roaming yuppies from Hong Kong to venture into China as investors in the past decade and to approach the mainland as an economic frontier. Probably for the first time in the history of Chinese migration overseas, these Hong Kong migrants are not returning to China as their home. Unlike the sojourners before them, they are not going back to their native villages to have their status confirmed and achievements celebrated. They do not feel the urge to display their wealth and glorify their ancestors. They are free from the heavy bondage of kinship and community obligations. Thus they are able to combine cultural affinity with economic rationality. They can mobilize social networks with flexibility, as these networks are no longer firmly embedded in strong attachments. Moving into China as entrepreneurs, they can look for economic opportunities dispassionately, unclouded by emotional bonds and insulated by psychological distance. We may say that they are engaging in a form of secular rather than sacred return. China is no longer the normative center of their cultural universe. As a result, they are able to forge a cosmopolitan form of Chineseness and entrepreneurship that is emerging as a potent, transnational force in the global economy today.

CONCLUSION

Emigration is nothing new to Hong Kong. Since it became a British colony in 1842, Hong Kong has been a port of embarkation for large numbers of people moving from China to other parts of the world. Throughout the modern era, Hong Kong has been a city of migrants. Historical transition is not new to the territory either. It has lived through the Chinese Revolutions of 1911 and 1949 but still managed to survive.

When Hong Kong confronted the last transition in 1949, the agonizing decision many Chinese had to make was whether to stay on the mainland or flee to the territory for shelter. At that time, the historian Chen Yin-ke made a fateful decision. He rejected the option of seeking refuge in Hong Kong because he could not bear the humiliation of living under British colonialism. He chose to stay in Guangzhou, as far away from Beijing as possible but still on Chinese soil. That did not spare him, however, and he died a tragic death in 1969 during the Cultural Revolution.

But as a historian of great vision and integrity, he held the unfashionable conviction, as early as 1919 during the May Fourth movement, that the modernization of China can succeed only by building on the strengths of traditional culture, such as respect for the family and the refined art of handling human relations. He predicted that as industrial enterprises developed in China, the commercial skills of the Chinese would flourish, "and the Chinese should be able to become the rich merchants of the world." (Wu Xue-zhao 1992: 9) That prediction, on the rise of capitalism with Chinese characteristics, seems to be coming true at long last. Yet, he did not anticipate that one of the main forces propelling that form of capitalism would be unleashed from Hong Kong, a place he spurned, a place tainted with colonialism, a place that is not quite genuinely Chinese but that has become rather cosmopolitan, and a place that permits its inhabitants the liberty to indulge in the agonies of deciding whether to leave or to stay, or to move back and forth without making a final decision.

NOTES

1.   This paper draws on the research findings of the project "Emigration from Hong Kong: Families, Networks, and Returnees," funded by the Hong Kong Research Grants Council from 1994 to 1997. I wish to thank the other members of the research team, in particular Janet Salaff, Ronald Skeldon, Fung Mei-ling, and Chiu Yue-tat, for their contributions and support. An earlier version of this paper was presented at the University of Washington on May 6, 1997, less than two months before Hong Kong's reversion to China. I have preserved the tone of the paper as it was delivered on that occasion.

2.   This section draws on my forthcoming article, co-authored with Janet Salaff, entitled "Network Capital: Emigration from Hong Kong" in *The British Journal of Sociology*.

REFERENCES

Bourdieu, P. 1986. "The Forms of Capital." In *Handbook of Theory and Research for the Sociology of Education*, edited by J. Richarson. New York:

Greenwood Press.

Burt, Ronald. 1992. *Structural Holes: The Social Structure of Competition.* Cambridge, Mass.: Harvard University Press.

Chan, Wendy W.Y. 1996. "Home But Not Home: A Case Study of Some Canadian Returnees in Hong Kong." Unpublished M.A. thesis, Hong Kong University of Science and Technology.

Cheung, Yuen-ting. 1997. "Director's Notes." Mimeographed leaflet on the gala premiere of *The Soong Sisters.* Hong Kong: University of Hong Kong Foundation for Educational Development and Research.

Chu, G.C., and Ju, Y. 1993. *The Great Wall in Ruins: Communication and Cultural Change in China.* Albany: State University of New York Press.

Coleman, J. S., 1988. "Social Capital in the Creation of Human Capital," *American Journal of Sociology* 94 (supplement): S95–S120.

Granovetter, Mark. 1982. "The Strength of Weak Ties: A Network Theory Revisited," In *Social Structure and Network Analysis*, edited by Peter V. Marsden and Nan Lin. Beverly Hills, Cali.: Sage.

Hamilton, Gary G. 1996. "Overseas Chinese Capitalism," in *Confucian Traditions in East Asian Modernity*, edited by Tu Wei-ming. Cambridge, Mass.: Harvard University Press.

Kee, P.K., and R. Skeldon. 1994. "The Migration and Settlement of Hong Kong Chinese in Australia," in *Reluctant Exiles? Migration from Hong Kong and the New Overseas Chinese*, edited by R. Skeldon. New York and Hong Kong: M. E. Sharpe and Hong Kong University Press.

Kwong, Paul C.K. 1993. "Internationalization of Population and Globalization of Families," in *The Other Hong Kong Report*, edited by Choi Po-king and Ho Lok-sang. Hong Kong: Chinese University Press.

Lam, Kit-chun, Yiu-kwan Fan, and Ronald Skeldon. 1995. "The Tendency to Emigrate From Hong Kong," in *Emigration from Hong Kong*, edited by Ronald Skeldon. Hong Kong: The Chinese University Press.

Lever-Tracy, C., et al. 1991. *Asian Entrepreneurs in Australia: Ethnic Small Business in the Indian and Chinese Communities of Brisbane and Sydney.* Canberra: Australian Government Publishing Service.

Luhmann, Niklas. 1979. *Trust and Power.* New York: John Wiley & Sons.

Ong, Aihwa. 1992. "Limits to Cultural Accumulation: Chinese Capitalists on the American Pacific Rim." *Annals of the New York Academy of Sciences* 645: 125–143.

Sinn, Elizabeth. 1989. *Power and Charity: The Early History of the Tung Wah Hospital, Hong Kong* Hong Kong: Oxford University Press.

Sit, Victor F.S., and Siu-lun Wong. 1989. *Small and Medium Industries in an Export-Oriented Economy: The Case of Hong Kong.* Hong Kong: Centre of Asian Studies, University of Hong Kong.

Skinner, G. William. 1971. "Chinese Peasants and the Closed Community: An Open and Shut Case." *Comparative Studies in Society and History* 13 no. 3:

271–281.

Smart, Josephine. 1994. "Business Immigration to Canada: Deception and Exploitation," in *Reluctant Exiles? Migration from Hong Kong and the New Overseas Chinese*, edited by Ronald Skeldon. Hong Kong: Hong Kong University Press.

Smart, Josephine, and Alan Smart. 1991. "Personal Relations and Divergent Economies: A Case Study of Hong Kong Investment in South China," *International Journal of Urban and Regional Research* 15: 216–233.

Wang Gungwu. 1993. "Migration and Its Enemies," in *Conceptualizing Global History*, edited by Bruce Mazlish and Ralph Buultjens. Boulder, Colo.: Westview Press.

Wong Siu-lun. 1988. *Emigrant Entrepreneurs: Shanghai Industrialists in Hong Kong*. Hong Kong: Oxford University Press.

Wong Siu-lun. 1991. "Chinese Entrepreneurs and Business Trust," in *Business Networks and Economic Development in East and Southeast Asia*, edited by Gary G. Hamilton. Hong Kong: Centre of Asian Studies, University of Hong Kong.

———. 1992. "Emigration and Stability in Hong Kong." *Asian Survey*, 32 no. 10: 918–933.

———. 1994a. "Roaming Yuppies: Hong Kong Migration to Australia." *Asian and Pacific Migration Journal* 3 nos. 2–3: 373–392.

———. 1994b. "Business and Politics in Hong Kong during the Transition," in *25 Years of Social and Economic Development in Hong Kong*, edited by B.K.P. Leung and T.Y.C. Wong. Hong Kong: Centre of Asian Studies, University of Hong Kong.

———. 1995. "Business Networks, Cultural Values and the State in Hong Kong and Singapore," in *Chinese Business Enterprise in Asia*, edited by R. A. Brown. London and New York: Routledge.

Wong, Thomas W.P. 1991. "Inequality, Stratification and Mobility," in *Indicators of Social Development: Hong Kong 1988*, edited by Lau Siu-kai et. al. Hong Kong: Institute of Asia-Pacific Studies, The Chinese University of Hong Kong.

Wu, Xue-zhao. 1992. *Wu Mi yu Chen Yin-ke (Wu Mi and Chen Yin-ke)*. Beijing: Tsinghua Daxue Chubanshe.

Yang, Mayfair M.H. 1994. *Gifts, Favors and Banquets: The Art of Social Relationships in China*. Ithaca and London: Cornell University Press.

8 / Hong Kong Immigration and the Question of Democracy

Contemporary Struggles over Urban Politics in Vancouver, B.C.

KATHARYNE MITCHELL

In the last two decades, migration levels between Asia and western Canada have risen markedly. One of the most pronounced migration streams has run between the former colony of Hong Kong and the city of Vancouver, British Columbia. The contemporary movement of people between these regions is profoundly different from earlier waves, as it is characterized by large numbers of extremely wealthy migrants. Unlike earlier periods of migration, the current group has left the greater China region not to seek better business opportunities or to escape poverty and persecution but to secure citizenship abroad and to diversify financial portfolios. Leaving Hong Kong in advance of the handover to China in 1997, many of the wealthy migrants moved to Canada primarily as a safeguard against the potential negative ramifications that might result from the political change.

The different character of this migrant group has led to vastly different types of interactions with the pre-existing communities in Vancouver. The new migrants' status as successful businesspeople or professionals has given them an economic and cultural power that was not the case with earlier Chinese migrants. As Wickberg and Wong have shown in other chapters in this volume, prior waves of migrants from the southern China region were primarily poor rural laborers brought in to build railroads and work in labor-intensive jobs that no other group of people could do so well and so cheaply. By contrast, the contemporary business and professional migrants have arrived in Canada with a high degree of economic clout, cultural savvy, and "network" capital.

In this paper I discuss the arrival of these new migrants and examine their impact on the democratic values and political institutions of two established communities in Vancouver. The first community, Shaughnessy Heights, is composed of residents of primarily Anglo heritage. The second community, centered in the city's Chinatown, is composed primarily of ethnic Chinese residents. The discussion will concentrate particularly on an analysis of how these new immigrants are able to successfully occupy a western political sphere (in Shaughnessy Heights) yet, seemingly paradoxically, have trouble dominating established Chinese spheres (in Chinatown).

In order to show this, I will narrow my focus by looking at two separate incidents: the first, a series of public hearings on a downzoning amendment in Shaughnessy Heights in 1992; and the second, a vote for the election of new board members to a prominent cultural and political institution in the Chinese community called the Chinese Cultural Center, in 1993. These two moments in the city's recent political history can serve as condensation points for an examination of the differing cultural constructions of and challenges to the concept of democracy that have occurred in the two communities of Vancouver in the last decade.

Democracy, in the sense employed here, is more than just the right to vote and be represented by a government. In both the Shaughnessy Heights and the Chinatown cases, democracy is perceived as a process in which decisions can be made by members of the community as to the best future direction of that community. This type of popular democracy stems from liberal democratic traditions emphasizing the rights of citizens to freely pursue rational debates in a public forum. The public forum, also known as the public sphere, is a space for critical discourse that ideally is open to all citizens concerned with questions of general interest to the public.

In both the case studies discussed in this paper, it is this democratic understanding of a public sphere that is challenged by the new immigrants. In the case of Shaughnessy Heights, the Hong Kong immigrants claimed that they had been shut out of the democratic decision-making process regarding land use in the community, and they demanded and won the right to have a voice in a contemporary downzoning amendment decision. In this way, they succeeded in challenging some of racial and class distinctions that have historically operated to exclude certain citizens from participating on an equal basis in a public forum. They eventually prevented the amendment from passing. In the case of the Chinatown election, by contrast, the recent Hong Kong immigrants were unable to change a democratic system that excluded participation on the basis of particularistic community ties and relationships (a form of insider "nepotism"). Despite the call for more open democratic procedures and equal, rational debate, the immigrants were voted down, and the system of representation remains much as it was prior to the election.

In the following sections, I will briefly document the major movements of people and capital from Hong Kong to Vancouver in the late 1980s and early 1990s, and show some of the ramifications of this movement for the urban environment. Following that, I discuss the ways in which this particular migration wave has affected the political procedures and outcomes of the Shaughnessy Heights downzoning amendment and the Chinese Cultural Center election in the early 1990s. I then draw together these case studies with a more general analysis of the impact of recent Hong Kong immigration on democratic procedures in Vancouver within the two different communities.

MIGRATION AND URBAN TRANSFORMATION
IMMIGRATION

Many scholars have documented the major influx of Hong Kong immigrants into Canada in the last ten years. Immigration statistics show a major leap in immigration in the years following the introduction of a new (business) category of immigration in 1986, and again after the Tiananmen massacre in 1989 (see Table 1). Vancouver, in particular, has been a favorite landing point for Hong Kong immigrants, many of whom are drawn to the city because of the shorter geographical distance to Hong Kong, historical and family ties, and a highly touted quality of life.

An important new component of the immigration program in Canada is a category entitled "business immigration." This category allows investors to skip the processing queue for landed immigrant visas if, among other qualifications, they have a personal net worth of at least C$500,000. Those arriving within the "entrepreneur" category must promise to invest a minimum amount of capital in a Canadian business over a three-year period. For British Columbia, which is known as a "have" province, this amount is C$350,000. Hong Kong has consistently led in this immigration category since it was established in 1986, and Vancouver has once again been a primary recipient of both these business immigrants and their capital funds.

CAPITAL FLOWS

The exact amounts of capital flows between Hong Kong and Vancouver are not documented by statistical agencies in either city. The business immigrant statistics, however, provide one approximate measure. According to *Employment and Immigration Canada*, the amount of estimated funds brought to British Columbia in 1988 (most of the funds brought into the province wind up in Vancouver) was nearly 1.5 billion Canadian dollars. Figures from 1989 show an approximate capital flow of C$3.5 billion from Hong Kong to Canada, of which C$2.21 billion, or 63 percent was transferred by the business migration component (Nash 1992; Macdonald 1990).

I consider these figures conservative. Most applicants under-declare their actual resources by a significant margin for income tax purposes. I interviewed bankers

Table 1. Canada: Landed Immigrants by Country of Last Permanent Residence.

Region/Country of last residence	1980	1981	1982	1983	1984	1985	1986	1987	1988	1989	1990	1991	1992
Afghanistan	14	38	79	73	125	370	590	975	1,010	1,054	1,027	1,353	1,193
Bangladesh	76	73	58	78	84	94	449	473	454	337	534	1,063	1,591
Cambodia	3,265	1,337	1,378	1,542	1,727	1,803	1,745	1,612	1,543	2,041	766	424	337
China	4,936	6,551	3,572	2,217	2,214	1,883	1,902	2,625	2,778	4,430	7,989	13,915	10,420
Hong Kong	6,309	6,451	6,542	6,710	7,696	7,380	5,893	16,170	23,281	19,908	29,261	22,340	38,841
India	8,483	8,256	7,776	7,041	5,502	4,028	6,940	9,692	10,409	8,819	10,624	12,848	12,664
Indonesia	267	214	264	136	131	107	142	219	261	278	249	280	241
Iran	1,021	1,056	1,201	1,268	1,870	1,728	1,952	3,083	3,669	3,797	3,475	6,209	6,783
Japan	737	770	630	333	250	205	273	446	346	541	369	502	603
Laos	6,266	866	375	434	870	379	636	456	842	679	583	1,006	98
Malaysia	702	708	688	399	356	332	418	717	1,676	1,936	1,641	1,173	1,305
Myanmar	87	81	275	39	51	37	14	31	56	86	140	107	69
Nepal	10	6	7	1	2	5	12	8	14	4	20	34	28
Pakistan	881	731	868	836	611	479	643	991	1,242	2,007	2,114	2,883	3,822
Philippines	6,051	5,859	5,062	4,454	3,748	3,076	4,102	7,343	8,310	11,393	12,042	12,335	18,252
Singapore	290	389	435	241	176	166	220	489	1,141	1,634	1,077	807	616
South Korea	957	1,430	1,506	1,017	801	934	1,143	2,276	2,676	2,820	1,871	2,486	3,682
Sri Lanka	144	223	182	166	1,048	815	1,753	4,226	2,409	2,423	3,106	6,826	12,626
Taiwan	827	834	560	570	421	536	695	1,467	2,187	3,388	3,681	4,488	7,451
Thailand	396	123	201	128	125	73	86	118	154	194	181	262	229
Vietnam	25,541	8,251	5,935	6,451	10,950	10,404	6,622	5,668	6,196	9,425	9,081	8,963	7,674
Total Asia	71,602	48,834	41,624	36,906	41,896	38,597	41,600	67,327	81,136	93,213	90,798	101,140	123,525
Total	143,133	128,618	121,147	89,157	88,239	84,302	99,219	152,098	161,929	192,001	214,230	230,781	252,107

and immigration consultants in Hong Kong in 1991 who put the overall amount of funds being transferred from Hong Kong to Canada annually as high as 5 to 6 billion dollars in the late 1980s and early 1990s. Of that amount, nearly one-third would be destined for British Columbia.

IMPACT ON URBAN ENVIRONMENT

Many bank officials I interviewed in Hong Kong estimated that most of the funds transferred from Hong Kong to Canada in the late 1980s were invested in property. Despite government attempts to channel capital into productive sectors, the majority of business immigrant funds went into property investment, particularly in the early years of the program. The *Financial Post*, for example, estimated that in 1990, foreign investment in privately held real estate in Canada nearly tripled from the 1985 figure of US$1.2 billion. If bank financing is included in that figure, the total during 1990 would exceed US$13 billion (Fung 1991).

There have been several repercussions from this capital influx for the built environment. They include a rapid rise in house prices and apartment rates, numerous demolitions of older houses and apartment buildings, and the construction of quite large, boxy houses (termed "monster houses" by the media and local residents) in older neighborhoods (Mitchell 1993, 1997). Many of these houses (some studies show up to 80 percent) were purchased by Hong Kong Chinese buyers, so changes in the neighborhoods often became associated with the influx of people and capital from Hong Kong. These changes have occurred citywide but have been protested most vociferously in westside communities such as Shaughnessy Heights (see Map 1). Residents of this neighborhood have the highest average family income in Vancouver, and census tracks show that the area was almost composed exclusively of white residents of British heritage through the late 1970s.

EXCLUSIVE ZONING IN SHAUGHNESSY HEIGHTS

In the context of massive urban transformations throughout Vancouver in the 1980s, a number of westside community groups arose to resist these changes. The specific emphasis of a majority of these groups was the protection of trees and older houses, but it was part of a much broader struggle to retain the older "character" of the communities, a character predicated on the history, architecture, and values of a British tradition. Historically, Shaughnessy Heights was the most exclusive neighborhood in the city, with numerous specially designed zoning measures and protective covenants that effectively limited residence in the neighborhood to upper-income white families (Mitchell 1994; Ley 1995; Duncan and Duncan 1988). In 1992, there was a major attempt to provide even more protection for this area through further restrictive zoning for the neighborhoods of 2nd and 3rd Shaughnessy. This 1992 amendment would have limited the allowable floor space

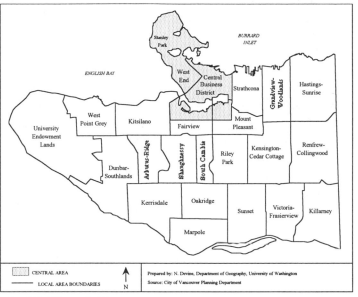

Figure 1. City of Vancouver Local Areas

Map 1. City of Vancouver and local areas.

ratio (FSR) for developers and placed numerous other restrictions on any redevelopment in the area. Before the City Council voted on this amendment, however, the Shaughnessy Heights Property Owners Association (SHPOA) sent out a survey soliciting neighborhood opinion on the amendment and called for a series of public hearings to discuss it.

THE PUBLIC HEARINGS OF 1992

I now turn to the most openly confrontational events between the older, Anglo-Canadian residents of Shaughnessy Heights and the more recent Hong Kong Chinese residents in the neighborhood. In six long and agonizing public hearings on the topic of downzoning in South Shaughnessy in 1992, the polarization of these two groups immediately became apparent. In the public hearings, a majority of Shaughnessy Heights Property Owners' Association (SHPOA) members advocated restrictions on future redevelopment in the area. A group composed almost entirely of recent Chinese immigrants from Hong Kong quickly formed an ad hoc committee in opposition to these proposed development restrictions. This ad hoc committee campaigned strenuously against the downzoning. Aided by a number of developers, most prominently Barry Hersh, a house-builder and president of the West Side Builders Association, the campaign used allegations of racism to discredit the SHPOA and its followers. They claimed that the downzoning amendment was actually a veiled effort to keep Chinese buyers from being interested in moving into the neighborhood.

After the first meeting in September, leaflets were sent to Chinese homeowners in the area, urging them to ask Chinese friends from the lower mainland to attend the rest of the hearings in a show of public alliance. These leaflets were written in Chinese, whereas the original survey questionnaire on the topic of downzoning had been written in English only. At the public hearings, Chinese speakers complained that the survey distributed by the Vancouver Planning Department had not been translated into Chinese, reducing the information that they needed to make informed decisions about the proposed change. (By contrast, a neighborhood garbage memorandum had been translated into six languages.) Some of these speakers spoke Cantonese at the hearing and used an interpreter. At several points, they were heckled by Anglo-Canadian members of the audience for not speaking English.

The widespread publicity of this racial polarization (The hearings were televised and reported globally) and the manipulation of the definitions of racism by both the Chinese residents and developers indicated new stakes in the battle over urban design and control of the Shaughnessy streetscape. Public hearings are generally presented as models of democratic debate and spaces of rational decision making. But historically most land use decisions have rarely been reached in this way. In Shaughnessy's past, for example, debates over appropriate land use generally led to restrictions based on class and race. The six hearings in 1992 represented the first time that a radically different interpretation of justice and the community good for a westside area was successfully promulgated by a group not composed primarily of Anglo-Canadian residents.

For the first time in the city's history, large numbers of wealthy capitalists who were perceived as "non-white" moved to westside neighborhoods that were formerly protected by virtue of their high prices and exclusive zoning covenants. This outside group was able to form alliances with local capitalists for a pro-growth agenda that threatened the carefully established symbolic value of westside neighborhoods. By raising the specter of racism, which could easily be buttressed by the historical evidence of racism in prior zoning measures, the Hong Kong Chinese and westside builders effectively controlled the public hearings and defeated the SHPOA-designed effort to restrict further development in the neighborhood.

In defense of their position against downzoning, many Chinese speakers extolled the virtues of a perceived Chinese way of life. Rather than contesting cultural differences, however, Chinese homeowners in Shaughnessy used them to their advantage, lecturing enthusiastically about family, respect for the elderly, communal closeness, education, and hard work—and contrasting these values with their representations of lazy, unfamilial, and undemocratic white Canadians. Similarly, they appropriated the meanings of racism and nationalism to their advantage, decrying English-only survey forms as inherently un-Canadian, and neighborhood rezoning proposals as manifestly racist.

The understanding of what constituted the community good became a major source of conflict. Definitions of what it meant to be "Canadian" or to "live in Shaughnessy" were opened up for interrogation and negotiation. Rather than simply contesting the Anglo definitions of "Chineseness" and appropriate places for Chinese to live, however, the financial power and cultural savvy of the new group gave them the power to completely invert this process of racial and spatial definition and allowed them to represent dominant Chinese definitions of "Angloness."

The new Chinese homeowners in Shaughnessy were able to ally themselves with developers, realtors, and politicians eager to combine capital in new, increasingly international, business ventures. This slight shifting of the economic and political power ballast in the neighborhood allowed public voicing and material representation of Anglo values and norms from the outsider's perspective. Through this process of contestation and inversion, the formerly undemocratic public forums on land use were exposed as traditional spaces of hegemonic production for an elite (white) group and were successfully transformed by the new immigrants.

To give final weight to this inversion, many of the Chinese residents voiced their concerns in Cantonese and deliberately employed the language of popular democracy in defense of their individual and economic rights. They further spoke of these rights as integral to the Canadian liberal and secular welfare state. In the hearings, much to the dismay of their Anglo-Canadian listeners, Chinese-Canadian speakers invoked notions of freedom, family, individual rights, property rights, and democracy itself in defense of their position. One Chinese-Canadian speaker (using an interpreter) said:

> "I live in Shaughnessy and we built a house very much to my liking. The new zoning would not allow enough space for me.... I strongly oppose this new proposal. Why do I have to be inconvenienced by so many regulations? This infringes my freedom. Canada is a democratic country and democracy should be returned to the people."[1]

The threat to established norms heralded by this position became clear in an interview with a SHPOA member. She said to me:

> "I can't describe to you how it feels to be lectured to about Canadian democracy by people who have to use an interpreter.... Lectured about laziness, how we don't need

big houses because we don't take care of our parents like the Chinese do.... I cannot understand how *anybody* could go to another country and insist they can build against the wishes of an old established neighborhood. The effrontery and the insolence take my breath away."[2]

Historic zoning patterns and landscape struggles in Shaughnessy Heights give some indication of how the construction of community spaces has been implicated in the reproduction of a dominant Anglo elite in Vancouver. The contemporary conflict over downzoning also demonstrates how the recent Chinese residents in the community were able to contest and even dominate this urban political sphere in the early 1990s by using alternative concepts of appropriate behavior and justice and by employing the language of individual rights and popular democracy.

THE POLITICAL SPACES OF THE CHINESE CULTURAL CENTER

My second case study focuses on the impact of recent immigrants from Hong Kong on the political struggle over an important institution within the Chinese community. In this struggle, the question of democracy is raised once again, as many of the new migrants challenge the institutional procedures used in electing new members to the executive board. In this case, the new immigrants again draw from their high economic status and cultural savvy as professionals and businesspeople to attempt to open a supposedly democratic process to more participants. Rather than an exclusivity based on class and race, as in the case of the primarily white neighborhood of Shaughnessy Heights, the Chinese Cultural Center reputedly excluded people on the basis of personal affiliations and other "ascribed" characteristics. In other words, rather than a "modern" democratic system based on principles of equality and achievement, the political system prevailing in the Chinese community was traditionalist in its operation, with authority resting on connection, consensus, and seniority.

In an effort to render the process more democratic and more professional, and thus open up the community to wider participation in a "neutral" public sphere, several recent migrants from Hong Kong and Taiwan ran for office on a platform of political renewal. In their platform, this group professed interest in the democratic reform of a system that they characterized as outmoded, exclusionary, and out of touch with modern organizational principles. Despite their high education and professional status, however, their effort failed. In the following section, I examine this failed effort to revolutionize democratic procedure and the political sphere in Chinatown, then conclude with an analysis comparing the differing community outcomes.

THE DEMOCRATIC BEGINNINGS OF THE
CHINESE CULTURAL CENTER

In order to understand how important the Chinese Cultural Center's 1993 election was to the board of directors, it is necessary to know something about the establishment of this institution and its early history. The Chinese Cultural Center (CCC) was established in the early 1970s as an organization that would introduce not just a new cultural forum but also new ways of managing and thinking about community institutions. It arrived on the Chinatown scene as a new political force in direct competition with the older Chinese Benevolent Association (CBA)—an association perceived as stagnant and undemocratic by many younger members of the community.

After it had garnered the support of several prominent professionals and 53 organizations in Chinatown, the early fund-raising efforts by the CCC were extremely successful. This early success, the ambitious plans for a large and central community space, and the democratic leadership style espoused by the founders of the new organization threatened the dominance and traditional authority of the CBA in the political and social affairs of the community. In response to this threat, a smear campaign against the CCC was launched in the Chinese press, in which the CCC was labeled an organization "belonging to the Communist Party."[3]

The rancorous debate between the CBA and the CCC spread through the community and began to hinge on the question of democratic representation. Several articles in the *Chinese Times*, the main Chinatown newspaper through the 1970s, questioned the process by which representatives were elected to the CBA. In these articles, democracy was described as an open, public process, one that was being subverted by a more traditionalist method of governing within the CBA.[4] In the 1970s, the early ideas and values surrounding the Chinese Cultural Center were thus formulated within the context of demands for greater political involvement and a transformation of old-style politics within the community.

THE 1993 ELECTIONS

In 1993 another major challenge was posed to the established leadership in Chinatown, but this time it was the directors of the Chinese Cultural Center who were attacked for their entrenched and non-democratic positions. Despite the Center's early support of the promotion of a more open and democratic process in association elections, by the late 1980s its own board was criticized for perceived insularity and traditionalism. Jane Chan, a lawyer who served on the board during this time period, characterized the CCC board as "not democratic," with "power held by a few."[5] Because of her desire to change these things, Chan, along with 24 other young professionals, campaigned for election to the board of directors in

1993. The group ran under the banner of the Chinese Cultural Center Renewal Committee.

The Renewal Committee, which claimed to be more open and responsive to recent changes in Chinatown (including problems associated with the major influx of people from Hong Kong and Taiwan), was composed entirely of professionals, eight of whom were recent Hong Kong and Taiwanese immigrants who had been in Canada less than 10 years. The Committee challenged the sitting directors of the CCC on two main points: first, the lack of an open, democratic, and professional organizational process (manifested most obviously in an attempt to amend the Center's constitution in 1992); and second, the Center's ongoing political allegiance with the People's Republic of China.

According to Jennifer Lim, a member of the board in 1996, the attempt to render the constitution less democratic was part of a general organizational mode in the CCC in the late 1980s and early 1990s, which was "very inward looking." She believed that "despite the increase in immigrants and new needs" of the community, most of the board was still controlled by elderly individuals who were "locked in" to older cultural values. Lim claimed that the new immigrants were more liberal and open-minded, and wanted to hire professional people and run the association more systematically, less on the basis of favoritism and ascribed relationships.[6] Nelson Tsui, a lawyer and member of the Renewal Committee, said in an interview, "We want the board to be directly accountable; we want the process to be open." He claimed that the politics in older Chinese-Canadian institutions had been based on the traditional Chinese model of respect for authority. But younger immigrants, living in democratic Canada, want "to see *that* context applied, rather than 5,000 years of Chinese history, which is not democracy."[7]

In turn, the Renewal Committee's public allegations of undemocratic procedures and shady financial dealings angered the CCC board, which labeled the new group "elitist social activists" and portrayed them as young, urban, wealthy professionals who were new to Canada, yet wanted to take over from the old pioneers who had built Chinatown. The board and its supporters formed a group called the Committee to Maintain the Community's Participation in the Cultural Center (Maintain). This group began a strong counterattack in which they depicted themselves as more traditional and respectful of history and authority; they claimed to be composed primarily of the older family and regional associations, the Chinatown merchants, and a working class core. In an article defending the CCC board, Executive Director Fred Mah upheld the leadership of the association and spoke against its increased politicization. He represented the CCC board as "moderate" and the Center's positions as "apolitical."[8]

Despite the CCC's early origins as a new, invigorating force in Chinatown, however, by the late 1980s it had become entrenched in old-style, traditional politics of authority and consensus. This emphasis culminated in 1992 in the attempt to limit the types of members who could be elected to positions of power on the Board of Directors. It was also evident in the strong desire to seem neutral and "apolitical" in the context of overseas politics. As many Renewal candidates pointed out, however, the decision to attend the PRC banquet in 1989 and not to erect a pro-democracy statue or plaque in the garden were themselves political statements. These kinds of statements were also contested by the Renewal group, which claimed that the Center's politics were not focused on local issues but on the maintenance of strong connections with China.

As with the earlier interrogation of the CBA leadership and its relations with the KMT, the board's economic connections with China were raised and its financial dealings questioned. In both these cases, the money links between regions and individuals and the connection of these links to the construction of a politics of home were brought to the fore by a group claiming some degree of "outsider" status. Their "outsider" status allowed members of the Renewal group to challenge the CCC's old-style politics and connections with China, but it eventually led to their defeat at the polls. Despite a fairly broad representation, Renewal candidates were positioned in campaign flyers, several CCC reports, and editorials as brash and wealthy new arrivals from Hong Kong. And although immigrants from Hong Kong represented a wide spectrum—including refugees, family class migrants, and the working class—the general view of Hong Kong immigrants as arrogant and wealthy was fueled by the influx of business migrants in the late 1980s. This undercurrent of negative feeling about new, "rootless" immigrants who only lived part-time in Vancouver and didn't respect the history of Chinatown or its working-class core was effectively manipulated by the Maintain group. At the prospect of a yuppie "takeover," the old guard of Chinatown closed ranks, upheld a more traditionalist vision of organizational authority, and moved away from the open and self-proclaimed "unselfish and democratic procedures" advocated by members of the Renewal Committee.

Thus, in the 1990s, a group with a large composition of recent Hong Kong and Taiwanese immigrants catalyzed a discussion about democracy and representation similar to the earlier debates of the 1970s, but in this case, the effort to "renew" Chinatown politics failed. The Renewal Committee voiced opposition to the non-democratic and violent authoritarianism of China. They also criticized members of the CCC board for continuing open relations with China in the context of this violence and questioned both the undemocratic political connections and the undemocratic political process they felt was characteristic of the association's leadership. In the context of *their* arrival in Vancouver, however, many long-term Chinatown residents perceived the challenge as a threat to the very character and history of the community's institutions. The influence of the wealthy business migrants was so great that the general perception of Hong Kong immigrants was largely tied to this group. And because this group represented economic power and urban change on an unprecedented scale, the fear of takeover within the community was correspondingly large.

CONCLUDING REMARKS

The Hong Kong emigration to Vancouver in the 1980s and early 1990s was one of many migration streams between Hong Kong and numerous sites around the world. In terms of the movement of a monied class of people, the scale of this migration is unprecedented. Many scholars have examined the economic ramifications as well as the physical and cultural changes that have resulted from the rapid influx of dominant-class fractions into specific areas. But few have begun to analyze the enormous implications for local political systems and outcomes.

One of the most important conclusions that can be drawn from my research to date is the finding that this qualitatively different type of migration does not only affect urban land decisions or the outcomes of political elections. Because of its enormous economic power, coupled with a cosmopolitan and strategic awareness of cultural and political differences worldwide, this migrant group has also been able to impact the democratic process itself in certain instances. Thus, in one neighborhood in Vancouver, the process by which land use decisions had historically been made, a process that was legitimized by reference to equal participation within the public sphere, was forever tarnished, then transformed, by allegations of racism from a group of recent Hong Kong immigrants. This group used the tools of democracy to demand a re-negotiation of the workings of democracy—something quite unusual if not unprecedented for such recent urban arrivals.

However, whereas money, power, network capital, and "outsider" status worked to the advantage of recent Hong Kong immigrants in the struggle over downzoning in Shaughnessy Heights, it appears to have worked to their disadvantage in the political election of the CCC board of directors. Here a key institution within the Chinese community, which had been established originally with specific reference to more open and representative democratic procedures in the 1970s, did not "renew" those democratic commitments in the 1990s. In this case, the perception of longtime Chinatown residents that recent Hong Kong immigrants were arrogant entrepreneurs uninterested in the historical memories and spiritual core of Chinatown was an important factor in the defeat of the Renewal Committee's campaign agenda.

But in juxtaposing these two case studies, let me offer an important caveat to the first conclusion. Although I believe it can be clearly demonstrated that transmigration flows from Hong Kong have had a major impact on urban politics in Vancouver, this impact has taken quite different forms within different communities. The fear of a loss of community "character" as well as the loss of control by an old, established group was expressed in both Shaughnessy Heights and Chinatown, but with differing outcomes. In the first case, a re-negotiation of democratic procedures was forced, partly as a result of a challenge that relied on references to the traditional ideals of a state founded on the principles of liberalism. In the face of evidence that these principles had not been upheld historically in the area of urban land designation, the contemporary challenge prevailed. In the latter case, there could be no reliance on an overarching principle of liberal democracy within the traditional Chinese community, nor could allegations of racism buttress the argument for reform. Despite the economic power of the new arrivals, they were unable to dislodge the old guard at the CCC, nor initiate a reworking of the ideas and institutions of democracy.

Social relations are *always* reworked in the context of spatial relations and vice versa. Thus, although the contemporary changes that have occurred in Vancouver in the context of major economic and demographic upheaval may be broad, they will also always exhibit specific community outcomes that reflect the histories and memories of specific places and institutions.

NOTES

1. This testimony at the public hearing of October 5, 1992, is cited in Ley (1995).

2. Author's interview, November 1992. Owing to the ongoing sensitivity of this case I have used pseudonyms to protect the identities of those I interviewed.

3. See, for example, the article in *Sing Tao Zhi Bao* (Sing Tao Daily), May 26, 1977.

4. See, for example, the editorial in *Da Han Gong Bao* (Chinese Times), May 24, 1973.

5. Author's interview, July 1996.

6. Author's interview, July 1996.

7. Quoted in Alison Appelbe, "Elders Maintain Hold on Chinese Centre," *Vancouver Courier*, May 5, 1993, p.10.

8. Fred Mah, *Chinese Cultural Centre Bulletin*, March 30, p. 2.

REFERENCES

Duncan, Jim. 1994. "Shaughnessy Heights: The Protection of Privilege," in *Neighborhood Organization and the Welfare State,* edited by Shlomo Hasson and David Ley, pp. 58–82. Toronto: University of Toronto Press.

Fung, V. 1991. "Hong Kong Investment Funds Pour into Canada," *Financial Post,* June 17, p. 18.

Ley, David. 1995. "Between Europe and Asia: the Case of the Missing Sequoias," *Ecumene* 2: 185–210.

Macdonald, P. 1990. "Canada to Trim Numbers of Independent Class Visas," *Hong Kong Standard,* January 26.

Mitchell, Katharyne. 1993. "Multiculturalism, or the United Colors of Capitalism?" *Antipode* 25 no. 4:263–294.

———. 1994. "Zoning Controversies in Shaughnessy Heights," *Canada and Hong Kong Update* 11(Winter): 11.

———. 1997. "Fast Capital, Modernity, Race and the Monster House," Forthcoming in *Burning Down the House: Recycling Domesticity*, edited by Rosemary George. New York: Harper Collins.

Nash, Alan. 1992. "The Emigration of Business People and Professionals from Hong Kong," *Canada and Hong Kong Update* (Winter): 2–4.

9 / From Colonial Rule to One Country, Two Systems

ROSANNA YICK-MING WONG

I am a Hongkonger, born and bred. Hong Kong is where my home is and where my heart is. My commitment is such that I have been actively involved in Hong Kong's political and public life since the mid-1980s, from around the time, in fact, of the Joint Declaration. It is on the basis of my personal observations and experience that I write this chapter on the politics of creating Hong Kong's future.

When I was a little girl, growing up in Hong Kong in the 1950s and 1960s, Hong Kong was in the throes of post-war recovery and renewal. In those years, the people of Hong Kong were concerned chiefly with improving their livelihood, repairing the damage done by the ravages of World War II, and coping with the hundreds of thousands of refugees who had fled from the newly established People's Republic of China (PRC) and who would become so important in making Hong Kong an economic success. At that time, for Hongkongers, the demands of the immediate present far outweighed their concerns about the future. They were so preoccupied with modernizing the economy and building an infrastructure that they could hardly envision the time when China would reclaim Hong Kong. For my school friends and me, that day seemed impossibly far away. Yet now, as though in the mere blink of an eye, the time has come and gone.

On the mainland, many people were very excited that Hong Kong would become part of China again. In Beijing they literally counted the days until the handover occurred. The sale of books about Hong Kong was big business. There was even an extremely popular quiz program in the PRC that tested people's knowledge of Hong Kong.

In Hong Kong itself, where the atmosphere could never, at any time, be called dull, the place positively brimmed over with nervous excitement and anticipation in the period leading up to the transition. Everyone was asking what this unique and unprecedented handover would mean. We wondered what would occur during this transformation of Hong Kong, from its colonial status to a Special Administrative Region of the People's Republic of China. So many people were and, for that matter, still are longing to know, and predictions and opinions abound. It is too early to make a definitive pronouncement, and I will not attempt to do so here. All I can do is give my own interpretation of events, based on my own experience in public life in Hong Kong.

The 150 years of British colonial rule has formed the foundation of what Hong Kong is today. In this chapter I will discuss to what extent some of these characteristics of Hong Kong can or will be retained. The transfer from colonial rule to a type of sovereignty called "one country, two systems" is unique in the history of mankind. Therefore, our path to the future has not been cleared by the actions of earlier governments; it will have to be created. One thing is certain, though, it will be us, we Hong Kong belongers who have witnessed this extraordinary moment in history, who will now be involved in making this new type of sovereignty work.

THE COLONIAL BACKGROUND

The fact that Hong Kong has never been an independent state is central to its new political status. Under British constitutional law, Hong Kong was a crown colony. It was ruled by the Governor and the Commander-in-Chief under instructions signed by the sovereign in London, that is to say, under basic empowering Letters Patent together with Royal Instructions on detail and procedure. To a large extent, the political legitimacy of the Hong Kong government was derived from the sovereign. But day-to-day administration remained the responsibility of the local government. The legitimacy required to maintain an effective administration rested with the system's ability to win the trust and support of the people.

When Hong Kong was ceded to Britain and became a British colony on 26 June 1843, the British government believed that, as in the other colonies, a very limited administration would meet the needs of the inhabitants of Hong Kong. The structure of the colonial authority was executive-led. The Legislative Council was not a representative assembly. Power basically rested with the bureaucratic elite in the civil service, and decisions were made behind closed doors. Britain was too far away to police the colony adequately, and the local colonial administration took a lenient view of its own shortcomings (*Hong Kong Annual Report* 1955). Public expenditures were confined to the bare essentials. Even the small amounts spent on community upkeep proved too much for the merchants who dominated the life of the territory. Indeed, for most of the nineteenth century, the central question that concerned the merchants in their relationship with government was the location of power. The merchants wanted to see the government run to their benefit, and they wanted control over finance. As the economy grew, the merchants became so politically powerful that they could no longer be ignored. They regarded themselves as the legitimate guardian of the public purse. They argued for representatives in the legislature and urged the government to create political links with Chinese notables and indirectly with the Chinese community (*Hong Kong: Report 1899*).

Before the Second World War, Hong Kong's economy was based largely on entrepôt trade. At the end of the war, by which time there was little left of the economy, local businessmen had to find new outlets for their activities. Increasingly, they moved into manufacturing, particularly textiles and garments. The Communist victory on the mainland produced unexpected bonuses for Hong Kong, mainly the influx of capital and entrepreneurs from Shanghai and cheap refugee labor. The values of hard work and frugality, and the willingness to change, experiment, and even gamble, values embodied by the refugees and the entrepreneurs, were all central to the process of industrialization and the establishment of a manufacturing base. The government at that time practiced a philosophy of laissez-faire. The Hong Kong government's own term is "positive non-intervention." This policy brought the British, other Western merchants, and a handful of local elites the advantages of a free port and a political regime that imposed few restrictions of any kind. The economic boom of the 1950s spawned a wealthy new elite that was absorbed into the system, but it also produced an exploited working class living and working in atrocious conditions.

Riots in 1966 and 1967 called the role of the government into question and provided the catalyst for change. A Commission of Inquiry was set up to investigate the causes of the unrest. The Commission Report addressed problems that were central to the social conditions and political structure of the territory and recommended many much-needed reforms. Even though the riots had posed a powerful threat to the legitimacy of the colonial state, many bureaucrats and traditional elites still opposed any radical new measures. The primary focus of reform in the period 1968–72, therefore, tended to be structural. Political reforms included the establishment of the City District Office, a local-level structure mediating between the government and the people; improvements in public relations within government departments; and an increased number of advisory committees and consultative forums. On the social and economic fronts, the major immediate change was labor legislation, particularly the promulgation of the Employment Act of 1968. The new order stressed "consultation" as the basis of its legitimacy, a more direct relationship with the population as its immediate goal, and improved social policies as its future objectives. Consultation meant the process by which the government, through advisory committees rather than democratic votes, arrived at a consensus on which it based its often predetermined decisions. While the structure of political authority was unaffected, the government responded to the crisis by developing a stronger relationship with the community and improving basic social services.

For over a hundred years, Hong Kong's progress has been substantially undisturbed by the kind of turmoil and violence that occurred elsewhere in Asia. Despite the 1966 and 1967 riots challenging the government and seeking change, the community has basically enjoyed peace and order for a long time. One wonders why this should be the case. Lucian Pye writes that a given political culture is the result not only of the life histories of individuals but also of the collective history of the system (Pye and Verba 1965). The Chinese community of Hong Kong is the descendant of two historical traditions, that of mainland China and that of a British colony. It can be assumed that both traditions have shaped attitudes towards government. Li Chien-ming (1966: 11) writes :

> "The traditional Chinese view of the ideal relationship between government and people...is analogous to that which should exist between parents and children...This traditional concept does not contemplate the direct participation of the population in the organization or processes of government. The Chinese people had characteristically remained aloof...from party politics for the last several thousands years, refraining from political action except during their most distressing moments."

The history of China would not encourage a Chinese, particularly a refugee from mainland China fleeing political oppression, to take an active part in making decisions for his community if he valued his peace of mind, his property, or his life. The traumatic experiences refugees have undergone predispose most of them to political quietism. As a Chinese Legislative Councilor colorfully put it, "Hong Kong is a lifeboat; China is the sea. Those who have climbed into the lifeboat naturally do not want to rock it" (Hoadley 1973: 613).

The history of Hong Kong itself also provides clues to the political conservatism of the colony's residents during most of its history. The fact that only a tiny minority of the present population is descended from the original inhabitants means that most residents from China see themselves as immigrants rather than natives. Consequently they perceive themselves as willing subjects of a foreign government, not involuntary slaves of a conquering colonial regime.

The distinctive political culture that developed under colonial rule was the result of an amalgam of circumstances attributable partly to history and partly to the need to keep controversy for controversy's sake to a minimum. The political socialization of Hong Kong residents favored consensus as the most appropriate goal of politics. A consensus, says one writer (Graham 1984: 111), is a "state of agreement, which varies in intensity and scope over time, incorporating the goals for society, the procedures for decision-making, and the particular policies." In

Hong Kong, such a consensus entailed a very careful political construction. In the period of reform after the 1966–67 riots, the British and Hong Kong governments wanted to create an institutional framework that would appear to simultaneously incorporate representatives of various sections of the community and maintain a strongly conservative bias preserving the executive powers of the colonial regime.

The resulting political reforms helped create the ensuing decade of growth and peaceful change. Political stability, economic prosperity, and greatly expanded social policy outputs in Hong Kong characterize this period. Targets were set for the construction of public housing and for an increased number of schools. Social welfare policies were drawn up, new towns were planned, medical facilities were improved, and an underground railway was built. Government centered its effort on reforming the civil service, improving the quality of life, and eliminating police corruption.

While improvements in the quality of social policy outputs were gradually incorporated into the government's plans, political change came very slowly. The political mechanism of co-optation and consultation continued and was further expanded at both the central and local levels. By the 1980s, however, at which time the future of Hong Kong was becoming a topic of discussion at every level, there was a demand for more open political participation. The reforms of the district administration in 1982 had involved more local people than ever before. The Legislative Council elections of 1985 were the first elections in Hong Kong, in which 24 members were indirectly elected. In 1991, there were direct elections to the Council. At that time, elected members, 18 directly and 21 indirectly elected, became the majority.

Throughout the decade leading up to the handover, there was pressure from the local community for more democratic representation and more accountability. This drive was offset by pressure from the Chinese government urging caution and the continuation of the status quo. The resulting tension between the British and the Chinese governments over this issue is well known.

HONG KONG INTO THE TRANSITION

China's official attitude on the future of Hong Kong was relatively simple and could be reduced to the proposition that the treaties had been unequal, Hong Kong was Chinese territory, and China would take back Hong Kong "sooner or later" when the time was ripe. Negotiations between the governments of the United Kingdom and the PRC over the future of Hong Kong started in Beijing in September 1982.

Representatives of the British and Chinese governments sat down to discuss the details of how Hong Kong could be administered by China, yet also preserve the distinctive features of the place. These included the successful free-market economy, freedom of speech, freedom of the press, and the rule of law. The result was Deng Xiaoping's unique and imaginative "one country, two systems," a slogan enshrined in the Sino-British Joint Declaration on the Question of Hong Kong. The Joint Declaration, as it is known, is a unique arrangement. It contains more than 8,000 words and is perhaps the second largest international agreement ever concluded by the PRC. Under the Declaration, sovereignty over the whole territory—most of Kowloon Peninsula and the New Territories (whose lease expired in 1997), plus Hong Kong Island and part of Kowloon (which were ceded outright)—would revert to China on 1 July 1997. Thereafter, Hong Kong would be a Special Administrative Region of the People's Republic of China. As such, Hong Kong would enjoy a high degree of autonomy, with executive, legislative, and independent judicial power, including that of final adjudication. The laws in force at the time of the handover, except for those that contravene the Basic Law, would remain the same, and the legal system would remain unchanged in many important respects. The significant legal principles underpinning the system would also remain in effect. These include the right to be tried by a jury, the presumption of innocence, freedom of speech, and freedom of religious beliefs. Hong Kong's present social and economic systems would continue unchanged for 50 years. Its status as a free port and international financial center would not change. An impressive array of rights and freedoms, including respect for private property, ownership of enterprise, and legitimate right of inheritance, would be protected by the Special Administrative Region government (Joint Declaration, 1984). The Chinese government pledged that the above basic policies would be valid for 50 years after 1997.

By and large, there was general consensus that the agreement reached in 1984 was the best the British government could expect to obtain and there was optimism, at least in the business classes, that stability and economic prosperity were assured. However, the events of 4 June 1989 in Tiananmen Square forced some in the community to reappraise the guarantees promised in the Joint Declaration. A new wave of uncertainty arose at that time over the future of the Territory after 1997. Although emigration has been a feature of life in Hong Kong for over a hundred years, the number of people leaving increased dramatically from an average of 20,000 per year in the early 1980s to over 60,000 in 1990.

In his study of transitional politics in non-Western countries, Lucian Pye shows that a shared characteristic of most colonial transitions is the general lack of consensus about the legitimate ends and means of political action. The fundamental fact that transitional societies are engrossed in a process of discontinuous social change precludes the possibility of a widely shared agreement about what is and is not an appropriate political activity (Pye 1992). In the political realm, where conscious choice and rational strategies should vie in promoting alternative human values, it becomes difficult to discern the possible choices and the truly held values of the people. This is certainly the case for Hong Kong's transition from colonialism, too. Conflicting views abound about how to continue prosperity and stability after 1997.

Broadly speaking, in the period leading up to the handover, there were two camps trying to capture the political marketplace. The view of one camp was that reform of Hong Kong's present system was necessary and the only logical approach was to develop a representative form of government, with its legitimacy and power rooted in Hong Kong. The British government took this position, as did most of the politically motivated pressure groups and democratic coalitions. The other camp, which the PRC government supported, was of the opinion that there should be "no big change" to the current political structure. Most of the capitalists and economic elites were and continue to be staunch exponents and supporters of the status quo.

The Chinese preference for preserving the political status quo in the wake of the transfer of sovereignty is publicly very clear. The Chinese want to see continued prosperity in Hong Kong after 1997. They estimate that their formula of "no big change" will bring Hong Kong the same "quality" and "quantity" of prosperity. If there are changes, they reason, Hong Kong might not be as they want it to be. Ji Peng-fei, the former head of Hong Kong and Macau Affairs for the Chinese government, openly expressed the view that the proposition of "prosperity plus reforms" is unacceptable and that "only those elements that run counter to the transfer of sovereignty, that exhibit colonial characteristics and that damage the honor of the Chinese people need to be changed while all others should remain unchanged" (Kuan and Lau 1987).

The transition has occurred. Stability, order, and prosperity remain intact for the moment, although the latter is a bit battered by the Asian financial crisis. To predict what will happen in the future, however, is no easy task. Throughout this decade, things have been changing very quickly, and things will continue to change in the future. Like it or not, the PRC government is observing these changes and is aware of their momentum. The *first* of these changes is the continuing quest for democracy. The emergence of a political market enables politicians representing different sectors of the population to be involved in the decision-making arena. The first direct election to the legislature in 1991 clearly demonstrated this change of atmosphere.

Another change resulted from the problem of the so-called brain drain. Ever since the negotiations began in 1982, Hong Kong has been losing a considerable number of managers and professionals every year. They are the elites and the middle class on which the colonial administration relied heavily for legitimacy in the past. Many stayed behind, and recent trends show that some are returning to Hong Kong to secure opportunities created by the brain drain. Nonetheless, it is a fact that the new government still needs to nurture new leaders who can provide a vision for the future; it must also cultivate political efficacy and self-identity among the expectant public. In order to do this, Hong Kong after 1997 must be a place where the public believes it has a secure future in a free and fair society with an accountable government and an independent judiciary.

The third change is the gradual development of an economic realism that acknowledges that Hong Kong's economy cannot operate under the international free-market system unless it has relatively free-market politics. Hong Kong is crucial to China's own development, particularly in terms of direct trade and inward investment, acting as a link with the world economic community. Any move by China that would damage Hong Kong's prosperity must, therefore, take account of the effect on the development of China and prospects for internal, regional, and international stability in the short-and long-term. The more China develops, the greater the need to fine-tune the relationship between the polity and the socioeconomic system in Hong Kong.

Finally, the change of sovereignty, which entails a change of ideology, means a new relationship must be developed with the Chinese government. Hong Kong will become an "internal" problem for Beijing's political leaders. The question of how to meet the challenge of "one country, two systems" for the future development of Hong Kong will continue to be on their minds for some time to come. The struggle between what is called "interference" by the sovereign and "participation" by the people of Hong Kong will require new political engineering.

THE KEY CHALLENGES

So, what is the future for Hong Kong? Will the "Pearl of the Orient" continue to remain an open and fair society, as well as a dynamic economy, as we move into a new millennium? Or will we see a decline in personal freedom, an erosion of the Hong Kong government's autonomy, the reemergence of corruption, and a general whittling away of those qualities that give Hong Kong its distinct, international identity?

In his book *Borrowed Place, Borrowed Time*, the veteran journalist Richard Hughes wrote : "Hong Kong *is* China. That was, is and remains the abiding corner-stone of survival for the unique territory." At midnight on 30 June 1977, this statement became literally true.

But is Hong Kong just another Chinese city? Certainly its people are predominantly Chinese, and profoundly proud to be so as I think all those of Chinese descent are, in whatever corner of the world they were born or dwell. Yet for us there is a dichotomy, one that I suspect those of you who are Chinese Americans feel as well. We are Chinese, but we are also Hong Kong people, and that, we feel, makes us a bit different. There are aspects to our culture, to our experience, that set us apart from the mainland. We have grown up, above all, in a "climate of freedom." That may sound odd to the ears of citizens of the country that was the first to cast off the "yoke" of British colonialism, but it is a fact that George Washington, Benjamin Franklin, and the other patriots might actually find quite a lot they approve of in Hong Kong today! We have grown used to the rule of law, to free speech, to a free press, to freedom of movement, and to a liberal education system. It is, of course, true that independence has never been in the cards for us, and that, until the 1980s, there wasn't much that could justly be described as democracy. Yet the colonial government was generally responsive to the wishes of the people, and this responsiveness grew in the last decade of the colony.

It is the "climate of freedom" that has allowed the Chinese citizens of Hong Kong to develop their talents and energies to the maximum extent. Our post-war record is particularly remarkable. In 1945, when Hong Kong was liberated at the end of the Second World War, the city was a ruin and the population had fallen to 600,000. Today, Hong Kong is one of the world's leading commercial and financial centers, with a thriving population of 6 million.

Hong Kong's Trade and Development Council lists a lot of "facts" about what Hong Kong has become in the last 50 years: "the world's freest economy," "the world's eighth largest trading economy in the world," "the world's second most competitive economy," "the world's busiest container port," to repeat only a few. As a result of this amazing expansion, Hong Kong enjoyed an average real GDP growth of 6.5 percent each year during the 10 years preceding the Asian business crisis. In 1997, Hong Kong's per capita GDP was US$23,200 , higher than many western countries, including Britain, Canada, and Australia.

But Hong Kong's story has not only been one of economic success. Our growing prosperity has also enabled us to finance ever-improving services for our community. Let me give some examples. In the midst of an economy that is labeled the world's freest, over half the population lives in subsidized public housing that they either rent or own. We aim to produce some 316,000 additional housing units in the public sector by the year 2001. Since 1978, nine years of free education have been provided for all our children. In addition, over 90 percent of Hong Kong's children now complete highly subsidized upper secondary education or the equivalent technical education, and there are first-year first- degree places in our universities for 18 percent of the relevant age group. We have comprehensive medical and health services that are provided either free or at very low charge. Our infant mortality is lower, and our life expectancy is longer, than that of the United States or the United Kingdom. And, finally, we have both a means-tested Comprehensive Social Security Assistance Scheme, and non means-tested allowances for people who are aged 70 and above or who have a disability. As rags-to-riches stories go, Hong Kong's isn't bad.

But will it, *can* it, go on beyond 1997? I say it *can* and *will*, but I do not say this out of a spirit of blind optimism. There are challenges, there will be problems, and we *shall* have to struggle. We shall have to use all our energies and determination if we are to retain our essential autonomy and identity and our place in the international community, while at the same time lending our weight (as we have lent it these last 15 years and more) to China's drive toward modernization and prosperity.

What basis is there for believing that Hong Kong will continue to enjoy a high degree of autonomy, our present lifestyle, and our social, legal, and economic systems—for at least 50 years after 1997?

There is, firstly, a *legal* basis, laid down in the Sino-British Joint Declaration, which was signed in 1984 and subsequently registered at the United Nations by both Britain and China. Annex I to the Joint Declaration sets out in detail the basic policies of the People's Republic of China toward the Hong Kong Special Administrative Region (SAR). It states that the SAR will be vested with executive, legislative, and independent judicial powers, including that of final adjudication. The government and legislature of the SAR will be composed of local inhabitants, in other words, *not* people sent from mainland China. The legislature will be constituted by elections, and the executive authorities will be accountable to it. Common law will continue to be practiced. In addition to Chinese, English may continue to be used by the government and in the courts.

The provisions of the Joint Declaration have been further enshrined in the Basic Law, the constitution that China has drafted, in consultation with Hong Kong people, for the Special Administrative Region. Together, the Joint Declaration and the Basic Law embody Deng Xiaoping's twin precepts of "one country, two systems" and "Hong Kong people to run Hong Kong." But what other reasons are there for confidence beyond these two "scraps of paper"?

You will often hear people say that Hong Kong will continue to prosper because it is in China's interest that it should. This is true. But I would go much further. It is in *everyone's* interest that it should—China, Britain, the international community, and, above all, the people of Hong Kong themselves. No one stands to gain anything from Hong Kong's collapse or slow disintegration.

However, there is debate as to what constitutes the fundamentals of Hong Kong's continuing stability and prosperity. There is a school of thought that says that Hong Kong people care about nothing but money, that when you land at Hong Kong's airport the first aroma that greets you is the smell of money, that life in Hong Kong revolves around boardroom battles and stockmarket wheeling and dealing, and that Hong Kong people have no use for democracy and liberty. I often hear this view put forward, sometimes by people I know pretty well. I always wonder whether they are talking about the place in which I have lived all my life and the many selfless, civilized, public-spirited citizens of all ranks who have many, many, priorities in life beyond making a fortune. Prosperity is crucial, certainly—no one would deny it. But freedom is the foundation of our economic success, not the other way around.

I fear that one sad proof of what freedom means to Hong Kong people has been the recent large efflux of emigrants heading for America, Canada, Australia, and elsewhere, particularly since the events of June 4, 1989. These people have not left Hong Kong to find fame and fortune. In most cases, they have left their fortunes behind and have had to settle for lower-paid jobs, or no jobs at all, in the countries where they have settled. They have left in search of a guarantee of freedom. This diaspora of Hong Kong talent is a tragedy. We should not minimize its significance. However, I do not believe that it will do Hong Kong fatal harm, and I am hopeful that many of the émigrés will return. Indeed, some of them already have, their confidence in the future restored.

So Hong Kong's future depends on more than prosperity. It rests on making a reality out of the terms of the Joint Declaration and the Basic Law. We cannot continue to have a free and vigorous economy unless we continue to enjoy the other fundamental facets of our traditional "climate of freedom."

I would stress in particular the importance of maintaining the rule of law overseen by an independent judiciary. In Hong Kong today, no one is above the law. Anyone can take the government to court, and in many cases he or she will receive legal aid with which to do so. The law-making process is open and transparent. And the government does not always get its own way in this process. All legislative proposals put forward by the government have to be approved by the Legislative Council, in which the government has no vote. The law is enforced impartially and fairly. The continuation of this system is underwritten by the Basic Law.

I would place the public accountability of the government next in importance, for this embraces both essential human freedoms and the need for a clean and efficient civil service. The people of Hong Kong have never been loath to criticize their government whenever its services failed to meet their expectations. Our press has been one of the most vigorous and outspoken in the world, although I would not deny that there is now some evidence of "self-censorship" over matters relating to China, which is a worrisome development. The Legislative Council, meanwhile, makes full use of its right to question the government on its policies, to examine draft legislation, and to scrutinize proposals for public expenditure. Again, the Joint Declaration and the Basic Law guarantee the continuation of this system.

Although international treaty and by the constitution of the Special Administrative Region guarantee Hong Kong freedom and a high degree of autonomy beyond 1997, we cannot simply sit back and wait for these good things to drop into our hands. When have such things ever come that easily?

Ensuring that we do enjoy freedom and autonomy after 1997 is both the challenge and the opportunity. I am confident that we have what it takes to face that challenge and seize that opportunity. The fundamentals of Hong Kong's past and present successes are so sound and so all-pervasive that, whatever debates and controversies may have raged, Hong Kong has come through the transition as Hong Kong.

Struggle and crisis have forged the robust qualities of the place and its people. The post-war success story that I outlined earlier was achieved in the face of many obstacles. But Hong Kong has always been good at making a virtue out of necessity. For example, the hundreds of thousands of refugees who fled to Hong Kong to escape political turmoil in China, and whose arrival created gigantic social challenges in housing, education, and health care, were the very people whose energy and enterprise helped create the wealth that overcame the social challenges. There were other obstacles: civil disturbance (most notably in 1967 when the Cultural Revolution spilled past the mainland Chinese border), periodic economic recessions (including the current one), and natural disasters, too—typhoons and landslides. Hong Kong survived and flourished in this post-war atmosphere of challenge. And it is this historical background that strengthens my confidence that we shall be equal to whatever challenges the future may throw out, and ready to grab whatever opportunities the future will certainly offer.

Working with young people has given me a deep faith in the power of youth. Hong Kong has a great reservoir of youthful talent and energy, young people who are proud to belong to Hong Kong, young people who want no other home and would live nowhere else, young people who will also be proud to contribute to the resurgence of the Chinese nation as a whole.

Hong Kong has gone back to China. In some spiritual sense it never left. Its political return has been an event of great historical significance. But what is even more significant is that the Hong Kong of 1 July was essentially the Hong Kong of 30 June. The continuum of political, social, and economic progress has and will be maintained. With a high degree of autonomy and its "climate of freedom," Hong Kong, a city of China, will remain a unique place, a place that exemplifies the triumph of the Chinese spirit better than any other, but that is also an international vortex welcoming people of all races who wish to work and live and drink deep of its vivid, vigorous, and varied atmosphere.

I can offer you no proof that all that I have written here will come true. But of this I am certain. The truths of which historians will someday write are the truths that we must now create. The people of Hong Kong can and must grasp their own future today and every day to come.

REFERENCES

Graham, George J. 1984. "Consensus," in *Social Science Concepts: A Systematic Analysis,* edited by Giovanni Sartori. Beverly Hills, Cali.: Sage Publications.

Hoadley, John S. 1973. "Political Participation of Hong Kong Chinese: Patterns and Trends," *Asia Survey* 13: 604–616.

Hong Kong Annual Report 1955. Hong Kong: Hong Kong Government Printer.

Hong Kong: Report 1899. 1901. London: His Majesty's Stationary Office.

Hughes, Richard. 1968. *Hong Kong: Borrowed Place, Borrowed Time.* New York: F. A. Praeger.

Kuan H.C., and Lau S.K. 1987. "Hong Kong's Search for a Consensus: Barriers and Prospects," in *The Future of Hong Kong: Toward 1997 and Beyond,* edited by Jungdah Chiu, Y.C. Jao, and Yuan-li Wu. New York: Quorum Books.

Li Chien-ming. 1966. *Report of the Working Party on Local Administration.* Hong Kong: Hong Kong Government Printer.

Pye, Lucian. 1992. *Politics, Personality, and Nation Building: Burma's Search for Identity.* Cambridge, Mass.: Center for International Studies, Massachusetts Institute of Technology.

Pye, Lucian, and Sidney Verba, eds. 1965. *Political Culture and Political Development.* Princeton, N.J.: Princeton University Press.

Contributors

GARY HAMILTON is Professor of Sociology at the University of Washington. He has written extensively on Chinese economic organization and is the author of current and forthcoming books on Chinese and Asian economies.

KATHARYNE MITCHELL is Assistant Professor of Geography at the University of Washington. She is the author of a forthcoming book on Hong Kong migration to Vancouver, B.C. (University of California Press) and is currently studying the lines of conflict and consensus between new and old Chinese migration communities of Vancouver.

BARRY NAUGHTON is a Professor in the Graduate School of International Relations and Pacific Studies. He is one of the foremost specialists on the Chinese economy and the author of a recently published book, *Growing Out of the Plan, Chinese Economic Reform, 1973–1993* (Cambridge University Press, 1996).

HELEN SIU is Professor of Anthropology and Chair of the Council on East Asian Studies at Yale University. A native Hongkonger, she is a leading specialist on the anthropology of South China.

G. WILLIAM SKINNER is Professor of Anthropology at the University of California. A distinguished anthropologist and former president of the Asian Studies Association, he is an authority on urban organization in Asia and the Chinese in overseas communities.

WANG GUNGWU is a distinguished historian, the foremost specialist on the Chinese in Southeast Asia, and former president of the University of Hong Kong. He is currently the Director of the East Asian Institute at the National University of Singapore and a Distinguished Senior Fellow at the Institute of Southeast Asian Studies.

EDGAR WICKBERG is Professor Emeritus of History at the University of British Columbia. He is one of the foremost specialists on the history of the Chinese in Southeast Asia and Canada.

WONG SIU-LUN is Professor of Sociology and Director of the Centre of Asian Studies, University of Hong Kong. He is the leading specialist on Chinese entrepreneurship and has just completed a very large study on recent migration from Hong Kong.

The Honorable ROSANNA YICK-MING WONG is currently Chair of the Hong Kong Housing Authority, a member of the Executive Council of the Hong Kong Government, and Executive Director of the Hong Kong Federation of Youth Groups.

Index